John Woolman and the Affairs of Truth

The Journalist's Essays, Epistles, and Ephemera

Edited by
James Proud

D0921451

Inner Light Books
San Francisco, California

JOHN WOOLMAN AND THE AFFAIRS OF TRUTH

The Journalist's Essays, Epistles, and Ephemera

Cover images: By permission of The Historical Society of Pennsylvania (HSP), from its John Woolman Papers (Collection #737, Box 2, MS A, pages 133 and 282).

Cover and book design: Charles Martin

Published by Inner Light Books,
San Francisco, California
www.innerlightbooks.com
editor@innerlightbooks.com

Library of Congress Control Number: 2010939658

ISBN 978-0-9797110-6-0 (hardcover)
ISBN 978-0-9797110-7-7 (paperback)

For all the souls sacrificed to
enslavement, impoverishment, and war

IN MEMORIAM

Table of Contents

PREFACE   *vii*

INTRODUCTION   *xi*

1   A Life of Letters   xi

2   Woolman's Holographs   xxxii

3   This Edition   xxxv

4   References and Abbreviations   xxxix

THE TEXTS
(in chronological order of writing)

1   Some Considerations on the Keeping of Negroes   1

2   An Epistle from our General Spring Meeting of
Ministers and Elders, etc., 1755
To Friends on the Continent of America   15

3   To Friends at their Monthly Meeting at New Garden
and Cane Creek in North Carolina   20

4   From our Yearly Meeting held at Philadelphia,
etc. 1759. To the Quarterly and Monthly
Meetings of Friends   24

5   Considerations on Keeping Negroes: Part Second   30

6   A Word of Remembrance & Caution to the Rich &c.   62

7   Ephemera (of various dates):
A   untitled parable on "a tax demanded
for evil ends"   87
B   account of peace mission dream   91
C   notes and commentaries on Anthony
Benezet's *A Caution and Warning
to Great Britain*   93
D   untitled fragment on patience and on
trusting in God   102

E copies of two letters on 'high living'
and 'expensive customs'   105
F thoughts on the customary use of silver
vessels   109

8   Considerations on Pure Wisdom, and Human Policy;
on Labor; on Schools; and on the Right
Use of the Lord's Outward Gifts   111

9   Serious Considerations on Trade   125

10   A First Book for Children   129

11   Considerations on the True Harmony of Mankind
& how it is to be maintained   146

12   Conversations on the True Harmony of Mankind &
how it may be promoted   166

13   1772 An Epistle to the Quarterly and Monthly
Meetings of Friends   180

14   [The final essays, written at sea and in England]   194

APPENDICES

1   A Guide to the Manuscripts of John Woolman's
Literary Works, Personal Business
Records, and Epistles from PYM to
other yearly meetings   217

2   Reformers of the mid-eighteenth century
American Quaker Church: Israel
Pemberton, Jr. and John Woolman   220

Table 1: John Woolman's missionary
journeys and his traveling
companions   241
Table 2: John Woolman's annual
appointments to the PYM
epistle committees writing to
other yearly meetings   243
Table 3: The PYM Overseers of the
Press between 1743 and 1771   245

v

Appendix Text 1: The Epistle of 1756
    from PYM to Long Island YM   249
Appendix Text 2: The Epistle of 1757
    from PYM to Virginia YM   251
Appendix Text 3: The Epistle of 1758
    from PYM to North Carolina YM 254
Appendix Text 4: The Epistle of 1760
    from PYM to Rhode Island YM   256
Appendix Text 5: The Epistle of 1761
    from PYM to Rhode Island YM   258
Appendix Text 6: The Epistle of 1762
    from PYM to Long Island YM   260
Appendix Text 7: The Epistle of 1763
    from PYM to Long Island YM   262
Appendix Text 8: The Epistle of 1764
    from PYM to London YM   264
Appendix Text 9: The Epistle of 1768
    from PYM to London YM   267
Appendix Text 10: The Epistle of 1770
    from PYM to London YM   270

3   John Woolman's memorial concerning his
brother Abner addressed to the Meeting
for Sufferings at Philadelphia   274

Appendix Text 11: The testament to
    Abner Woolman's children   280

INDEXES

Subject Index   297
Scripture Index   307

Preface

Many pilgrims on spiritual journeys since John Woolman's time have been drawn toward the irenic virtues and steadfast faith illuminating the pages of his *Journal*. It is a confessional work, painfully honest in its self-revelations, telling us much not only of the confessor's struggles in finding his true way through this earthly life but also of the pain he felt over the growing injustices of the society in which he lived. Woolman did not begin writing his *Journal* until he was nearing the midpoint of his career as a man of letters, a career he seldom mentions in those pages. While many of his general writings were published and widely-distributed in his lifetime, it was not until after Woolman's death that the *Journal* itself was revealed, edited by friends, and only then put in print. Today, his thought and influence chiefly come to us from the *Journal* while the main body of his lifetime writings—scattered and for the most part unknown—remain outside our ken.

This work collects the body of Woolman's general writings (other than the *Journal*) so that the record will be made more complete as to his concerns and thoughts, his experiences and prophetic witness, 'in the affairs of Truth'. While the intention has been to gather and put into a timely order all such writings that can be found, an early, and unconscious, assumption was made that it would simply result in filling out the picture of a plain, earnest man of local education and limited means, acting for the most part alone yet inspired with a Jeremiah-like mission to speak in a time when most people were too worldly to listen. The result, for the editor, has been surprisingly other than that simple expectation.

Woolman was a man of wide erudition and used the entire range of the Hebrew Bible and New Testament, as well as biblical literature, with the elegance of a connoisseur, exactly quoting on some occasions, freely paraphrasing in context on others. He was a master of scripture and thus of how to 'think and act biblically'. He also knew and used in his texts the published works of his day on church history, Quaker theology and foundations, and the practices and economics of the slave trade. Indeed, in several sketches herein touching on international trade, he looks wisely upon one of the besetting problems of his day and ours—that of securing the viability of local economies when confronted by powerful interests intent on promoting international trade and globalization.

Nor was Woolman a simple but poor man economically surviving on the margins through shopkeeping and tailoring. He had purposefully renounced his birth-right expectations of being the patriarch of his generation and the manorial lord of the family plantation, positions which would have secured for him wealth and local status. Instead, he chose to be in business for himself and, further, to reduce the 'cumber' of that business so far as would allow him to support his wife and daughter and himself and yet be free to teach, to travel on missions, to write, and, above all, to engage in a heavy schedule of attending local, regional, and provincial business and ministerial meetings under the aegis of the Philadelphia Yearly Meeting of Friends at a time when PYM was undergoing major reform—Woolman himself being a moving force behind that reform. Indeed, and most surprisingly, as evidenced in Appendix 2 Woolman first and foremost was a reformer, and reform shaped and molded the body of his writings and his legacy to succeeding generations. That he chose to live austerely and frugally, and to avoid luxuries and superfluities, arose out of his intentional witness to the gospel he preached and the reform he saw as essential to health in the church and to justice in society.

There is one overarching acknowledgment that must be made for the body of Woolman documents now before the reader, and that is to the collective genius which long ago determined that Quakers would record all their corporate transactions and carefully preserve all their records. The minutes of the meetings held on a monthly, quarterly, and yearly basis by Quaker bodies; the reports, epistles, and other documents considered and put forth by those bodies and their subordinate entities; and the diaries, manuscripts for publication, and countless other miscellaneous papers employed in the work of the Religious Society of Friends, from the earliest time until now, have been archived and kept in institutions where they are made available for use. This legacy of the past is now in the care of curators, keepers, and custodians, scholars in their own right. To those who have assisted in this project, and without whose unfailing help and kindness these writings could not have been gathered, I am gratefully indebted.

I have received invaluable assistance and guidance from Ann W. Upton and Diana Franzusoff Peterson of the Quaker Collection, Haverford College Library, and from Christopher Densmore, Patricia C. O'Donnell, and Susanna Morikowa of the Friends Historical Library, Swarthmore College Library. Sarah Heim of the Historical Society of Pennsylvania and Albert C. King of the Special Collections and University Archives, Rutgers University Libraries, have each kindly facilitated my access to their Woolman holdings. I am indebted to both Katie Terrell and my valued friend William A. Johnson for steadfast encouragement to persevere in bringing this work forward, as I am also to Don Malcolm for his unique patience in guiding me out of the challenging thickets of word processing whenever I was lost. The artistic hand of Charles Martin, assisted editorially and technically by Barbara Mays and Matt Kelsey, has produced a volume that I can only believe John Woolman would have lovingly shelved in his own library. To and for all these individuals I give thanks. To me alone belong the errors and omissions herein.

I was conscious throughout this work of my late father's presence, and have been thereby comforted. Above all I have been and am continually nourished and sustained by Kathleen, my wife and the companion of my life, who has shared with me the Quaker ethos over years through her faithful teaching in Friends' schools.

Introduction

1
A Life of Letters

The Prophet's Quest for Truth[1]

The nurturing of John Woolman as a man of spiritual letters began in the years of his upbringing in the heart of a plantation family living on the banks of the Rancocas River in West New Jersey during the second quarter of the eighteenth century. The first of seven sons and the eldest brother of six sisters, Woolman and his siblings were educated both at home and in the local school. Because of the fortuity of his birth as first son, Woolman could expect from his father Samuel something more than any of his brothers and sisters might receive, and that was the customary right of becoming, upon Samuel's death, the head of this extended family and the principal owner of its lands and other property. It was a weighty expectation, but it entailed the obligation of accepting the responsibility to manage and oversee the plantation during all of John's active adult years.

It was a responsibility and burden which Woolman decided not to carry, and "in the twenty-first year of my age"[2] (sometime between 19 October 1741 and 18 October 1742), and with his father's agreement, he moved out of the family home to live alone in a shop in Mount Holly, five miles away. There he tended the store and kept the books for the owner whose business was merchandising and baking and who knew tailoring as well. John was hired by the year[3] and his employment apparently lasted until about 1746, when the business closed following the death of his employer's wife.[4] During his years in the shop John wrote legal

---

[1] For Woolman, in a real sense Truth was another name for God. It was the ultimate reality, the Supreme Being, which in human affairs manifests itself through social justice, peace, and equity, the key issues at the core of all of Woolman's writings. Woolman well encapsulated the essential nature of Truth, as he understood it, in the titles of his two important "considerations" on ethics: pure wisdom, and true harmony.

[2] *Journal*, p. 29.

[3] *Ibid.*, pp. 32-33.

[4] *Ibid.*, p. 36.

instruments as part of his duties,[5] discovered that merchandising was "attended with much cumber,"[6] and learned the craft of tailoring from his master's servant so that "if I should settle, I might by this trade and a little retailing of goods get a living in a plain way without the load of great business."[7] Also during this employment John found the occasion, in 1743, to take his first missionary journey. It was into East New Jersey where he traveled for two weeks.[8]

Immediately after the termination of his store clerkship, as Woolman records in the *Journal*, "I then wrought at my trade as a tailor, carefully attended meetings for worship and discipline, and found an enlargement of gospel love in my mind and therein a concern to visit Friends in some of the back settlements of Pennsylvania and Virginia."[9] In that moment, his apprenticeship in the world of commerce being ended, he realized he could provide for his own material needs through self-employment as a tailor and be free to travel in the Quaker ministry, thereby gaining experience and recording his impressions of the people and their social and spiritual issues in the burgeoning colonies of America. He made arrangements for his venturing into the South. It was the commencement of his career as an author; and while beyond knowing, it was also the beginning of the second half of his short life.

Truth I: The ground of emancipation

Woolman's southern journey, made in 1746, resulted in his first major written work. As he briefly noted in the *Journal*, "[a]fter my return from Carolina I made some observations on keeping slaves. . ."[10] These observations were the essay he titled "Some Considerations on the Keeping of Negroes" (**Text 1** herein); below the title were the words: "Recommended to the Professors of Christianity of Every Denomination." The essay, which makes no reference to his journey and is written in an impersonal style, examines "by the infallible standard: Truth" the evil of possessing enslaved people. Its arguments are grounded in biblical theology, the author quoting in the text more than twenty passages from the Old and New Testaments. The single reference

---

5 *Ibid.*, p. 32.
6 *Ibid.*, p. 35.
7 *Ibid.*, p. 35.
8 *Ibid.*, p. 34.
9 *Ibid.*, p. 36.
10 *Ibid.*, p. 44.

other than the Bible that Woolman makes is to *Some Considerations Relating to the Present State of the Christian Religion* by Alexander Arscott, an English Quaker. It had been printed in Philadelphia in the 1730s.

Woolman waited almost eight years to submit his manuscript to the Overseers of the Press of the Philadelphia Yearly Meeting of Friends.[11] In 1754, the Overseers "having examined and made some small alterations in it, ordered a number of copies thereof to be published by the yearly meeting stock and dispersed amongst Friends."[12] Near the same time yearly meeting, in its "Epistle of Caution and Advice, Concerning the Buying and Keeping of Slaves" testified to its "uneasiness and disunity with the importation and purchasing of negroes and other slaves".[13] In a specific word to Friends "who by inheritance have slaves born in your families" they wrote: "we beseech you to consider them as souls committed to your trust, whom the Lord will require at your hands. . ."[14]

Yearly meeting again addressed the issue of "importing, buying, selling, or keeping slaves for a term of life" in 1758 with a view to putting a stop to its increase. In an epistle that year it held that if "any professing with us should persist to vindicate it" then their monthly meetings

> should manifest their disunion with such persons, by refusing to permit them to sit in Meetings for Discipline, or to be employed in the affairs of Truth, or to receive from them any contributions towards the relief of the poor, or other services of the meeting.[15]

Moreover, the 1758 epistle also named Woolman, together with John Churchman, John Scarborough, John Sykes, and Daniel Stanton, as being willing, as well as approved by PYM, to "visit and treat with all such Friends who have any slaves." Thus what Woolman and PYM had achieved in 1754 began slowly to have wider impact. In 1780 Pennsylvania adopted America's first abolition act. But it was a gradual emancipation and the total abolition of enslavement did not come to the Commonwealth until 1847.

---

[11] See herein the Historical Notes which are part of Table 3: The PYM Overseers of the Press between 1743 and 1771.

[12] *Journal*, p. 47.

[13] Michener, p. 342.

[14] *Ibid.*, p. 345.

[15] *Ibid.*, pp. 346-47.

In the eight years of waiting to see "Some Considerations on the Keeping of Negroes" in print and before writing his second important work, Woolman experienced major changes in his personal life. In 1749 he married Sarah Ellis. The next year his father Samuel died and his daughter Mary was born. In the momentous year of 1754 came the birth and then the death, at the age of two months, of William, his only other child. And there was the constant necessity to establish and support himself and his young family, as evidenced throughout his years of entrepreneurship by the personal account books he kept.[16]

Notwithstanding all the changing circumstances of his life, John continued in most of these years between his first two major writings to journey from home on visits to other Quaker communities. Less than two months after returning from the southern journey in 1746, he spent twenty-two days visiting Friends on the East New Jersey seacoast. In 1747 he traveled four months in Long Island and New England. In 1748 he spent six weeks journeying in New Jersey and Delaware. The first recorded travel after his 1749 marriage occurred in 1751 when he was away in upper West New Jersey for nine days. In 1753 he was away on a visit in Bucks County, Pennsylvania lasting about two weeks. Through these travels he remained a keen observer of the issues, as he perceived them, confronting the American colonies in the years before the Revolution.

Truth II: The testimony of peace

When the peace of the colonies was broken in western Pennsylvania in early 1754, signaling the commencement of the French and Indian War, Woolman was stirred to write his second major work, the "Epistle from our General Spring Meeting of Ministers and Elders, etc., 1755" (**Text 2** herein). It was drafted by Woolman in advance of this meeting of Quaker ministers and elders where it was inspected, revised, and signed. The war itself is directly alluded to only once in the "Epistle":

> And now dear Friends, with respect to the commotions and stirrings of the powers of the earth at this time near us, we are desirous that none of us may be moved thereat; (par. 4)

---

[16] See pp. xx-xxii hereafter.

As with the earlier essay on enslavement, the "Epistle" is grounded in the profession of Truth. It urges trust in God's gracious design to break the earthly powers that oppose his spiritual kingdom. Also as in the earlier essay, all the references save one are to the Bible and those chiefly to the prophets of ancient Israel. Interestingly, the only non-biblical author quoted is Stephen Crisp, the English Quaker, writing in 1666 of the tribulations of Friends during the Restoration, the very tribulations Woolman's paternal grandfather and great-grandfather would have witnessed before leaving England for America in 1678.

As the war progressed it became increasingly difficult for Friends in the colonial government to practice the principles of peace which Woolman enunciated in this epistle. The exigencies of the day for the defense of the colony were overwhelming them. From the Philadelphia Yearly Meeting of 1758 came this exhortation and judgment:

> As the maintaining inviolate the liberty of conscience, which is essential to our union and well-being as a religious society, evidently appears to be an indispensable duty, this meeting doth, with fervent and sincere desires for the present and future prosperity of Truth among us. . .caution, advise, and exhort Friends to beware of accepting of, or continuing in office, or station in civil society or government, by which they may be in any respect engaged in. . .and if any professing with us should. . .persist in a conduct so repugnant to that sincerity, uprightness, and self-denial, incumbent on us, it is the sense and judgment of this meeting, that such persons should not be allowed to sit in our Meetings for Discipline, nor be employed in the affairs of Truth, until they are brought to a sense and acknowledgment of their error.[17]

In these personally difficult years following the death of his son and the beginning of the French and Indian War, Woolman confined his brief missionary travels to New Jersey. In 1754 he visited Quaker families belonging to Chesterfield Monthly Meeting in nearby Crosswicks; the following winter he was among families in Shrewsbury. Then in 1756 he made pivotal changes in his life. He returned to making longer and further journeys, spending twenty-four days in the 5th and 6th months of that year visiting Friends on Long Island. He lessened his retail

---

[17] Michener, p. 274.

merchandising and directed his business activities to working as a tailor without an apprentice and to keeping a nursery of apple trees in which he did the "hoeing, grafting, trimming, and inoculating"[18] himself. And it was "in the thirty-sixth year of my age",[19] (sometime between 19 October 1756 and 18 October 1757), that he began writing his *Journal*. The consequences of those changes soon became apparent.

In the 5th month of 1757 Woolman began his second major journey into the American South. He was gone from his wife and young daughter, his home and livelihood, for almost two months. This, his longest outing in ten years, is the subject of chapter IV of the *Journal*.[20] In that chapter he refers to this time as a "deep and painful exercise," a "weighty work," a "deep trial" in which his mind was "almost overwhelmed" because of the "weight of distress upon me." He described the heaviness he felt when beholding the southern churches as follows:

> It appeared to me that through the prevailing of the spirit of this world the minds of many were brought to an inward desolation, and instead of the spirit of meekness, gentleness, and heavenly wisdom, which are the necessary companions of the true sheep of Christ, a spirit of fierceness and the love of dominion too generally prevailed.[21]

While four years would pass before Woolman completed an essay based on these difficult experiences, the work immediately issuing from this travel, however, was his warm and loving pastoral epistle "To Friends at their Monthly Meeting at New Garden and Cane Creek in North Carolina" (**Text 3** herein), which was included in the *Journal*.[22]

In 1758 Woolman stayed close to home by limiting his travels to Friends' meetings in and around Philadelphia, absenting himself from family and business for only brief periods. In the time between the yearly meetings of 1758 and 1759, Woolman recorded in his *Journal* having made six visits in the homes of Friends "who had slaves." These visits were pursuant to the 1758 PYM Epistle described above, authorizing Woolman and four other Friends opposed to enslavement "to visit and treat" with those Quakers who held others in their power. On five such

---

[18] *Journal*, p. 54.
[19] *Ibid.*, p. 23.
[20] *Ibid.*, pp. 58-74.
[21] *Ibid.*, p. 64.
[22] *Ibid.*, pp. 67-69.

occasions Woolman was with one or more of his authorized colleagues; once he made the visit alone.[23]

In 1759 Woolman again stayed near home and limited his travels to Friends in Philadelphia, in Salem, New Jersey, and in Bucks County, Pennsylvania. And as in 1755 he again went to the yearly meeting held in Philadelphia with grave concerns about the French and Indian War and armed with a draft epistle for the meeting to consider, revise, and adopt.[24] In what became the "Epistle from the 1759 Yearly Meeting of Friends for Pennsylvania and New-Jersey" (**Text 4** herein) he enumerated the calamities of the war visited upon Pennsylvania.

[M]any of our fellow subjects have suffered on and near our frontiers, some have been slain in battle, some killed in their houses and some in their fields, some wounded and left in great misery, and others separated from their wives and little children, who have been carried captives among the Indians. We have seen men and women who have been witnesses of these scenes of sorrow and, being reduced to want, have come to our houses asking relief.[25]

In 1760 Woolman was away from home between 17th day 4th month, and 10th day 8th month on the longest journey undertaken since his marriage. This travel, described in the whole of Chapter VII of the *Journal*, took him through northern New Jersey to Long Island and New England,[26] areas he had visited in 1747, similarly for four months. He recorded his concern that at Newport, Rhode Island "a large number of slaves were imported from Africa and then [put] on sale by a member of our Society. . .I saw that this trade was a great evil and tended to multiply troubles and bring distresses on the people in those parts."[27] He was moved to prepare an essay in the form of a petition to the legislature, and then to address the meeting for business of the Rhode Island Yearly Meeting. In the *Journal* he summarized his opening statement to the meeting as follows:

---

[23] *Ibid.*, pp. 94-97.
[24] Moulton, p. 295.
[25] *Journal*, p. 100.
[26] *Ibid.*, pp. 106-16.
[27] *Ibid.*, p. 109.

I have been under a concern for some time on account of the great number of slaves which are imported into this colony. I am aware that it is a tender point to speak to, but apprehend I am not clear in the sight of heaven without speaking to it. I have prepared an essay of a petition proposed, if way open, to be presented to the Legislature.[28]

In the end, he left the essay with Friends, for them to proceed as they determined, while he held private conversations with enslaving Friends in the area.

By November 1761 Woolman had completed the sequel to his great work on enslavement, "Considerations on Keeping Negroes: Part Second" (**Text 5** herein). His preserved correspondence at that time with Israel Pemberton, who was an influential friend of Woolman and a leading Quaker in Philadelphia,[29] shows how scrupulous Woolman was in having his work examined and approved by the Overseers of the Press of the Yearly Meeting. This essay builds on the initial essay and surely reflects the author's laborious experiences in both the second southern journey made in 1757 and the two New England journeys made in 1747 and 1760. As before, he adopts a formal writing style and makes many references to the Bible, most to the Old Testament and therein to the five books of Moses. He also makes chilling and extensive use of published firsthand accounts of the contemporaneous enslavement trade on the western coast of Africa. At the very end he wrote:

Negroes are our fellow creatures and their present condition among us requires our serious consideration. . . .[W]herever gain is preferred to equity, and wrong things publicly encouraged, to that degree that wickedness takes root and spreads wide among the inhabitants of a country, there is real cause for sorrow to all such whose love to mankind stands on a true principle and wisely consider the end and event of things.[30]

---

[28] *Ibid.*, p. 109.
[29] HSP: Pemberton Papers, Collection #484A, Vol. XV pp. 74, 111, 112. See also Gummere, pp. 348-49; Moulton, pp. 195-96.
[30] Text 5, par. 115.

Truth III: The humbled spirit of an exiled native people

In his *Journal* Woolman describes only short periods away from home for meetings with Friends from 1761 through early 1763. Then in 6ᵗʰ month 1763 he journeyed into northeastern Pennsylvania as far as Wyalusing to be among the Native Americans

> whose ancestors were the owners and possessors of the land where we dwell, and who for a very small consideration assigned their inheritance to us. . .³¹

It was a perilous time to be in that wilderness as Indians reportedly had taken an English fort at some "westward" place from where Woolman and his party were traveling and there was word that a number of English people had been slain and scalped. The people living not far from Wyalusing heard that "[i]t was war with the English."³² Yet Woolman's party pushed forward, he being concerned

> to spend some time with the Indians, that I might feel and understand their life and the spirit they live in, if haply I might receive some instruction from them, or they be in any degree helped forward by my following the leadings of Truth among them.³³

And he meditated upon "the alterations of the circumstances of the natives of this land since the coming in of the English."³⁴ As he noted, they had lost their lands near to the sea and the tidal rivers and thereby their access to fertile fishing and crop harvests; the wild game was now over-hunted; and the means of their subsistence, skins and furs, too often lost "in purchasing a liquor which tends to the ruin of them and their families."³⁵ Out of these meditations he gave voice to his prophetic understanding and anguish:

> My own will and desires being now very much broken and my heart with much earnestness turned to the Lord. . .I had

---

³¹ *Journal*, p. 122.
³² *Ibid.*, p. 129.
³³ *Ibid.*, p. 127.
³⁴ *Ibid.*, p. 128.
³⁵ *Ibid.*, p. 128.

a prospect of the English along the coast for upward of nine hundred miles where I have traveled. And the favorable situation of the English and the difficulties attending the natives in many places, and the Negroes, were open before me.[36]

Woolman began, probably later in 1763 after returning home from Wyalusing, to compose "A Word of Remembrance & Caution to the Rich &c" (**Text 6** herein). For one of the rare times in his writings Woolman numbered the chapters, and in Chapter XII he describes the situation of the natives of North America. The work, while formal in style, avoids citation to authority, even using scripture not by direct quotation but in Woolman's free paraphrase manner. It is a heartfelt work addressed not to the problems of Indians or enslaved Africans, but to poverty and to the misuse of wealth.

After completing this his longest essay the author then rested from his literary labors. He had, between 1746 and 1763, written six general essays and epistles in which he considered three of his major concerns about the future of American society. He had addressed the issue of enslavement in three of those works (Texts 1, 3, and 5). He had twice, in a time of war, given utterance on behalf of all Friends in Pennsylvania and New Jersey to the peace testimony (Texts 2 and 4). And he had, yet again, looked at the issues surrounding enslavement, added to it fresh considerations on the plight of disinherited Native Americans, and saw the whole as the impoverishment of non-English peoples by many colonists who were using power to accumulate wealth for themselves (Text 6). It would be approximately five years before he wrote again for the public.

The Entrepreneurial Woolman

While Woolman saw American colonial society through the lens of God's Truth, his prophetic inner spiritual vision did not blind him to the practical necessities of living in this world. Although he gave himself liberty to travel and to write, he depended entirely on his own resources for providing everything necessary to support his wife, his daughter, and himself. From the days of his commercial apprenticeship (and probably even from his childhood) he knew the importance for men of business to

---

[36] *Ibid.*, p. 128.

keep accurate books of account. Woolman the businessman kept such books, and four have survived.

These account books are preserved in the John Woolman Collection held by The Historical Society of Pennsylvania.[37] They span, with some gaps, his working life from 1743 to 1772. Herein the author recorded his life in business. The first is an untitled book recording day labor and tailoring work that Woolman performed, with the first entry made on the 8th month 21st day 1743 and the last on the 6th month 2nd day 1746. Each line showed, in the same order: date; then either "To work done for" or "To making [or mending or quilting or altering]" a named garment; then the customer's name; then whether paid in cash or "X" (presumably either an exchange or a charge to Woolman's credit); then the amount. Woolman's day labor rate almost always was 1 shilling 6 pence. The book was handmade by folding over white parchment sheets, each page having a width of 8 1/8 inches and a height of 6 ½ inches. It was covered with a blue parchment page of like dimensions and bound by stitching, presumably Woolman's handiwork, at the centerfold.

About the time Woolman made his last entry for day labor and tailoring in this small account book he turned it upside down and began using it to record his management of five estates in which he served, either alone or jointly with another, as the fiduciary of a decedent's assets. On the cover of this reversed book he wrote *John Woolman's Book of Executorship*. The estates were those of his sister Elizabeth, Thomas Shinn, Peter Fearon, Samuel Haines, and "Negro Maria." The entries began in 1746 and ended in 1765. For his fiduciary labors he was compensated for his time which he justified in such entries as "going to Haddonfield," "proving the Will," "collecting money from," "writing advertisements," "tracing lot lines," or "attendance at." For these labors he charged a day rate of four shillings or more.

There is a gap in Woolman's work record from 6th month 2nd day 1746, the date of the last entry in his initial small day labor and tailoring account book, to 4th month 20th day 1752, the first entry in his third preserved regular business account book. It is a bound hard cover volume that Woolman titled *Ledger B 1753* in which he entered running debits and credits in each customer's account. There is an alphabetical index of customers' surnames in the front but it is only for the letters F, S, R, and W, in that order. Notwithstanding, the customers debited and credited in

---

37 HSP: Collection #737, Boxes 1 & 2. See herein Appendix 1: A Guide to the Manuscripts of John Woolman's Literary Works, Personal Business Records, and Epistles from PYM to other yearly meetings.

these pages, including all six of his brothers, range the alphabet. The open double pages were numbered by Woolman consecutively in the upper right hand corner of the right side page only, and he numbered them from pages 2 to 40 and then from pages 199 to 244. The missing numbers are not explained even though the index refers to entries on pages from 41 to 198. Some customer entries commence with the notation "1753 To account from Book A fol [number]" but no Book, or Ledger, A has been found. Woolman's usual pattern for a client with many transactions was to show the customer's name and debits on the left page and credits, whether of cash payments, of labor done for Woolman or supplies provided to him, on the right page. The entries appear to have continued until 1768 when they ceased, at which time Woolman began to use the fourth and last of his surviving account books.

This fourth book was a large bound covered volume titled *John Woolman's Book 1769* (hereafter referred to as *Account Book 1769*) which, following a complete alphabetical index in the front, Woolman had paginated on the right side page only from 1 to 175. The account entries end at page 76; the subsequent pages are blank. This 1769 account book was continued in use by Woolman's son-in-law and agent, John Comfort, after Woolman left America, and even after his death.

It is *Ledger B 1753* that reveals both the extent to which Woolman had taken up general retailing and the variety of his merchandise, which included molasses and rum, hay, wood by the cord, meats, spices, tea, supplies and tools, utensils, cloth goods and sewing supplies, paper by the quire and parchment by the sheet. In it he also detailed, beginning in 1755, data concerning an orchard of fruit trees he planted [*Ledger B*, p. 217 reverse side]. Included in these accounts were the preparation of legal instruments such as leases, deeds, wills, and land surveys. There were also occasional charges for services such as "use of my meadow" and "pasturing your cow," and for labor such as ditching, grubbing, picking brush, thrashing, and plowing. And beginning in 1765 in *Ledger B 1753* and continuing in *Account Book 1769* there are a number of charges for "schooling thy child." While the 1753 and 1769 account books show that from about 1756 Woolman may have begun restricting his retail merchandising, he certainly did not end it.

Journeying Nearer Home, Muting the Written Word

After returning from the visit among Native Americans at Wyalusing Woolman undertook no travel further from home than Maryland until embarking for England. In some of those intervening years between 1763 and 1772 he traveled not at all. In other years he remained in New Jersey and the areas around Philadelphia. The furthest travel occurred when he made three consecutive springtime walking journeys into Maryland, beginning in 1766.

In the 5th month of 1766 he visited Friends in and around Wilmington, Delaware and went on from there to Maryland's Eastern Shore, traveling northerly from Choptank to Third Haven to Queen Anne. As he wrote in his *Journal*, before this visit he was moved

> to travel on foot. . .that by so traveling I might have a more lively feeling of the condition of the oppressed slaves, set an example of lowliness before the eyes of their masters, and be more out of the way of temptation to unprofitable familiarities.[38]

In the 4th month of 1767 he walked southwestwardly from Philadelphia to meetings at Nottingham and Little Britain in Pennsylvania and thence crossed the Susquehanna River into Maryland for meetings in the northern and western regions well beyond Baltimore.

And in the 5th month of 1768 he traveled not only without a horse but without a companion for thirty-seven days to attend the yearly meeting at West River, Maryland, located below Annapolis.

No published work resulted from any of the eight missionary journeys described in the *Journal* during this time. Indeed, the only preserved writings in the period following "A Word of Remembrance and Caution to the Rich" and before 1768, are some unpublished notes, fragments, and fair copies of letters (**Texts 7 B, C, and E** herein). Text 7 B, dated by Woolman in 1764, is his brief note of a dream about a peace mission he conducted while "on a religious visit beyond the sea." Visiting in one kingdom he became aware of preparations for war with its neighbor. Just as he met the neighboring chief man to "try to prevail on him to stop fighting," he awakened. Text 7 C consists of three long quotations Woolman has taken from his friend Anthony Benezet's *A Caution and Warning to Great Britain*, published in 1766, a collection of first hand accounts by observers of the trade in enslaving native people. After each quotation Woolman has added his own extensive commentary. It shows him wrestling with the horrors of enslavement, beginning with

---

[38] *Journal*, p. 145.

the natives' capture in Africa to their transportation and then to their hardship, misery, and death. Text 7 D is an undated fragment on patience and on trusting in God. Possibly part of an essay, it is another of the few times in his manuscripts Woolman has marked the beginning of a chapter or section. In this fragment, after two paragraphs on patience, the notation "V" precedes the last two paragraphs on trusting in God. Text 7 E consists of an undated letter of six paragraphs, numbered by Woolman, written to a "Beloved friend," on the presence of ostentatious wealth among Quakers; and another letter, dated in 1769, to "My dear friend," expressing concerns on the conduct "in our meeting of ministers and elders."

Thoughts of home and family—of keeping the eye "single" to God and therein finding the "true medium of labor," the right education of children, and the proper use of material things—seemed to engage his spiritual concern and became the subjects of his published work in 1768, "Considerations on Pure Wisdom, and Human Policy; on Labor; on Schools; and on the Right Use of the Lord's Outward Gifts" (**Text 8** herein). The opening words of the Introduction set forth his concern:

> My mind has often been affected with sorrow on account of the prevailing of that spirit, which leads from an humble waiting on the inward teaching of Christ, to pursue ways of living attended with unnecessary labor, and which draws forth the minds of many people to seek after outward power, and to strive for riches, which frequently introduce oppression, and bring forth wars and grievous calamities.

All the references in this essay are biblical and most are drawn from the New Testament. The work is an extended commentary on a verse in the General Epistle of James, which is the source of the title:

> But the wisdom that is from above is first pure, then peaceable, gentle, and easy to be intreated, full of mercy and good fruits, without partiality, and without hypocrisy.[39]

Woolman had written an additional chapter for "Considerations on Pure Wisdom, &c." but its inclusion was deferred by the Overseers of the Press. Entitled "Serious Considerations on Trade" (**Text 9** herein) it

---

[39] James 3:17.

survived separately among Woolman's holographs but was not published until 1922.

The *Journal* reveals Woolman's concerns beginning in 1769 regarding "a visit to some part of the West Indies."[40] The concerns continue into 1770 when he almost took passage to Barbados[41] but which in the end, and after much distress, he did not.

> I felt what I esteemed a fresh confirmation that it was the Lord's will that I should pass through some further exercises near home. So I went home and still felt like a sojourner with my family. . .[42]

Some of these exercises concerned his health. After a few weeks at home he was stricken with pleurisy, and in that bodily distress contemplated his own death.[43] Even before that time he had been concerned with "a lump gathering on my nose" and as a result of dieting to relieve the condition he had grown weak in body.[44]

An important ministry keeping Woolman close to Mount Holly in the years from 1765 to 1769—but nowhere mentioned in his *Journal*—was giving instruction to the young. He "schooled" children, even boarding some, during those years, and entered the charges in his business records, *Ledger B 1753* and *Account Book 1769*. An outgrowth of this ministry was his major—and only known—publication during that time, the children's primer, *A First Book for Children*. (**Text 10** herein). It was first printed and sold by no later than 1769 as witnessed by Woolman debiting that year in *Account Book 1769* the sale of six copies to his brother Abraham. Today, the only known copy is of the third edition which is held in the Library of Friends House, London.

In the last month of 1770 Woolman published another work on Christian ethics, this one entitled "Considerations on the True Harmony of Mankind & how it is to be maintained" (**Text 11** herein).[45] It was divided into four chapters, the author's headings well describing the contents: on serving the Lord in our outward employments; on the example of Christ;

---

[40] *Journal*, p. 153.
[41] *Ibid.*, pp. 155-56.
[42] *Ibid.*, pp. 158-59.
[43] *Ibid.*, pp. 159, 185.
[44] *Ibid.*, p. 155.
[45] It appears this manuscript also was approved by the Overseers of the Press. See Gummere, pp. 438, 440.

on merchandizing; and on divine admonitions. The themes and treatment were familiar, but the growing wealth, materialism, and ostentation in his church and society, especially in the face of the enslavement, impoverishment, and territorial displacement he had witnessed and prophetically spoken to, seemed to bring Woolman to a new level of despair. He voiced it in the final paragraph of the work (Ch. IV, par. 8):

When blood shed unrighteously remains unatoned for, and the inhabitants are not effectually purged from it, when they do not wash their hands in innocency. . .but seek for gain arising from scenes of violence and oppression, "here the land is polluted with blood." Moreover when the earth is planted and tilled and fruits brought forth are applied to support unrighteous purposes, here the gracious design of infinite goodness, in these his gifts being perverted, the earth is defiled; and the complaint formerly uttered becomes applicable: "Thou hast made me to serve with thy sins, thou hast wearied me with thine iniquities" (Isa. 43:24).

The *Journal* makes no reference either to the children's primer or the work on the true harmony of mankind. And in the most significant omission of all, the *Journal* moves directly from the end of chapter 10 (an account of a dream in the 5th month of 1770) to the beginning of chapter 11 (late in the 4th month of 1772 when Woolman is considering boarding the *Mary and Elizabeth*, the vessel which will convey him to England). During the almost two years not mentioned in this journaling gap between chapters 10 and 11 Woolman experienced fresh and major changes in his personal life, after which he began a rush of literary activity and planning that signaled his departure on the final journey.

Death and New Life

The year 1771 brought several major family events to Woolman, the first an occasion of joy, the others of sorrow. On 6 May his only child, Mary, was married to John Comfort, a Friend from Bucks County, Pennsylvania. The groom, a farmer and the eldest of nine children, moved to Mount Holly following the marriage and farmed there until the death in 1787 of Sarah Woolman, Mary's widowed mother. Thereupon John and Mary Woolman Comfort, with their children (in all they had ten, born between 1772 and 1794), returned to the Comfort family farm in Pennsylvania.

On 9 October 1771 came the death of Peter Harvey (1721-1771), Woolman's first cousin and a fellow minister in the Society of Friends. His mother, Elizabeth Woolman Harvey, was the first Woolman born in America and the eldest of the journalist's five paternal aunts. The final entry made by Woolman in his *Journal*[46] (dated 9th month 28th day 1772 and signed by him after dictation) related to a dream told him by "[a]n honest-hearted Friend in America, who departed this life a little less than a year ago." Henry Cadbury has identified this Friend as Peter.[47] Woolman wrote a memorial minute on Peter's death in which he stated "I was twice with him in his last sickness."

And then on 4 November 1771 Woolman's brother Abner (1724-1771) died after a long illness during which John had often been at his bedside. The journalist even wrote the final entries in the testament which Abner had been composing, in which he expressed a father's loving thoughts for his children as he neared his life's end.[48] Abner was survived by four children, two of whom John had "schooled" and "boarded," as shown in his account books. Two years after the birth and death of Woolman's only son, William, in 1754, Abner's second oldest son, John Aaronson Woolman, was born. The close affection the journalist felt for this young man is evident in the letter he addressed "For John Woolman, Junr." written six days after Woolman arrived in London in June 1772:

I have often felt tender desires that my cousin, John Woolman, may be preserved in a watchful frame of mind, and know that which supports innocent young people against the snares of the wicked.

The deep trials of thy Father and his inward care for you are often in my remembrance, with some concern that you, his children, may be acquainted with that inward life to which his mind, whilst among us, was often gathered.

John Woolman

---

[46] Gummere, pp. 191-92.
[47] Henry J. Cadbury, *John Woolman in England 1772: A documentary supplement* (Supplement No. 31 to the Journal of the Friends Historical Society, London, 1971), p. 112.
[48] See Appendix Text 11 herein.

In the early months of 1772 Woolman was stirred into what must have been unremitting literary activity, impressive both for its volume as well as for his references—albeit guarded—to very personal matters. He prepared a memorial concerning Abner which he addressed to the Meeting for Sufferings at Philadelphia. In it he included two "pieces" by Abner as well as Abner's testament to his children, a work of which John may have been the principal author. (**Appendix Text 11** herein). It was simply dated "1772"—and the entire submission was in John's hand.

In the 3rd month of 1772 he wrote "Conversations on the True Harmony of Mankind & how it may be promoted" (**Text 12** herein) in which he continued the themes of his earlier work, "Considerations on the True Harmony of Mankind & how it is to be maintained" (see Text 11). "Conversations," as the title indicates, is in dialogue form and consists of two discussions by a "laboring man" (who rings of Woolman himself) with, first, a "man rich in money," and then with a "thrifty land-holder." The discussions, reflecting on the economic hardships endured by the poor in Woolman's day, are direct, honest, and without heat. In paragraph 15 is this heart-felt passage:

I have known grain and hay so scarce that I could not any where near get so much as my family and creatures had need of, being then sparing in feeding our cow she has grown poor. In her pineing condition she has called aloud, I knew her voice, and the sound thereof was the cry of hunger. I have known snowy stormy weather of long continuance. I have seen poor creatures in distress for want of good shelter and plentiful feeding when it did not appear to be in the power of their owners to do much better for them, being straitened in answering the demands of the wealthy.

In the 4th month of 1772 he wrote "An Epistle to the Quarterly and Monthly Meetings of Friends" (**Text 13** herein) in which he expressed his concerns for the state of what he called the "visible gathered church" among Friends. At the time of writing Woolman would surely have known that his daughter was expecting her first child and his thoughts on his role in the succession of the generations may have informed this passage in paragraph 18:

My mind is often (drawn) towards children in the Truth. . .
The thoughts of such being entangled with customs

(contrary to pure wisdom) conveyed to them through our hands, does often very tenderly and movingly affect my heart; while I look towards and think on a succeeding generation, fervent desires are raised in me that yielding to that Holy Spirit which leads into all Truth, may not do the work of the Lord deceitfully, may not live against the purity of our own principles, but as faithful laborers in our age, may be instrumental in removing stumbling blocks out of the way of such who may succeed us.

And in reflecting on the religious liberty which the Friends in America had obtained through the "great and manifold afflictions of those who lived before us" he reminded his readers in paragraph 35: "There is gratitude due from us to our heavenly Father. There is justice due to our posterity."

Additionally, in the early months of 1772, before his departure for England, Woolman had three important personal matters to care for. In the 4ᵗʰ month he placed in the hands of John Comfort, his son-in-law, *Account Book 1769* which contained the record of all of Woolman's outstanding business credits and debits with others. It was, indeed, the record of his own and his family's ongoing livelihood. On the first page, which had theretofore been blank, he wrote:

All due to me from people on Accompt I commit to the Care of John Comfort to him to collect the same in a neighborly way and apply it to the use of my Wife and his Wife and the rest of our Family, as he may find Occasion.
4ᵗʰ month 1772   John Woolman

And on the 27ᵗʰ day of the 4ᵗʰ month of 1772, within a week before his departure for England, Woolman executed and delivered to Stephen Comfort, the father of his son-in-law, a deed of trust whereby he conveyed the ownership of all of his lands, buildings, and improvements "in trust for my use and for the use of my beloved wife Sarah during the time that we and the survivor of us may live in this world." In the deed he wrote:

(H)aving it in my heart to prepare for a voyage to Great Britain on a religious visit [I] do not see any way in which I may dispose of the lands and buildings which I possess more to my own peace than to commit them to the said Stephen Comfort.

Woolman further directed that Stephen:

> may convey or devise all the lands which I now possess to his son John or to our daughter Mary or to either of them and to their heirs and assigns forever as he in the fear of the Lord may believe right.

The third care was the disposition of the final manuscript of his *Journal*. Since 1770 Woolman had been revising it and preparing a clean copy for eventual publication.[49] In the period prior to his departure he "sealed up" that and "some other manuscripts" and directed them to his friend John Pemberton for safekeeping during his absence abroad.[50]

The draught to the North

On 1 May Woolman sailed from Chester, Pennsylvania—just below Philadelphia on the Delaware River—aboard the *Mary and Elizabeth*, for London, England, where he disembarked on 8 June. He traveled the entire way in steerage with the crew. Until his death in York on 7 October, just four months after his arrival in England, he walked northwards making missionary visits among Friends. Meanwhile at home, his first grandchild, John Comfort, was born on 20 June.

During the period Woolman was at sea and in England, he completed several short writings. These last chapters (**Text 14** herein) were first printed, with some of his earlier works, in London in 1773 under the collective title "Remarks on Sundry Subjects" given them by their Quaker publisher, Mary Hinde.

In Chapter I, "On loving our neighbors as ourselves," come these two paragraphs (50 and 51) on wealth and the burdens of maintaining luxurious living, subjects of intense concern for Woolman beginning with his first printed work:

> Many are the vanities and luxuries of the present age, and in laboring to support a way of living conformable to the

---

[49] See Moulton, pp. 273, 283-84.
[50] See Appendix 2, Reformers of the mid-eighteenth century American Quaker Church: Israel Pemberton, Jr. and John Woolman, at p. 236.

present world the departure from that wisdom that is pure and peaceable has been great.

Under the sense of a deep revolt and an overflowing stream of unrighteousness my life has been often a life of mourning, and tender desires are raised in me that the nature of this practice may be laid to heart.

Chapter I concludes with this paragraph (104), which must have had personal resonance for Woolman at the time he wrote it:

Where customs contrary to pure wisdom are transmitted to posterity it appears to be an injury committed against them, and I often feel tender compassion toward a young generation and desires that their difficulties may not be increased through unfaithfulness in us of the present age.

+++

Notwithstanding all of Woolman's written labors, in the end we are left with the questions of why did he make this pilgrimage to England, especially at such a significant time in his life? What was he seeking? Why did he not express his purpose in the *Journal*, or elsewhere? Or did he explain himself, somewhere in his writings, even guardedly?

There can only be tentative answers. Surely his spirit was heavy because of the recent deaths in his generation of Abner Woolman and Peter Harvey, even though the generation of his grandchildren, bringing the promise of new life, was just commencing. And surely his spirit was afflicted because he had been witness for so long to the sufferings of the enslaved at the hands of their 'owners', to the impoverishment of Native Americans after trading their land and cultural heritage for European 'superfluities', and to the scourge of the colonists' wars brought into the American wilderness. He said so in the *Journal* when he reported his decision given to the owner of the *Mary and Elizabeth* that he would travel in steerage and not in the cabin so as not to support the expense of the "carved work and imagery. . .[and the] superfluity of workmanship":

I told the owner that I had at several times in my travels seen great oppressions on this continent, at which my heart had been much affected and brought into a feeling of the state of the sufferers.[51]

---

[51] *Journal*, pp. 164-65.

And surely his spirit needed renewal at the source where his religious society drew its strength. The account of Woolman's final illness, kept by those who cared for him in York, indicates as much. One week before he died he said he had long wanted to visit England and he reported a past dream

> in which he saw himself in the northern parts of it, and that the spring of the gospel was opened in him much as in the beginning of Friends. . .At another time said, "My draught seemed strongest to the north, and I mentioned in my own Monthly Meeting that attending the Quarterly Meeting at York, and being there, looked like home to me."[52]

It is also likely that his earthly spirit was wearied to death by all the human unwisdom and disharmony he had witnessed in both America and England, and that at the last he felt himself, a sojourning prophet, ready to return to the Truth, his real home.

Eleven days before Woolman died, he asked a Friend to record this deathbed prayer:

> O Lord my God! The amazing horrors of darkness were gathered around me and covered me all over, and I saw no way to go forth. I felt the depth and extent of the misery of my fellow creatures separated from the divine harmony, and it was heavier than I could bear, and I was crushed down under it. I lifted up my hand and I stretched out my arm, but there was none to help me. I looked around and was amazed in the depths of misery, O Lord!. . .[53]

2
Woolman's Holographs[54]

John Woolman's great gift to his own age and to ours was the body of his literary work in which he recorded his spiritual insights into the relationship between Truth and the human condition. In writing at the

---

[52] *Ibid.*, p. 304.
[53] Moulton, pp. 302-03.
[54] For the following MSS references, see Appendix 1: A Guide to the Manuscripts of John Woolman's Literary Works, Personal Business Records, and Epistles from PYM to other yearly meetings.

time that condition was being shaped and given custom and institutional structure in colonial America, Woolman also recorded the plasticity of the historical moment—and evidenced his personal courage in showing a wiser and more harmonious path to follow. Yet he made no collection, nor kept either formal records or files, of his literary work. It is doubtful he even preserved copies of all his writings in view of the several orphaned fragments that have been found. He appointed no literary executor, and made no testamentary provision for any of his property other than his lands, buildings, and accounts receivable. No discrete testamentary disposition was made of his books, papers, personal effects, or household goods. Except for the manuscripts left with John Pemberton or with the first printer, presumably all others remained in his home and with his widow.

Even the provisions that Woolman made for the ownership of his lands and buildings in the deed of trust appointing Stephen Comfort as trustee came close to being frustrated, for Comfort himself died in December, only weeks after John's death in York. However, in late September 1772 Comfort, "being sick and weak in body yet sound [in] mind and memory", made his own Last Will and Testament. In it he provided:

> I give and bequeath unto my son John Comfort and Mary his wife to them their heirs and assigns forever all that Estate of John Woolman lying in the Jerseys or anywhere else, that I have any right to by will or otherwise.[55]

John and Mary continued living in Mount Holly until the death of Sarah Woolman, the journalist's widow and Mary's mother, in March 1787. There it was that their first seven children—all sons—were born, and that two of them died. In November 1785 Sarah Woolman executed her own Will[56] in which, after the gifts of her wearing apparel to her daughter and of her chest of drawers to John Comfort, her first grandson and the only one born in Woolman's lifetime, she left the rest of her estate "wheresoever to be found" to five grandsons whom she named. They were John, Stephen, Samuel, William, and Joseph Comfort. William died in 1786, after Sarah made her Will but before her own death. And she omitted naming Ira, who was born in 1785. Whatever books, papers, holographs, and other evidence of Woolman's literary work remained at the death of

---

55 Gummere, p. 605.
56 Copy found at Gummere, pp. 606-07.

Sarah, by virtue of her Will or of family possession—more likely both— came into the ownership of, and were to be divided with all the other assets equally among, share and share alike, the four surviving Comfort brothers whom Sarah had named: John, Stephen, Samuel, and Joseph. There was provision that their respective shares not be paid until each attained the age of twenty-one years, and contingencies were provided for in the event any of them died before that age.

In time some, and perhaps all, of the Woolman holographs held by the descendants of the Comfort family were gifted to learned institutions, thereby making the works available for public research. The first gift was made in 1912 to The Historical Society of Pennsylvania by Major Samuel Comfort, the grandson of that Samuel Comfort who was the third-born of Woolman's grandsons. The gift included MSS A, 1A, 1B, 3, some of Woolman's correspondence, and other miscellaneous family items. In the following year Major Comfort's first cousin, Elizabeth Comfort Lawrence Dudley, a great-great-granddaughter of Woolman, made a gift of MSS B, C, M, P, S, S1, and other brief manuscripts, correspondence, and miscellaneous papers to Friends Historical Library at Swarthmore College on behalf of herself and of members of the Wharton and Dudley families. In 1929 Mrs. Dudley's daughter gave a statement to Swarthmore in which she noted that Woolman's grandson Samuel Comfort

> was the one who remained in the family [i.e. Mount Holly] home and raised his children there. In the next generation Samuel's son, George, likewise remained in the home and raised his family there, so that the Woolman papers came directly to Samuel Comfort's children. . . This brother and sister inherited all the Woolman manuscripts, which were divided between the two.[57]

Some Woolman holographs were received by learned institutions from sources other than the Comfort family. By 1975 Philadelphia Yearly Meeting had sent all of its records, in which were some Woolman holographs, to the archives of the Friends Historical Library of Swarthmore College and the Quaker Collection of Haverford College.[58] In 1927 J. Wilmer Lundy, a Quaker businessman and writer who was born

---

[57] See letter of Florence Elizabeth Dudley Wharton dated December 10, 1929, in the Swarthmore College FHL Correspondence files, Series 1, Box 2.

[58] Guide, p. vi. Thus it was that Appendix Texts 1 through 11 came to the Quaker Collection at Haverford College.

and raised in Rancocas, New Jersey, the place of the original proprietary seat of the Woolman family in America, gave MS 2 to The Historical Society of Pennsylvania. In 1936 Rutgers University acquired, by purchase from a dealer, MSS R1, R2, and R3, the only Woolman holographs now known to be in a public institution in the journalist's home state. And about 1970 there was discovered, in private hands, MS W which was, through the offices of Henry J. Cadbury, deposited in Haverford College's Quaker Collection.

Some Woolman holographs cannot now be located. These are the manuscripts for "Some Considerations on the Keeping of Negroes" (**Text 1** herein), "Considerations on Keeping Negroes: Part Second"(**Text 5** herein), "Considerations on Pure Wisdom, and Human Policy; etc." (**Text 8** herein), *A First Book for Children* (**Text 10** herein), and [The final essays, written at sea and in England] (**Text 14** herein). Further, while the holographs for the peace epistles which Woolman authored on behalf of the PYM Meeting of Ministers and Elders and of PYM (**Texts 2** and **4** herein) are missing, he wrote directions to the printer in MS B of the *Journal* where to insert the PYM printed texts. And the personal epistle he wrote to the Monthly Meeting at New Garden and Cane Creek, North Carolina (**Text 3** herein), although lost, was copied in his own hand into MS B of the *Journal*. The holographs of Texts 1, 5, and 8 having been submitted to the Overseers of the Press for their approval and thereafter sent to the printers, probably were never returned to the author. And strangely, not only is the holograph of Text 10 missing, there is but one known printed copy extant—and that of the 3rd edition.

For several of the texts there are multiple and variant holographs. Moulton has explained this in detail as to the *Journal* itself.[59] The same phenomenon is found in the case of **Text 6** herein, which in one holograph (that used in this edition) is titled "A Word of Remembrance & Caution to the Rich &c" and in another (that used in Moulton) is titled "A Plea for the Poor."

3
This Edition

The primary reason for bringing forth this new edition of John Woolman's general writings (other than the *Journal*) is the need in these troubled years at the beginning of the twenty-first century for concerned

---

[59] Moulton, pp. 283-87.

people everywhere to have the texts of all of Woolman's works available for studying his written understanding of Truth in relationship to the human condition. The interrelated problems of enslavement, impoverishment, and war which Woolman witnessed and spent his life addressing in colonial America have only grown larger and become increasingly compounded in the United States and the world beyond its borders in the more than 235 years since his death.

This edition gathers into one convenient volume and in chronological order all of the known essays, epistles, and other works which Woolman intended for general readers. While some, but not all, of the essays have been published at various times, and while several of the epistles in the Texts have been incorporated into printed versions of the *Journal*, most of the ephemera in Texts 7 A, B, C, D, E, and F have never before been published and the children's primer in Text 10, as well as all eleven of the Appendix texts, have barely been known in modern times. Further, by placing this body of Woolman's literary work in chronological order, the development of his thought in the context of his life experiences seems best revealed. The editor's introduction to each of the texts is intended to explain the context for each work in its historical moment.

One of the joys of reading Woolman is for the sweetness and simplicity of his prose style. He wrote with an eloquent honesty rooted in both his personal integrity and his ongoing and passionate, spiritual conversation with God. The God with whom Woolman conversed was the Truth as revealed in holy scripture. Woolman intimately knew the Old and New Testaments and in his writings either quoted from them exactly (often giving the citation to the Authorized, or King James, Version) or paraphrased them. Woolman's style could be formal and biblical; it could also be warm and personal. Always it was direct and unaffected, grounded in the Holy Spirit.

Notwithstanding the gracefulness of his prose, for the twenty-first century reader there are some eighteenth century problems to be overcome in Woolman's manuscripts. A recent biographer of Woolman's younger contemporary Thomas Paine described such problems thus:

> Writers of the eighteenth century did not believe that consistency in spelling, capitalization, punctuation, or italics was a mark of literacy. I have used modern versions of their work so that today's reader will not imagine them

fusty, old-fashioned, or poorly educated, opinions that would have horrified them.[60]

To which should be added that the quaintness of Woolman's seeming idiosyncrasies should not be allowed to distract the reader from the profound relevance of his message to our times. In any event, the richness of his holographs can only be known in a facsimile edition, and even then one would miss the texture and aroma of the papers and, in some instances, the hand-stitched binding, which undoubtedly was the work of the tailor of Mount Holly himself.

The texts in this edition are newly transcribed from Woolman's known holographs. Except in the case of **Text 10,** for those texts without holographs, the first printed versions have been revised to the extent that the following general rules of revision could be used. These rules have been applied to repair certain peculiar usages—as well as ambiguous or hasty penmanship—found in Woolman's texts. The intention has been to apply all these rules consistently across all the texts herein so as to render them more accessible to twenty-first century readers.

Capitalization. Initial capital letters have been used for all divine names, e.g. God, Christ, Holy Spirit; and for Truth when used in Woolman's special sense of God in his pure wisdom and true harmony as revealed in the Bible.

Citations. Woolman's citations of biblical and other authorities have been left 'as is' and 'in place'; and in every instance they are in parentheses, whether Woolman used parentheses, brackets, or neither.

Grammar. Except for subject-verb agreement, no attempt has been made to repair any grammatical issues, not even that of long run-on, yet incomplete, sentences.

Paragraphing. Identifying paragraphs is a major issue when reading the holographs because Woolman variously marked their beginnings—sometimes by indentation, sometimes by skipping space on the same line where the last paragraph ended and the next began, and sometimes by

---

[60] Craig Nelson, *Thomas Paine: Enlightenment, Revolution and the Birth of Modern Nations* (New York: Viking, 2006), unnumbered front page captioned "A Note."

just running-on. His paragraphing is problematical and thus becomes a matter of editorial judgment. It has also seemed important to supply numbers to the paragraphs for ease of reference. Woolman himself numbered paragraphs only once (for **Text 9** herein), and even his numbering of chapters (found only in **Texts 6, 7 E, and 11** herein) was rare.

Parentheses and brackets. Throughout the texts all parentheses now contain Woolman's work; all brackets contain editorial matter.

Punctuation. The use of colons, semicolons, and periods has been conformed to modern style.

Spelling. Modern American, rather than colonial British, usage has been used, resulting in, e.g., labor, 'honor', etc. rather than 'labour', 'honour', etc.; 'among', 'while', etc. rather than 'amongst', 'whilst', etc.; 'has', 'says', etc. rather than 'hath', 'saith', etc.

4
References and Abbreviations

Journal	All references to the Journal of John Woolman are to be found in *The Journal and Major Essays of John Woolman*, ed. Phillips P. Moulton (Richmond, Ind.: Friends United Press, 1971)

+

Guide	*Guide to the Records of Philadelphia Yearly Meeting*, comp. Jack Eckert (Philadelphia: Haverford College, Records Committee of Philadelphia Yearly Meeting, Swarthmore College, 1989)
Gummere	*The Journal and Essays of John Woolman*, ed. Amelia Mott Gummere (New York: Macmillan Co., 1922)
Marietta	Jack D. Marietta, *The Reformation of American Quakerism, 1748-1783* (Philadelphia: University of Pennsylvania Press, 1984)
Michener	Ezra Michener, *A Retrospect of Early Quakerism* (Philadelphia, T. Ellwood Zell, 1860; reprinted Washington, D.C., Cool Spring Pub. Co., 1991)
Moulton	*The Journal and Major Essays of John Woolman*, ed. Phillips P. Moulton (Richmond, Ind.: Friends United Press, 1971)
Smith	Joseph Smith, *A Descriptive Catalogue of Friends' Books*, 2 vols. (London: J. Smith, 1867)

+

HC	Haverford College Quaker Collection, Haverford College, Haverford, PA
HSP	The Historical Society of Pennsylvania, Philadelphia, PA
MM	Monthly Meeting
PYM	Philadelphia Yearly Meeting of the Society of Friends (Quakers). In Woolman's time the formal title was "The General Yearly Meeting for Friends of Pennsylvania, East and West Jersey, and of the adjacent Provinces".[61]
QM	Quarterly Meeting

---

[61] Michener, p. 24.

SC   Swarthmore College Friends Historical Library,
          Swarthmore College, Swarthmore, PA

Abbreviated Bible references

OLD TESTAMENT		NEW TESTAMENT	
Gen.	Genesis	Matt.	Matthew
Exod.	Exodus	Rom.	Romans
Lev.	Leviticus	1 Cor.	1 Corinthians
Num.	Numbers	2 Cor.	2 Corinthians
Deut.	Deuteronomy	Gal.	Galatians
Josh.	Joshua	Eph.	Ephesians
Judg.	Judges	Phil.	Philippians
1 Chron.	1 Chronicles	Col.	Colossians
Neh.	Nehemiah	1 Tim.	1 Timothy
Ps.	Psalms	Heb.	Hebrews
Prov.	Proverbs	1 Pet.	1 Peter
Eccles.	Ecclesiastes	Rev.	Revelation
Isa.	Isaiah		
Jer.	Jeremiah		
Lam.	Lamentations		
Ezek.	Ezekiel		
Hos.	Hosea		
Jon.	Jonah		
Mic.	Micah		
Nah.	Nahum		
Hab.	Habakkuk		
Zeph.	Zephaniah		
Zech.	Zechariah		
Mal.	Malachi		

Some Considerations on the Keeping of Negroes

Written 1746; 1st printed 1754

Editor's Introduction

"Some Considerations on the Keeping of Negroes" was John Woolman's initial major writing. He composed the essay in 1746 after returning from his first visit as a recorded missionary to Friends outside New Jersey. The journey, made with his fellow Quaker minister and Mount Holly neighbor Isaac Andrews, began on 12th day, 3rd month, 1746. Together they traveled in Pennsylvania, Maryland, Virginia, and North Carolina before coming home three months and four days later, having covered approximately 1500 miles. Some ten years thereafter, when Woolman described this experience in the *Journal*[1] (which he began writing about 1756), he concluded with a concern about those "who lived in ease on the hard labor of their slaves," and with a prophetic view of the slave trade "as a dark gloominess hanging over the land . . . the consequence [of which] will be grievous to posterity!" It was, as he put it in the *Journal*, "a matter fixed on my mind."[2]

After completion Woolman showed the manuscript to his father, Samuel, who "proposed a few alterations." Samuel during his last illness in 1750, inquired when John expected to "offer it to the Overseers of the Press [of the Philadelphia Yearly Meeting]."[3] Further withholding the work until 1754—the delay from 1746 probably being due to Woolman's waiting for a change in the majority of the Overseers from slaveholders to abolitionists[4]—it was at last offered to these supervisors of publications

---

[1] *Journal*, pp. 36-38.
[2] Ibid., p. 38.
[3] Ibid., pp. 44-45.
[4] See herein Historical Notes: (1) The PYM Overseers of the Press in Table 3, pp. 246-48. See also Jean R. Soderlund, *Quakers and Slavery: A Divided Spirit* (Princeton: Princeton University Press, 1985), pp. 26-27, 32-35, 46.; and Gary B. Nash and Jean R. Soderlund, *Freedom by Degrees: Emancipation in Pennsylvania and its Aftermath* (New York: Oxford University Press, 1991), p. 51.

and after they "examined and made some small alterations in it" ordered it published.[5]

The essay, the holograph of which is missing,[6] was first printed in 1754 by James Chattin of Philadelphia; the following is based on that edition. In the same year PYM issued, and James Chattin printed, "An Epistle of Caution and Advice, Concerning the Buying and Keeping of Slaves" in which it addressed Friends on the evils of importing and buying Negro slaves and on the necessity of ending their bondage.[7]

+++

Text

Some Considerations on the Keeping of Negroes

Recommended to the Professors of Christianity of Every Denomination

Introduction

1   Customs generally approved and opinions received by youth from their superiors become like the natural produce of a soil, especially when they are suited to favorite inclinations. But as the judgments of God are without partiality, by which the state of the soul must be tried, it would be the highest wisdom to forego customs and popular opinions, and try the treasures of the soul by the infallible standard Truth.

2   Natural affection needs a careful examination. Operating upon us in a soft manner, it kindles desires of love and tenderness, and there is danger of taking it for something higher. To me it appears an instinct like that which inferior creatures have; each of them, we see, by the ties of

---

5 *Journal*, p. 47.
6 Moulton, p. 283.
7 While Moulton and other scholars hold that JW was the author of this PYM Epistle, there is indisputable evidence in the archived official record that the germinal idea for this Epistle was presented to Philadelphia Monthly Meeting by Anthony Benezet, that a committee of PMM worked for months to draft its "Epistle of Advice and Caution" [*sic*], that PMM presented it to Philadelphia QM which then, after its "solid consideration," presented it to PYM, which adopted it as its own and ordered it printed and distributed. The record does not name JW with the work. (See Appendix 2 herein, the 1754 chronological entries.)

nature love self best. That which is a part of self they love by the same tie or instinct. In them it in some measure does the offices of reason, by which, among other things, they watchfully keep and orderly feed their helpless offspring. Thus natural affection appears to be a branch of self-love, good in the animal race, in us likewise with proper limitations, but otherwise is productive of evil by exciting desires to promote some by means prejudicial to others.

3   Our blessed Savior seems to give a check to this irregular fondness in nature and, at the same time, a precedent for us: "Who is my mother, and who are my brethren?"—thereby intimating that the earthly ties of relationship are, comparatively, inconsiderable to such who, through a steady course of obedience, have come to the happy experience of the Spirit of God bearing witness with their spirits that they are his children: "And he stretched forth his hands towards his disciples and said, 'Behold my mother and my brethren; for whosoever shall do the will of my Father which is in heaven (arrives at the more noble part of true relationship) the same is my brother, and sister, and mother'" (Matt. 12:48[-50]).

4   This doctrine agrees well with a state truly complete, where love necessarily operates according to the agreeableness of things on principles unalterable and in themselves perfect.

5   If endeavoring to have my children eminent among men after my death be that which no reasons grounded on those principles can be brought to support, then to be temperate in my pursuit after gain and to keep always within the bounds of those principles is an indispensable duty, and to depart from it a dark unfruitful toil.

6   In our present condition, to love our children is needful; but except this love proceeds from the true heavenly principle which sees beyond earthly treasures, it will rather be injurious than of any real advantage to them. Where the fountain is corrupt, the streams must necessarily be impure.

7   That important injunction of our Savior (Matt. 6:33), with the promise annexed, contains a short but comprehensive view of our duty and happiness. If then the business of mankind in this life is to first seek another, if this cannot be done but by attending to the means, if a summary of the means is not to do that to another which (in like circumstances) we would not have done unto us, then these are points of moment and worthy of our most serious consideration.

8   What I write on this subject is with reluctance, and the hints given are in as general terms as my concern would allow. I know it is a point about which in all its branches men that appear to aim well are not generally agreed, and for that reason I chose to avoid being very particular. If I may happily have let drop anything that may excite such as are concerned in the practice to a close thinking on the subject treated of, the candid among them may easily do the subject such further justice as, on an impartial enquiry, it may appear to deserve; and such an enquiry I would earnestly recommend.

Some Considerations on the Keeping of Negroes

Forasmuch as ye did it to the least of these
my brethren, ye did it unto me (Matt. 25:40).

1   As many times there are different motives to the same actions, and one does that from a generous heart which another does for selfish ends, the like may be said in this case.

2   There are various circumstances among them that keep Negroes, and different ways by which they fall under their care; and, I doubt not, there are many well-disposed persons among them who desire rather to manage wisely and justly in this difficult matter than to make gain of it.

3   But the general disadvantage which these poor Africans lie under in an enlightened Christian country having often filled me with real sadness, and been like undigested matter on my mind, I now think it my duty, through divine aid, to offer some thoughts thereon to the consideration of others.

4   When we remember that all nations are of one blood (Gen. 3:20); that in this world we are but sojourners; that we are subject to the like afflictions and infirmities of body, the like disorders and frailties in mind, the like temptations, the same death, and the same judgment; and that the All-wise Being is judge and Lord over us all, it seems to raise an idea of a general brotherhood and a disposition easy to be touched with a feeling of each other's afflictions. But when we forget those things and look chiefly at our outward circumstances, in this and some ages past, constantly retaining in our minds the distinction between us and them with respect to our knowledge and improvement in things divine, natural, and artificial, our breasts being apt to be filled with fond notions of superiority, there is danger of erring in our conduct toward them.

4

5   We allow them to be of the same species with ourselves; the odds are we are in a higher station and enjoy greater favors than they. And when it is thus that our heavenly Father endows some of his children with distinguished gifts, they are intended for good ends. But if those thus gifted are thereby lifted up above their brothers, not considering themselves as debtors to the weak nor behaving themselves as faithful stewards, none who judge impartially can suppose them free from ingratitude.

6   When a people dwell under the liberal distribution of favors from heaven, it behooves them carefully to inspect their ways and consider the purposes for which those favors were bestowed, lest through forgetfulness of God and misusing his gifts they incur his heavy displeasure, whose judgments are just and equal, who exalts and humbles to the dust as he sees meet.

7   It appears by Holy Record that men under high favors have been apt to err in their opinions concerning others. Thus Israel, according to the description of the prophet (Isa. 65:5), when exceedingly corrupted and degenerated, yet remembered they were the chosen people of God and could say, "Stand by thyself, come not near me, for I am holier than thou." That this was no chance language, but their common opinion of other people, more fully appears by considering the circumstances which attended when God was beginning to fulfill his precious promises concerning the gathering of the Gentiles.

8   The Most High, in a vision, undeceived Peter, first prepared his heart to believe, and at the house of Cornelius showed him of a certainty that God was no respecter of persons.

9   The effusion of the Holy Ghost upon a people with whom they, the Jewish Christians, would not so much as eat was strange to them. All they of the circumcision were astonished to see it, and the apostles and brothers of Judea contended with Peter about it, till he having rehearsed the whole matter and fully shown that the Father's love was unlimited, they are thereat struck with admiration and cry out, "Then hath God also to the Gentiles granted repentance unto life!" [Acts 11:18].

10   The opinion of peculiar favors being confined to them was deeply rooted, or else the above instance had been less strange to them, for these reasons: First, they were generally acquainted with the writings of the prophets, by whom this time was repeatedly spoken of and pointed at. Secondly, our blessed Lord shortly before expressly said, "I have other

sheep, not of this fold; them also must I bring," etc. [John 10:16]. Lastly, his words to them after his resurrection, at the very time of his ascension, "Ye shall be witnesses to me not only in Jerusalem, Judea, and Samaria, but to the uttermost parts of the earth" [Acts 1:8].

11   Those concurring circumstances, one would think, might have raised a strong expectation of seeing such a time. Yet when it came, it proved matter of offense and astonishment.

12   To consider mankind otherwise than brothers, to think favors are peculiar to one nation and exclude others, plainly presupposes a darkness in the understanding. For as God's love is universal, so where the mind is sufficiently influenced by it, it begets a likeness of itself and the heart is enlarged towards all men. Again, to conclude a people froward,[8] perverse, and worse by nature than others (who ungratefully receive favors and apply them to bad ends), this will excite a behavior toward them unbecoming the excellence of true religion.

13   To prevent such error let us calmly consider their circumstance, and, the better to do it, make their case ours. Suppose, then, that our ancestors and we had been exposed to constant servitude in the more servile and inferior employments of life; that we had been destitute of the help of reading and good company; that among ourselves we had had few wise and pious instructors; that the religious among our superiors seldom took notice of us; that while others in ease have plentifully heaped up the fruit of our labor, we had received barely enough to relieve nature, and being wholly at the command of others had generally been treated as a contemptible, ignorant part of mankind. Should we, in that case, be less abject than they now are? Again, if oppression be so hard to bear that a wise man is made mad by it (Eccles. 7:7), then a series of those things altering the behavior and manners of a people is what may reasonably be expected.

14   When our property is taken contrary to our mind by means appearing to us unjust, it is only through divine influence and the enlargement of heart from thence proceeding that we can love our reputed oppressors. If the Negroes fall short in this, an uneasy, if not a disconsolate, disposition will be awakened and remain like seeds in their minds, producing sloth and many other habits appearing odious to us, with which being free men they perhaps had not been chargeable. These and

---

[8] [Froward: to be obstinately willful and prone to disobedience.]

other circumstances, rightly considered, will lessen that too great disparity which some make between us and them.

15   Integrity of heart has appeared in some of them, so that if we continue in the word of Christ (previous to discipleship, John 8:31) and our conduct towards them be seasoned with his love, we may hope to see the good effect of it, the which, in a good degree, is the case with some into whose hands they have fallen. But that too many treat them otherwise, not seeming conscious of any neglect, is, alas! too evident.

16   When self-love presides in our minds our opinions are biased in our own favor. In this condition, being concerned with a people so situated that they have no voice to plead their own cause, there's danger of using ourselves to an undisturbed partiality till, by long custom, the mind becomes reconciled with it and the judgment itself infected.

17   To humbly apply to God for wisdom, that we may thereby be enabled to see things as they are and ought to be, is very needful; hereby the hidden things of darkness may be brought to light and the judgment made clear. We shall then consider mankind as brethren. Though different degrees and a variety of qualifications and abilities, one dependent on another, be admitted, yet high thoughts will be laid aside, and all men treated as becomes the sons of one Father, agreeable to the doctrine of Christ Jesus.

18

> He hath laid down the best criterion by which mankind ought to judge of their own conduct, and others judge for them of theirs, one towards another—viz., "Whatsoever ye would that men should do unto you, do ye even so to them." I take it that all men by nature are equally entitled to the equity of this rule and under the indispensable obligations of it. One man ought not to look upon another man or society of men as so far beneath him but that he should put himself in their place in all his actions towards them, and bring all to this test—viz., How should I approve of this conduct were I in their circumstance and they in mine?—Arscott's *Considerations*, Part III, Fol. 107.[9]

---

9   [The reference is to Alexander Arscott, *Some Considerations Relating to the Present State of the Christian Religion*, 3 parts (London: Sowle, 1730- 1734), Part III at p. 78.]

19 This doctrine, being of a moral unchangeable nature, has been likewise inculcated in the former dispensation: "If a stranger sojourn with thee in your land, ye shall not vex him; but the stranger that dwelleth with you shall be as one born amongst you, and thou shalt love him as thyself" (Lev. 19:33, 34). Had these people come voluntarily and dwelt among us, to have called them strangers would be proper. And their being brought by force, with regret and a languishing mind, may well raise compassion in a heart rightly disposed. But there is nothing in such treatment which upon a wise and judicious consideration will any ways lessen their right of being treated as strangers. If the treatment which many of them meet with be rightly examined and compared with those precepts, "Thou shalt not vex him nor oppress him; he shall be as one born amongst you, and thou shalt love him as thyself" (Lev. 19:33, [34]; Deut. 27:19), there will appear an important difference between them.

20 It may be objected there is cost of purchase and risk of their lives to them who possess them, and therefore needful that they make the best use of their time. In a practice just and reasonable such objections may have weight; but if the work be wrong from the beginning, there's little or no force in them. If I purchase a man who has never forfeited his liberty, the natural right of freedom is in him. And shall I keep him and his posterity in servitude and ignorance? How should I approve of this conduct were I in his circumstances and he in mine? It may be thought that to treat them as we would willingly be treated, our gain by them would be inconsiderable; and it were, in diverse respects, better that there were none in our country.

21 We may further consider that they are now among us and those of our nation the cause of their being here, that whatsoever difficulty accrues thereon we are justly chargeable with, and to bear all inconveniences attending it with a serious and weighty concern of mind to do our duty by them is the best we can do. To seek a remedy by continuing the oppression because we have power to do it and see others do it, will, I apprehend, not be doing as we would be done by.

22 How deeply soever men are involved in the most exquisite difficulties, sincerity of heart and upright walking before God, freely submitting to his providence, is the most sure remedy. He only is able to relieve not only persons but nations in their greatest calamities.

23 David, in a great strait when the sense of his past error and the full expectation of an impending calamity as the reward of it were united to the

aggravating his distress, after some deliberation, said, "Let me fall now into the hand of the Lord, for very great are his mercies; let me not fall into the hand of man" (1 Chron. 21:13).

24 To act continually with integrity of heart above all narrow or selfish motives is a sure token of our being partakers of that salvation which God has appointed for walls and bulwarks (Isa. [26:1]), and is, beyond all contradiction, a more happy situation than can ever be promised by the utmost reach of art and power united, not proceeding from heavenly wisdom.

25 A supply to nature's lawful wants, joined with a peaceful, humble mind, is the truest happiness in this life. And if here we arrive to this and remain to walk in the path of the just, our case will be truly happy. And though herein we may part with or miss of some glaring shows of riches and leave our children little else but wise instructions, a good example, and the knowledge of some honest employment, these, with the blessing of providence, are sufficient for their happiness, and are more likely to prove so than laying up treasures for them which are often rather a snare than any real benefit, especially to them who, instead of being exampled to temperance, are in all things taught to prefer the getting of riches and to eye the temporal distinctions they give as the principal business of this life. These readily overlook the true happiness of man as it results from the enjoyment of all things in the fear of God, and miserably substituting an inferior good, dangerous in the acquiring and uncertain in the fruition, they are subject to many disappointments; and every sweet carries its sting.

26 It is the conclusion of our blessed Lord and his apostles, as appears by their lives and doctrines, that the highest delights of sense or most pleasing objects visible ought ever to be accounted infinitely inferior to that real intellectual happiness suited to man in his primitive innocence and now to be found in true renovation of mind, and that the comforts of our present life, the things most grateful to us, ought always to be received with temperance and never made the chief objects of our desire, hope, or love, but that our whole heart and affections be principally looking to that city "which hath foundations, whose maker and builder is God" [Heb. 11:10]. Did we so improve the gifts bestowed on us that our children might have an education suited to these doctrines, and our example to confirm it, we might rejoice in hopes of their being heirs of an inheritance incorruptible.

27   This inheritance, as Christians, we esteem the most valuable; and how then can we fail to desire it for our children? Oh, that we were consistent with ourselves in pursuing means necessary to obtain it!

28   It appears by experience that where children are educated in fullness, ease, and idleness, evil habits are more prevalent than is common among such who are prudently employed in the necessary affairs of life. And if children are not only educated in the way of so great temptation, but have also the opportunity of lording it over their fellow creatures and being masters of men in their childhood, how can we hope otherwise than that their tender minds will be possessed with thoughts too high for them?— which by continuance, gaining strength, will prove like a slow current, gradually separating them from (or keeping from acquaintance with) that humility and meekness in which alone lasting happiness can be enjoyed.

29   Man is born to labor, and experience abundantly shows that it is for our good. But where the powerful lay the burden on the inferior, without affording a Christian education and suitable opportunity of improving the mind, and a treatment which we in their case should approve—that themselves may live at ease and fare sumptuously and lay up riches for their posterity—this seems to contradict the design of Providence and, I doubt [not], is sometimes the effect of a perverted mind. For while the life of one is made grievous by the rigor of another, it entails misery on both.

30   Among the manifold works of Providence displayed in the different ages of the world, these which follow (with many others) may afford instruction:

31   Abraham was called of God to leave his country and kindred, to sojourn among strangers. Through famine and danger of death he was forced to flee from one kingdom to another. He at length not only had assurance of being the father of many nations, but became a mighty prince (Gen. 23:6).

32   Remarkable were the dealings of God with Jacob in a low estate. The just sense he retained of them after his advancement appears by his words: "I am not worthy of the least of all thy mercies" (Gen. 32:10; 48:15).

33   The numerous afflictions of Joseph are very singular, the particular providence of God therein no less manifest. He at length became governor of Egypt and famous for wisdom and virtue.

34   The series of troubles David passed through, few among us are ignorant of; and yet he afterwards became as one of the great men of the earth.

35   Some evidences of the divine wisdom appear in those things, in that such who are intended for high stations have first been very low and dejected, that Truth might be sealed on their hearts, and that the characters there imprinted by bitterness and adversity might in after years remain, suggesting compassionate ideas and, in their prosperity, quicken their regard to those in the like condition, which yet further appears in the case of Israel. They were well acquainted with grievous sufferings, a long and rigorous servitude, then through many notable events were made chief among the nations. To them we find a repetition of precepts to the purpose above-said. Though for ends agreeable to infinite wisdom they were chosen as a peculiar people for a time, yet the Most High acquaints them that his love is not confined, but extends to the stranger, and to excite their compassion, reminds them of times past: "Ye were strangers in the land of Egypt" (Deut. 10:19). Again, "Thou shalt not oppress a stranger, for ye know the heart of a stranger, seeing ye were strangers in the land of Egypt" (Exod. 23:9).

36   If we call to mind our beginning, some of us may find a time wherein our fathers were under afflictions, reproaches, and manifold sufferings.

37   Respecting our progress in this land, the time is short since our beginning was small and number few, compared with the native inhabitants. He that sleeps not by day nor night has watched over us and kept us as the apple of his eye. His almighty arm has been round about us and saved us from dangers.

38   The wilderness and solitary deserts in which our fathers passed the days of their pilgrimage are now turned into pleasant fields. The natives are gone from before us, and we established peaceably in the possession of the land, enjoying our civil and religious liberties. And while many parts of the world have groaned under the heavy calamities of war, our habitation remains quiet and our land fruitful.

39   When we trace back the steps we have trodden and see how the Lord has opened a way in the wilderness for us, to the wise it will easily appear that all this was not done to be buried in oblivion, but to prepare a people for more fruitful returns, and the remembrance thereof ought to

humble us in prosperity and excite in us a Christian benevolence towards our inferiors.

40 If we do not consider these things aright, but through a stupid indolence conceive views of interest separate from the general good of the great brotherhood, and in pursuance thereof treat our inferiors with rigor, to increase our wealth and gain riches for our children, what then shall we do when God rises up; and when he visits, what shall we answer him? Did not he that made us make them, and "did not one fashion us in the womb?" (Job 31:14[-15]).

41 To our great Master we stand or fall [Rom. 14:4]; to judge or condemn is most suitable to his wisdom and authority. My inclination is to persuade and entreat, and simply give hints of my way of thinking.

42 If the Christian religion be considered, both respecting its doctrines and the happy influence which it has on the minds and manners of all real Christians, it looks reasonable to think that the miraculous manifestation thereof to the world is a kindness beyond expression.

43 Are we the people thus favored? Are we they whose minds are opened, influenced, and governed by the Spirit of Christ and thereby made sons of God? Is it not a fair conclusion that we, like our heavenly Father, ought in our degree to be active in the same great cause—of the eternal happiness of at least our whole families, and more, if thereto capacitated?

44 If we, by the operation of the Spirit of Christ, become heirs with him in the kingdom of his Father, and are redeemed from the alluring counterfeit joys of this world, and the joy of Christ remains in us, to suppose that one remaining in this happy condition can, for the sake of earthly riches, not only deprive his fellow creatures of the sweetness of freedom (which, rightly used, is one of the greatest temporal blessings), but therewith neglect using proper means for their acquaintance with the Holy Scriptures and the advantage of true religion, seems, at least, a contradiction to reason.

45 Whoever rightly advocates the cause of some thereby promotes the good of all. The state of mankind was harmonious in the beginning; and though sin has introduced discord, yet through the wonderful love of God in Christ Jesus our Lord, the way is open for our redemption, and means appointed to restore us to primitive harmony. That if one suffer by the unfaithfulness of another, the mind, the most noble part of him that occasions the discord, is thereby alienated from its true and real happiness.

46   Our duty and interest are inseparably united, and when we neglect or misuse our talents we necessarily depart from the heavenly fellowship and are in the way to the greatest of evils.

47   Therefore, to examine and prove ourselves, to find what harmony the power presiding in us bears with the divine nature, is a duty not more incumbent and necessary than it would be beneficial.

48   In Holy Writ the Divine Being says of himself, "I am the Lord, which exercise loving-kindness, judgment, and righteousness in the earth; for in these things I delight,' saith the Lord" (Jer. 9:24). Again, speaking in the way of man to show his compassion to Israel, whose wickedness had occasioned a calamity, and then being humbled under it, it is said, "His soul was grieved for their miseries" (Judg. 10:16). If we consider the life of our blessed Savior when on earth, as it is recorded by his followers, we shall find that one uniform desire for the eternal and temporal good of mankind discovered itself in all his actions.

49   If we observe men, both apostles and others in many different ages, who have really come to the unity of the Spirit and the fellowship of the saints, there still appears the like disposition; and in them the desire of the real happiness of mankind has out-balanced the desire of ease, liberty, and, many times, life itself.

50   If upon a true search we find that our natures are so far renewed that to exercise righteousness and loving-kindness (according to our ability) towards all men, without respect of persons, is easy to us or is our delight; if our love be so orderly and regular that he who does the will of our Father who is in heaven appears in our view to be our nearest relation, our brother and sister and mother; if this be our case, there is a good foundation to hope that the blessing of God will sweeten our treasures during our stay in this life, and our memory be savory when we are entered into rest.

51   To conclude, 'tis a truth most certain that a life guided by wisdom from above, agreeable with justice, equity, and mercy, is throughout consistent and amiable, and truly beneficial to society. The serenity and calmness of mind in it affords an unparalleled comfort in this life, and the end of it is blessed.

52   And, no less true, that they who in the midst of high favors remain ungrateful, and under all the advantages that a Christian can desire are selfish, earthly, and sensual, do miss the true fountain of happiness and

13

wander in a maze of dark anxiety, where all their treasures are insufficient to quiet their minds. Hence, from an insatiable craving, they neglect doing good with what they have acquired, and too often add oppression to vanity, that they may compass more.

Oh, that they were wise, that they understood this, that they would consider their latter end! (Deut. 32:29).

THE END

An Epistle from our General Spring Meeting of Ministers and Elders, etc., 1755. To Friends on the Continent of America

Written 1755; 1st printed 1755

Editor's Introduction

Beginning in the spring of 1754, "[f]rom a disagreement between the powers of England and France, it was now a time of trouble on this continent."[1] That "trouble" was the French and Indian War, the last of the four major colonial wars in North America among the British and the French and their respective Native American allies. The war began in western Pennsylvania and in its first season was limited to engagements there. By the war's end seven engagements had been fought in that area but the theater had expanded into upper New York and eastern Canada. Most of the fighting ended in September 1760 with the French surrender of Montreal—and thereby all of Canada—to the British. Hostilities were formally ended with the Treaty of Paris in September 1763 by which France lost all of its continental North American possessions east of the Mississippi River save for the islands of St. Pierre and Miquelon off the southern coast of Newfoundland in the Gulf of St. Lawrence and at the gateway to the fisheries of the Grand Banks.

At the General Spring Meeting of Quaker Ministers and Elders for Pennsylvania and New Jersey held in 1755, the issues raised by this importation of European wars into these Quaker colonies were of high concern. Woolman wrote in early drafts of his *Journal* (but later edited out):

> It came upon me to write an epistle to Friends, the which I took to our General Spring Meeting and proposed to some elderly Friends to have it inspected and signed by a number of brethren in behalf of the meeting, which, with some amendments, was agreed to . . .[2]

---

[1] *Journal*, p. 47.
[2] *Ibid.*, p. 48, footnote 9.

Prior to this moment in history, the Quaker peace testimony in Pennsylvania had been given in an era of peace. That era was suddenly gone and Woolman needed to frame a doctrine proclaiming the peace testimony in a time of war and of war's uncertainty. Penn's territory, a Quaker historian wrote,

had been stained by the blood of the battle-field; and now that the desolations of war had actually entered the province, the cry for means of defense became loud and overwhelming. Quaker principles were denounced as visionary and absurd; and, taking advantage of this state of things, the war party, at the election which followed in 1756, carried twenty-four out of the thirty-six representatives which composed the Assembly. From this date Pennsylvania ceased to be governed in accordance with the principles of the Society of Friends. It was now no longer the Arcadia of peace.[3]

For Woolman it was clear that God alone "rules in the army of heaven, and in the kingdoms of men" and that there must be "a faithful continuance to depend wholly upon the almighty arm" in order to establish the peaceable kingdom.[4]

The Epistle published by the meeting was "signed in and on [its] behalf" by fourteen Friends, of which Woolman was one. The holograph of this document is missing, and in MS B of the *Journal*, after the address "To Friends on the Continent of America," Woolman has written "here add the Epistle," presumably referring to the printed version issued by the meeting. The following text is the editor's modernization of that officially issued version, in which the biblical references were in the margin, not in the text.

---

3 James Bowden, *The History of the Society of Friends in America*, 2 vols. (London: W. & F. G. Cash, 1854), Vol. II at p. 161.
4 Woolman directly addressed the issues raised by the French and Indian War in two more writings: his unpublished 1756 "Ephemera: untitled parable on 'a tax demanded for evil ends'" (Text 7 A herein), and his 1759 PYM epistle (Text 4 herein). Additionally, one hears his authorial voice within the 1755 "An Epistle of Tender Love and Caution to Friends in Pennsylvania" of which he was a signer and the text of which he included in the *Journal* (at pp. 85-86). (See Appendix 2 herein, the 1755 chronological entries.)

+++
Text

An Epistle from our General Spring Meeting of Ministers and Elders for Pennsylvania and New-Jersey, held at Philadelphia, from the 29ᵗʰ of the Third Month, to the 1st of the Fourth Month, inclusive, 1755.

To Friends on the Continent of America

Dear Friends,

1   In an humble sense of divine goodness, and the gracious continuation of God's love to his people, we tenderly salute you; and are at this time therein engaged in mind, that all of us who profess the Truth, as held forth and published by our worthy predecessors in this latter age of the world, may keep near to that life which is the light of men, and be strengthened to hold fast the profession of our faith without wavering, that our trust may not be in man, but in the LORD alone, who rules in the army of heaven, and in the kingdoms of men, before whom the earth is *as the dust of the balance, and her inhabitants as grasshoppers* (Isa. 40:[15,]22).

2   We (being convinced that the gracious design of the Almighty in sending his Son into the world, was to repair the breach made by disobedience, to finish sin and transgression, that his kingdom might come, and his will be done on earth as it is in heaven) have found it to be our duty to cease from those national contests productive of misery and bloodshed, and submit our cause to him the Most High, whose tender love to his children exceeds the most warm affections of natural parents, and who has promised to his seed throughout the earth, as to one individual, *I will never leave thee, nor forsake thee* (Heb. 13:5). And as we, through the gracious dealings of the LORD our God, have had experience of that work which is carried on, *not by earthly might, nor power, but by my spirit, saith the Lord of hosts* (Zech. 4:6): by which operation that spiritual kingdom is set up, which is to subdue and break in pieces all kingdoms that oppose it, and shall stand for ever. In a deep sense thereof, and of the safety, stability and peace there is in it, we are desirous that all who profess the Truth, may be inwardly acquainted with it, and thereby be qualified to

conduct in all parts of our life as becomes our peaceable profession: And we trust, as there is a faithful continuance to depend wholly upon the almighty arm, from one generation to another, the peaceable kingdom will gradually be extended *from sea to sea, and from the river to the ends of the earth* (Zech. 9:10), to the completion of those prophecies already begun, that *nation shall not lift up sword against nation, nor learn war any more* (Isa. 2:4; Mic. 4:3).

3   And, dearly beloved Friends, seeing we have these promises, and believe that God is beginning to fulfill them, let us constantly endeavor to have our minds sufficiently disentangled from the surfeiting cares of this life, and redeemed from the love of the world, that no earthly possessions nor enjoyments may bias our judgments, or turn us from that resignation, and entire trust in God, to which his blessing is most surely annexed; then may we say, *Our redeemer is mighty, He will plead our cause for us* (Jer. 50:34). And if, for the further promoting his most gracious purposes in the earth, he should give us to taste of that bitter cup which his faithful ones have often partook of, O that we may be rightly prepared to receive it!

4   And now dear Friends, with respect to the commotions and stirrings of the powers of the earth at this time near us, we are desirous that none of us may be moved thereat; "But repose ourselves in the munition of that rock that all these shakings shall not move, even in the knowledge and feeling of the eternal power of God keeping us subjectly given up to his heavenly will, and feel it daily to mortify that which remains in any of us which is of this world: For the worldly part in any, is the changeable part, and that is up and down, full and empty, joyful and sorrowful, as things go well or ill in this world; for as the Truth is but one, and many are made partakers of its spirit, so the world is but one, and many are made partakers of the spirit of it, and so many as do partake of it, so many will be straitened and perplexed with it; but they who are single to the Truth, waiting daily to feel the life and virtue of it in their hearts, these shall rejoice in the midst of adversity,"5 and have to experience with the prophet, that, *Although the fig tree shall not blossom, neither shall fruit be in the vines, the labor of the olive shall fail, and the fields shall yield no meat, the flock shall be cut off from the fold, and there shall be no herd in the stalls, yet will they rejoice in the LORD, and joy in the GOD of their salvation* (Hab. 3:17,18).

---

5 [Stephen Crisp (1628-1692), "An Epistle to Friends concerning the present and succeeding times" (London: 1666), p. 22.]

5   If, contrary to this, we profess the Truth and not living under the power and influence of it are producing fruits disagreeable to the purity thereof, and trust to the strength of man to support ourselves, therein our confidence will be vain. For he, who removed the hedge from his vineyard and gave it to be trodden under foot by reason of the wild grapes it produced (Isa. 5[:1-7]), remains unchangeable: And if for the chastisement of wickedness and the further promoting his own glory he does arise, even to shake terribly the earth, who then may oppose him, and prosper!

We remain, in the love of the gospel, your friends and brethren.

Signed in and on behalf of our said meeting,
By

Jacob Howell,	John Evans,
James Bartram,	Mordecai Yarnall,
Joseph White,	Daniel Stanton,
John Scarbrough,	John Churchman.
John Woolman,	William Morris,
Josiah Foster,	Isaac Andrews,
Joseph Tomlinson,	Samuel Abbott.

3

To Friends at their Monthly Meeting at New Garden and Cane[1] Creek in North Carolina

Written 1757; 1st printed 1774

Editor's Introduction

In the Spring of 1757, "[f]eeling an exercise in relation to a visit to the southern parts to increase upon me,"[2] Woolman set out on his second missionary journey to Maryland, Virginia, and North Carolina. His companion was his brother Uriah, the fourth of seven brothers, John being the eldest. John had scrupled whether to accept Uriah's proposal that they travel together because Uriah "had a view of some outward affairs."[3] Uriah had business to attend to in North Carolina, while John's concern in this journey was the plight of the enslaved. As he expressed it, he needed to "attend with singleness of heart to the voice of the True Shepherd"[4] while traveling among the oppressed and their oppressors. When the brothers had been out about a month and were attending the Virginia Yearly Meeting near Norfolk, John wrote this epistle to Friends "in the back settlements of North Carolina."[5] Several days after the letter was written, the brothers parted company, Uriah joining "with some Friends from New Garden who were going homeward. . ."[6] Presumably they carried the epistle home with them to New Garden (near Greensboro). As John noted at journey's end, he had been "out about two months and rode about 1150 miles."[7]

This pastoral epistle, which Woolman incorporated into his *Journal*,[8] was written to a meeting of Quakers who were building a new community in a wilderness too far away for him to visit. The letter, although brief, is filled with his gentle, loving advice that they live in humility, shun the

---

[1] In MS B at p. 121 JW has spelled the place name "Cain."
[2] *Journal*, p. 58.
[3] *Ibid.*
[4] *Ibid.*, p. 59.
[5] *Ibid.*, p. 67.
[6] *Ibid.*, p. 70.
[7] *Ibid.*, p. 74 footnote 29.
[8] *Ibid.*, pp. 67-69.

pursuit of wealth, care for each other, help the youth preserve the ornament of virtue, set wise customs as they improve the wilderness, avoid the purchase of slaves, and that they pass on to their successors the blessings God has bestowed on them. "Dwell here, my dear Friends, and then in remote and solitary deserts you may find true peace and satisfaction."[9]

The author's holograph of this document is found in MS B (at pp. 121-27) of the *Journal* and the following revision is based thereon.

+++

Text

To Friends at their Monthly Meeting at New Garden and Cane Creek in North Carolina

Dear Friends,

1   It having pleased the Lord to draw me forth on a visit to some parts of Virginia and Carolina you have often been in my mind, and though my way is not clear to come in person to visit you, yet I feel it in my heart to communicate a few things as they arise in the love of Truth. First, my dear Friends, dwell in humility and take heed that no views of outward gain get too deep hold of you, that so your eyes being single to the Lord you may be preserved in the way of safety.

2   Where people let loose their minds after the love of outward things and are more engaged in pursuing the profits and seeking the friendships of this world than to be inwardly acquainted with the way of true peace, such walk in a vain shadow while the true comfort of life is wanting. Their examples are often hurtful to others, and their treasures thus collected do many times prove dangerous snares to their children.

3   But where people are sincerely devoted to follow Christ and dwell under the influence of his Holy Spirit, their stability and firmness through a divine blessing is at times like dew on the tender plants round about them, and the weightiness of their spirits secretly works on the minds of others; and in this condition, through the spreading influence of divine love, they feel a care over the flock and way is opened for maintaining good

---

[9] Par. 10.

order in the Society. And though we meet with opposition from another spirit, yet as there is a dwelling in meekness, feeling our spirits subject and moving only in the gentle, peaceable wisdom, the inward reward of quietness will be greater than all our difficulties. Where the pure life is kept to and meetings of discipline are held in the authority of it, we find by experience that they are comfortable and tend to the health of the body.

4   While I write, the youth comes fresh in my way. Dear young people, choose God for your portion; love his Truth and be not ashamed of it. Choose for your company such who serve him in uprightness, and shun as most dangerous the conversation of those whose lives are of an ill savor; for by frequenting such company some hopeful young people have come to great loss and been drawn from less evils to greater, to their utter ruin. In the bloom of youth no ornament is so lovely as that of virtue, nor any enjoyments equal to those which we partake of in fully resigning ourselves to the divine will. These enjoyments add sweetness to all other comforts and give true satisfaction in company and conversation where people are mutually acquainted with it, and as your minds are thus seasoned with the Truth you will find strength to abide steadfast to the testimony of it and be prepared for services in the church.

5   And now, dear Friends and brethren, as you are improving a wilderness and may be numbered among the first planters in one part of a province, I beseech you in the love of Jesus Christ to wisely consider the force of your examples and think how much your successors may be thereby affected. It is a help in a country, yea, a great favor and a blessing, when customs first settled are agreeable to sound wisdom; so when they are otherwise, the effect of them is grievous, and children feel themselves encompassed with difficulties prepared for them by their predecessors.

6   As moderate care and exercise under the direction of true wisdom is useful both to mind and body, so by this means in general the real wants of life are easily attained,[10] our gracious Father having so proportioned one to the other that keeping in the true medium we may pass on quietly. Where slaves are purchased to do our labor, numerous difficulties attend it. To rational creatures bondage is uneasy and frequently occasions sourness and discontent in them, which affects the family and such who claim the mastery over them, and thus people and their children are many

---

[10]   [In the holograph the word "supplied" is written above the word "attained" which is not stricken.]

times encompassed with vexations which arise from their applying to wrong methods to get a living.

7   I have been informed that there are a large number of Friends in your parts who have no slaves, and in tender and most affectionate love I beseech you to keep clear from purchasing any. Look, my dear Friends, to divine providence, and follow in simplicity that exercise of body, that plainness and frugality which true wisdom leads to; so may you be preserved from those dangers which attend such who are aiming at outward ease and greatness.

8   Treasures though small, attained on a true principle of virtue are sweet in the possession, and while we walk in the light of the Lord there is true comfort and satisfaction. Here neither the murmurs of an oppressed people, nor throbbing, uneasy conscience, nor anxious thoughts about the event of things hinder the enjoyment of it.

9   When we look toward the end of life and think on the division of our substance among our successors, if we know that it was collected in the fear of the Lord, in honesty, in equity, and in uprightness of heart before him, we may consider it as his gift to us and with a single eye to his blessing bestow it on those we leave behind us. Such is the happiness of the plain ways of true virtue. The work of righteousness shall be peace, and the effect of righteousness quietness and assurance forever (Isa. 32:17).

10   Dwell here, my dear Friends, and then in remote and solitary deserts you may find true peace and satisfaction. If the Lord be our God in Truth and reality, there is safety for us; for he is a stronghold in the day of trouble, and knows them that trust in him [Nah. 1:7].

Isle of Wight County in Virginia
29th day 5th month 1757

4

From our Yearly Meeting held at Philadelphia, for Pennsylvania and New-Jersey, from the 22ᵈ Day of the Ninth Month, to the 28ᵗʰ of the same (inclusive) 1759.

To the Quarterly and Monthly Meetings of Friends belonging to the said Yearly Meeting

Written 1759; 1ˢᵗ printed 1759

Editor's Introduction

Shortly before attending the 1759 Yearly Meeting for Friends in Pennsylvania and New Jersey held in Philadelphia, Woolman was moved to draft his second major epistle regarding the issues raised by the French and Indian War (1754-1763). Although the Friends attending this meeting could not know it, no further battles of that conflict were to be fought on the soil of Pennsylvania. At the time they met, however, Penn's Quaker plantation had already suffered greatly: the war had begun in the western part of the province; the prior year's campaign season had finished with two engagements around Pittsburgh; and, except for 1757, western Pennsylvania had endured and suffered in every year of the war. Those attending this yearly meeting undoubtedly were concerned about the calamities already experienced within Pennsylvania's borders, calamities that Woolman describes in this epistle.

The author had his work "examined and corrected by the committee on the epistle, [and] signed by a number of Friends in behalf of the Meeting . . ."[1] With typical modesty, Woolman was not one of the seven signatories.

The holograph of this document is missing. However, in MS B of the *Journal*[2] just after the comment "An epistle went forth from this Yearly Meeting which I thought good to give a place in this Journal, which is as

---

[1] Moulton, p. 295.
[2] MS B, p. 77.

follows:", Woolman has written: "here take in the printed Epistle of 1759." The following text is the editor's modernization of the printed version issued by the Meeting.

+++
Text

From our Yearly Meeting held at Philadelphia, for Pennsylvania and New-Jersey, from the 22ᵈ Day of the Ninth Month, to the 28ᵗʰ of the same (inclusive) 1759.

To the Quarterly and Monthly Meetings of Friends belonging to the said Yearly Meeting

Dearly beloved Friends and Brethren;

1 In an awful sense of the wisdom and goodness of the Lord our God, whose tender mercies have long been continued to us in this land, we affectionately salute you, with sincere and fervent desires, that we may reverently regard the dispensations of his providence and improve under them.

2 The empires and kingdoms of the earth are subject to his almighty power; he is the God of the spirits of all flesh, and deals with his people agreeable to that wisdom, the depth whereof is to us unsearchable. We in these provinces may say he has, as a gracious and tender parent, dealt bountifully with us, even from the days of our fathers. It was he who strengthened them to labor through the difficulties attending the improvement of a wilderness and made way for them in the hearts of the natives, so that by them they were comforted in times of want and distress. It was by the gracious influences of his Holy Spirit that they were disposed to work righteousness and walk uprightly one towards another and towards the natives, and in life and conversation to manifest the excellency of the principles and doctrines of the Christian religion, and thereby they retained their esteem and friendship. While they were laboring for the

necessaries of life, many of them were fervently engaged to promote piety and virtue in the earth and educate their children in the fear of the Lord.

3   If we carefully consider the peaceable measures pursued in the first settlement of the land, and that freedom from the desolations of war which for a long time we enjoyed, we shall find ourselves under strong obligations to the Almighty who, when the earth is so generally polluted with wickedness, gave us a being in a part so signally favored with tranquility and plenty, and in which the glad tidings of the gospel of Christ are so freely published, that we may justly say with the Psalmist, *"What shall we render unto the Lord for all His benefits?"* [Ps. 116:12].

4   Our own real good and the good of our posterity in some measure depends on the part we act, and it nearly concerns us to try our foundations impartially. Such are the different rewards of the just and unjust in a future state that to attend diligently to the dictates of the Spirit of Christ, to devote ourselves to his service and engage fervently in his cause, during our short stay in this world, is a choice well becoming a free intelligent creature. We shall thus clearly see and consider that the dealings of God with mankind in a national capacity, as recorded in Holy Writ, do sufficiently evidence the truth of that saying, *"it is righteousness which exalteth a nation"* [Prov. 14:34], and although he does not at all times suddenly execute his judgments on a sinful people in this life, yet we see many instances that where *"men follow lying vanities they forsake their own mercies"* [Jon. 2:8], and as a proud selfish spirit prevails and spreads among a people, so partial judgment, oppression, discord, envy, and confusions increase, and provinces and kingdoms are made to drink the cup of adversity as a reward of their own doings. Thus the inspired prophet reasoning with the degenerated Jews says, *"Thine own wickedness shall correct thee and thy backslidings shall reprove thee; know therefore that it is an evil thing and bitter, that thou hast forsaken the Lord thy God, and that my fear is not in thee, saith the Lord of Hosts"* (Jer. 2:19).

5   The God of our fathers who has bestowed on us many benefits, furnished a table for us in the wilderness and made the deserts and solitary places to rejoice, he does now mercifully call upon us to serve him more faithfully. We may truly say with the Prophet, *"it is his voice which cries to the city, and men of wisdom see his name: they regard the rod and him who has appointed it"* [Mic. 6:9]. People who look chiefly at things outward, too little consider the original cause of the present troubles, but such who fear the Lord and think often upon his name, they see and feel

26

that a wrong spirit is spreading among the inhabitants of our country; that the hearts of many are waxed fat and their ears dull of hearing, that the Most High in his visitations to us, instead of calling, he lifts up his voice and cries; he cries to our country and his voice waxes louder and louder. In former wars between the English and other nations, since the settlement of our provinces, the calamities attending them have fallen chiefly on other places, but now of late they have reached to our borders; many of our fellow subjects have suffered on and near our frontiers, some have been slain in battle, some killed in their houses, and some in their fields, some wounded and left in great misery, and others separated from their wives and little children, who have been carried captives among the Indians. We have seen men and women who have been witnesses of these scenes of sorrow, and being reduced to want, have come to our houses asking relief. It is not long since it was the case of many young men in one of these provinces to be drafted, in order to be taken as soldiers; some were at that time in great distress and had occasion to consider that their lives had been too little conformable to the purity and spirituality of that religion which we profess, and found themselves too little acquainted with that inward humility, in which true fortitude to endure hardness for the Truth's sake is experienced. Many parents were concerned for their children and in that time of trial were led to consider that their care to get outward treasure for them had been greater than their care for their settlement in that religion which crucifies to the world, and enables to bear a clear testimony to the peaceable government of the Messiah. These troubles are removed and for a time we are released from them.

6   Let us not forget that the Most High has his way in the deep, in clouds and in thick darkness, that it is his voice which cries to the city and to the country, and Oh! that these loud and awakening cries may have a proper effect upon us, that heavier chastisement may not become necessary! For although things as to the outward may for a short time afford a pleasing prospect, yet while a selfish spirit that is not subject to the Cross of Christ continues to spread and prevail, there can be no long continuance in outward peace and tranquility. If we desire an inheritance incorruptible and to be at rest in that state of peace and happiness, which ever continues; if we desire in this life to dwell under the favor and protection of that Almighty Being, whose habitation is in holiness, whose ways are all equal and whose anger is now kindled because of our backslidings—let us then awfully regard these beginnings of his fore judgments, and with abasement and humiliation turn to him, whom we have offended.

7   Contending with one equal in strength is an uneasy exercise, but if the Lord is become our enemy, if we persist to contend with him who is omnipotent, our overthrow will be unavoidable.

8   Do we feel an affectionate regard to posterity and are we employed to promote their happiness? Do our minds in things outward look beyond our own dissolution, and are we contriving for the prosperity of our children after us? Let us then like wise builders lay the foundation deep, and by our constant, uniform regard to an inward piety and virtue, let them see that we really value it; let us labor in the fear of the Lord that their innocent minds, while young and tender, may be preserved from corruptions, that as they advance in age they may rightly understand their true interest, may consider the uncertainty of temporal things, and above all have their hope and confidence firmly settled in the blessing of that Almighty Being who inhabits eternity and preserves and supports the world.

9   In all our cares about worldly treasures let us steadily bear in mind that riches possessed by children, who do not truly serve God, are likely to prove snares that may more grievously entangle them in that spirit of selfishness and exaltation which stands in opposition to real peace and happiness, and renders them enemies to the Cross of Christ, who submit to the influence of it.

10   To keep a watchful eye towards real objects of charity, to visit the poor in their lonesome dwelling places, to comfort them who through the dispensations of divine providence are in strait and painful circumstances in this life, and steadily to endeavor to honor God with our substance from a real sense of the love of Christ influencing our minds thereto, is more likely to bring a blessing to our children and will afford more satisfaction to a Christian favored with plenty, than an earnest desire to collect much wealth to leave behind us, for *here we have no continuing city* [Heb. 13:14], may we therefore diligently *seek one that is to come whose builder and maker is God* [Heb. 11:10].

11   *Finally, Brethren, whatsoever things are True, whatsoever things are Just, whatsoever things are Pure, whatsoever things are Lovely, whatsoever things are of good Report; if there be any Virtue, if there be*

any Praise, think on these things and do them, and the God of Peace shall be with you [Phil. 4:8-9].[3]

Signed by appointment and on behalf of our said Meeting by

MORDECAI YARNALL,
THOMAS MASSEY,
JOHN CHURCHMAN,
JOHN SCARBOROUGH,
PETER FEARON,
THOMAS EVANS,
JOSEPH PARKER.

---

[3] [The capitalizations are those of the draftsman.]

5

Considerations on Keeping Negroes
Part Second

Completed 1761; 1ˢᵗ printed 1762

Editor's Introduction

"Considerations on Keeping Negroes: Part Second" was Woolman's second major essay. Finished in 1761 and printed in 1762, here he continues the subject of Text 1, which had been published eight years earlier and was grounded in the experience of his 1746 missionary journey into the slaveholding provinces of Virginia and North Carolina. In this second part the author concludes that the institution of enslavement is stopping up "channels of justice" in the land and that it "stands in opposition to the God of love and spreads discord, trouble, and vexation."[1]

By the time he wrote this essay Woolman not only had made the second of his two missionary journeys into Maryland, Virginia, and North Carolina (in 1757) but had also witnessed trading in, and owning of, the enslaved in New England (on journeys made in 1747 and 1760). As before, he observed the hardships imposed on African natives by their American—including Quaker—"owners," and felt the burden to speak God's Truth to those who gained by such oppression.

The original holograph of this essay is missing.[2] The work was reviewed by the PYM Overseers of the Press and then printed in Philadelphia at the author's expense, not that of the yearly meeting, Woolman having scruples that some Friends would not be comfortable with his arguments and therefore should not involuntarily pay for "books being spread amongst a people where many of the slaves are learned to read, and especially not at their [the owners'] expense."[3]

The following text is the editor's modernization of the 1762 first printing made in Philadelphia by B. Franklin and D. Hall.

---

[1] Par. 114.
[2] Moulton, p. 283.
[3] *Journal*, pp. 117-18.

+++
Text

Considerations on Keeping Negroes

Recommended to the Professors of Christianity of Every Denomination

PART SECOND

> Ye shall not respect persons in judgment, but you shall hear the small as well as the great. You shall not be afraid of the face of man, for the judgment is God's (Deut. 1:17).

The Preface

1   All our actions are of like nature with their root, and the Most High weighs them more skillfully than men can weigh them one from another.

2   I believe that one Supreme Being made and supports the world, nor can I worship any other deity without being an idolater and guilty of wickedness.

3   Many nations have believed in and worshipped a plurality of deities, but I do not believe they were therefore all wicked. Idolatry indeed is wickedness, but it is the thing, not the name, which is so. Real idolatry is to pay that adoration to a creature which is known to be due only to the true God.

4   He who professes to believe in one Almighty Creator and in his son Jesus Christ, and is yet more intent on the honors, profits, and friendships of the world than he is in singleness of heart to stand faithful to the Christian religion is in the channel of idolatry, while the Gentile who under some mistaken opinions is notwithstanding established in the true principle of virtue, and humbly adores an almighty power, may be of that number who fear God and work righteousness.

5   I believe the Bishop of Rome assumes a power that does not belong to any officer in the church of Christ; and if I should knowingly do

anything tending to strengthen him in that capacity it would be great iniquity. There are many thousands of people who by their profession acknowledge him to be the representative of Jesus Christ on earth, and to say that none of them are upright in heart would be contrary to my sentiments.

6   Men who sincerely apply their minds to true virtue and find an inward support from above by which all vicious inclinations are made subject, that they love God sincerely and prefer the real good of mankind universally to their own private interest, though these through the strength of education and tradition may remain under some speculative and great errors, it would be uncharitable to say that therefore God rejects them. He who creates, supports, and gives understanding to all men, his knowledge and goodness is superior to the various cases and circumstances of his creatures which to us appear the most difficult.

7   The apostles and primitive Christians did not censure all the Gentiles as wicked men (Rom. 2:14; Col. 3:[11]), but as they were favored with a gift to discern things more clearly respecting the worship of the true God, they with much firmness declared against the worshipping of idols and with true patience endured many sufferings on that account.

8   Great numbers of faithful Protestants have contended for the Truth in opposition to papal errors and with true fortitude laid down their lives in the conflict, without saying that no man was saved who made profession of that religion.

9   While we have no right to keep men as servants for term of life but that of superior power, to do this with design by their labor to profit ourselves and our families I believe is wrong. But I do not believe that all who have kept slaves have therefore been chargeable with guilt. If their motives thereto were free from selfishness and their slaves content, they were a sort of freemen, which I believe has sometimes been the case.

10   Whatever a man does in the spirit of charity, to him it is not sin; and while he lives and acts in this spirit, he learns all things essential to his happiness as an individual. And if he does not see that any injury or injustice to any other person is necessarily promoted by any part of his form of government, I believe the merciful Judge will not lay iniquity to his charge. Yet others who live in the same spirit of charity from a clear convincement may see the relation of one thing to another and the necessary tendency of each, and hence it may be absolutely binding on

32

them to desist from some parts of conduct which some good men have been in.

Considerations on Keeping Negroes, &c.

1   As some in most religious Societies among the English are concerned in importing or purchasing the inhabitants of Africa as slaves, and as the professors of Christianity of several other nations do the like, these circumstances tend to make people less apt to examine the practice so closely as they would if such a thing had not been, but was now proposed to be entered upon. It is, however, our duty and what concerns us individually, as creatures accountable to our Creator, to employ rightly the understanding which he has given us, in humbly endeavoring to be acquainted with his will concerning us and with the nature and tendency of those things which we practice. For as justice remains to be justice, so many people of reputation in the world joining with wrong things do not excuse others in joining with them nor make the consequence of their proceedings less dreadful in the final issue than it would be otherwise.

2   Where unrighteousness is justified from one age to another, it is like dark matter gathering into clouds over us. We may know that this gloom will remain till the cause be removed by a reformation or change of times and may feel a desire, from a love of equity, to speak on the occasion; yet where error is so strong that it may not be spoken against without some prospect of inconvenience to the speaker, this difficulty is likely to operate on our weakness and quench the good desires in us, except we dwell so steadily under the weight of it as to be made willing to endure hardness on that account.

3   Where men exert their talents against vices generally accounted such, the ill effects whereof are presently perceived in a government, all men who regard their own temporal good are likely to approve the work. But when that which is inconsistent with perfect equity has the law or countenance of the great in its favor, though the tendency thereof be quite contrary to the true happiness of mankind in an equal, if not greater, degree than many things accounted reproachful to Christians, yet as these ill effects are not generally perceived, they who labor to dissuade from such things which people believe accord with their interest have many difficulties to encounter.

4   The repeated charges which God gave to his prophets imply the danger they were in of erring on this hand: "Be not afraid of their faces; for

33

I am with thee to deliver thee, saith the Lord" (Jer. 1:8). "Speak . . . all the words that I command thee to speak to them, diminish not a word" (Jer. 26:2). "And thou, son of man, be not afraid of them . . . nor dismayed at their looks. Speak my words to them, whether they will hear or forbear" (Ezek. 2:6[-7]).

5   Under an apprehension of duty, I offer some further considerations on this subject, having endeavored some years to consider it candidly. I have observed people of our own color whose abilities have been inferior to the affairs which relate to their convenient subsistence, who have been taken care of by others, and the profit of such work as they could do applied toward their support. I believe there are such among Negroes and that some people in whose hands they are keep them with no view of outward profit, do not consider them as black men who, as such, ought to serve white men, but account them persons who have need of guardians, and as such take care of them. Yet where equal care is taken in all parts of education, I do not apprehend cases of this sort are likely to occur more frequently among one sort of people than another.

6   It looks to me that the slave trade was founded and has generally been carried on in a wrong spirit, that the effects of it are detrimental to the real prosperity of our country, and will be more so except we cease from the common motives of keeping them and treat them in future agreeable to Truth and pure justice.

7   Negroes may be imported who, for their cruelty to their countrymen and the evil disposition of their minds, may be unfit to be at liberty; and if we, as lovers of righteousness, undertake the management of them, we should have a full and clear knowledge of their crimes and of those circumstances which might operate in their favor; but the difficulty of obtaining this is so great that we have great reason to be cautious therein. But should it plainly appear that absolute subjection were a condition the most proper for the person who is purchased, yet the innocent children ought not to be made slaves because their parents sinned.

8   We have account in Holy Scripture of some families suffering where mention is only made of the heads of the family committing wickedness; and it is likely that the degenerate Jews, misunderstanding some occurrences of this kind, took occasion to charge God with being unequal, so that a saying became common: "The fathers have eaten sour

grapes, and the children's teeth are set on edge" (Ezek. 18:2). Jeremiah and Ezekiel, two of the inspired prophets who lived near the same time, were concerned to correct this error. Ezekiel is large on the subject. First, he reproves them for their error: "What mean ye, that ye do so?" (Chap. 18, verse 1-3). "'As I live,' saith the Lord God, 'ye shall not have occasion any more to use this proverb in Israel.'" The words "any more" have reference to time past, intimating that though they had not rightly understood some things they had heard or seen, and thence supposed the proverb to be well grounded, yet henceforth they might know of a certainty that the ways of God are all equal—that as sure as the Most High lives, so sure men are only answerable for their own sins. He thus sums up the matter: "The soul that sinneth, it shall die. The son shall not bear the iniquity of the father; neither shall the father bear the iniquity of the son. The righteousness of the righteous shall be upon him, and the wickedness of the wicked shall be upon him" [Ezek. 18:20].

9   Where men are wicked they commonly are a means of corrupting the succeeding age and thereby hasten those outward calamities which fall on nations when their iniquities are full.

10   Men may pursue means which are not agreeable to perfect purity, with a view to increase the wealth and happiness of their offspring, and thereby make the way of virtue more difficult to them. And though the ill example of a parent or a multitude does not excuse a man in doing evil, yet the mind being early impressed with vicious notions and practices and nurtured up in ways of getting treasure which are not the ways of Truth, this wrong spirit getting first possession and being thus strengthened frequently prevents due attention to the true spirit of wisdom, so that they exceed in wickedness those before them. And in this channel, though parents labor as they think to forward the happiness of their children, it proves a means of forwarding their calamity. This being the case in the age next before the grievous calamity in the siege of Jerusalem, and carrying Judah captive to Babylon, they might say with propriety: "This came upon us because our fathers forsook God and because we did worse than our fathers" [Judg. 2:12,19].

11   As the generation next before them inwardly turned away from God, who yet waited to be gracious, and as they in that age continued in those things which necessarily separated from perfect goodness, growing more stubborn till the judgments of God were poured out upon them, they might properly say, "Our fathers have sinned and we have borne their

iniquities" [Lam. 5:7]. And yet, wicked as their fathers were, had they not succeeded them in their wickedness, they had not borne their iniquities.

12   To suppose it right that an innocent man shall at this day be excluded from the common rules of justice, be deprived of that liberty which is the natural right of human creatures, and be a slave to others during life on account of a sin committed by his immediate parents or a sin committed by Ham, the son of Noah, is a supposition too gross to be admitted into the mind of any person who sincerely desires to be governed by solid principles.

13   It is alleged in favor of the practice that Joshua made slaves of the Gibeonites.

14   What men do by the command of God and what comes to pass as a consequence of their neglect are different, such as the latter case now mentioned was.

15   It was the express command of the Almighty to Israel concerning the inhabitants of the promised land: "Thou shalt make no covenant with them, nor with their gods. They shall not dwell in thy land" (Exod. 23:32[-33]). Those Gibeonites came craftily, telling Joshua that they were come from a far country, that their elders had sent them to make a league with the people of Israel, and as an evidence of their being foreigners showed their old clothes, etc. "And the men took of their victuals and asked not counsel at the mouth of the Lord; and Joshua made peace with them and made a league with them to let them live; and the princes swore to them" [Josh. 9:14, 15].

16   When the imposition was discovered, the congregation murmured against the princes. But all the princes said to all the congregation: "We have sworn to them by the Lord God of Israel; now therefore, we may not touch them; . . . we will even let them live, lest wrath be upon us; . . . but let them be hewers of wood and drawers of water unto the congregation" [Josh. 9:19-21].

17   Omitting to ask counsel involved them in great difficulty. The Gibeonites were of those cities of which the Lord said: "Thou shalt save alive nothing that breatheth" [Deut. 20:16], and of the stock of the Hivites, concerning whom he commanded by name: "Thou shalt smite them and utterly destroy them. Thou shalt make no covenant with them, nor show mercy unto them" (Deut. 7:[2]). Thus Joshua and the princes, not knowing

them, had made a league with them to let them live, and in this strait they resolve to make them servants. Joshua and the princes suspected them to be deceivers: "Peradventure you dwell amongst us; and how shall we make league with you?" [Josh. 9:7], which words show that they remembered the command beforementioned, and yet did not enquire at the mouth of the Lord, as Moses directed Joshua when he gave him a charge respecting his duty as chief man among that people (Num. 27:21). By this omission things became so situated that Joshua and the princes could not execute the judgments of God on them without violating the oath which they had made.

18 Moses did amiss at the waters of Meribah and doubtless he soon repented, for the Lord was with him. And it is likely that Joshua was deeply humbled under a sense of his omission, for it appears that God continued him in his office and spared the lives of those people for the sake of the league and oath made in his name.

19 The wickedness of these people was great, and they worthy to die, or perfect justice had not passed sentence of death upon them; and as their execution was prevented by this league and oath, they appear content to be servants: "As it seemeth good and right unto thee to do unto us, do" [Josh. 9:25].

20 These criminals, instead of death, had the sentence of servitude pronounced on them in these words: "Now therefore ye are cursed; and there shall none of you be freed from being bondmen and hewers of food and drawers of water for the house of my God" [Josh. 9:23].

21 We find (Deut. 20:10[-11]) that there were cities far distant from Canaan against which Israel went to battle, to whom they were to proclaim peace; and if the inhabitants made answer of peace and opened their gates, they were not to destroy them but make them tributaries.

22 The children of Israel were then the Lord's host and executioners of his judgments on people hardened in wickedness. They were not to go to battle but by his appointment. The men who were chief in his army had their instructions from the Almighty, sometimes immediately and sometimes by the ministry of angels. Of these, among others, were Moses, Joshua, Othniel, and Gideon (see Exod. 3:2 and 18:19; Josh. 5:13). These people far off from Canaan against whom Israel was sent to battle were so corrupt that the Creator of the universe saw it good to change their situation; and in case of their opening their gates and coming under

tribute, this their subjection, though probably more mild than absolute slavery, was to last little or no longer than while Israel remained in the true spirit of government.

23 It was pronounced by Moses the prophet as a consequence of their wickedness: "The stranger that is within thee shall get above thee very high; and thou shalt come down very low. He shall be the head and thou the tail [Deut. 28:43-44].

24 This we find in some measure verified in their being made tributaries to the Moabites, Midianites, Amorites, and Philistines.

25 It is alleged in favor of the practice of slavekeeping that the Jews by their law made slaves of the heathen (Lev. 25:45[-46]). "Moreover, of the children of the strangers that do sojourn amongst you, of them shall ye buy and of their children which are with you which they beget in your land. And they shall be your possession; and you shall take them as an inheritance for your children after you, to inherit them as a possession; they shall be your bondmen forever." It is difficult for us to have any certain knowledge of the mind of Moses in regard to keeping slaves, any other way than by looking upon him as a true servant of God, whose mind and conduct were regulated by an inward principle of justice and equity. To admit a supposition that he in that case was drawn from perfect equity by the alliance of outward kindred would be to disown his authority.

26 Abraham had servants born in his house and bought with his money. And the Almighty said of Abraham: "I know him, that he will order his house after him" [Gen. 18:19], which implies that he was as a father, an instructor, and a good governor over his people. And Moses, considered as a man of God, must necessarily have had a prospect of some real advantage in the strangers and heathens being servants to the Israelites for a time.

27 As mankind had received and established many erroneous opinions and hurtful customs, their living and conversing with the Jews while the Jews stood faithful to their principles might be helpful to remove those errors and reform their manners. But for men with private views to assume an absolute power over the persons and properties of others and continue it from age to age in the line of natural generation, without regard to the virtues and vices of their successors, as it is manifestly contrary to true universal love and attended with great evils, there requires the clearest evidence to beget a belief in us that Moses intended that the strangers should as such be slaves to the Jews.

28　He directed them to buy strangers and sojourners. It appears that there were strangers in Israel who were free men, and considering with what tenderness and humanity the Jews by their law were obliged to use their servants and what care was to be taken to instruct them in the true religion, it is not unlikely that some strangers in poverty and distress were willing to enter into bonds to serve the Jews as long as they lived; and in such case the Jews by their law had a right to their service during life.

29　When the awl was bored through the ear of the Hebrew servant, the text says: "He shall serve forever" [Exod. 21:6]. Yet we do not suppose that by the word "forever" it was intended that none of his posterity should afterwards be free. When it is said in regard to the strangers which they bought: "They shall be your possession" [Lev. 25:45], it may be well understood to mean only the persons so purchased. All preceding relates to buying them, and what follows to the continuance of their service: "You shall take them as an inheritance to your children after you; they shall be your bondmen forever" [Lev. 25:46]. It may be well understood to stand limited to those they purchased.

30　Moses, directing Aaron and his sons to wash their hands and feet when they went into the tabernacle of the congregation, says: "It shall be a statute forever to them, even to him and his seed throughout all generations" [see Exod. 40:12,15]. And to express the continuance of the Law, it was his common language: "It shall be a statute forever throughout your generations" [see Lev. 3:17]; so that had he intended the posterity of the strangers so purchased to continue in slavery to the Jews it looks likely that he would have used some terms clearly to express it. The Jews undoubtedly had slaves whom they kept as such from one age to another. But that this was agreeable to the genuine design of their inspired Lawgiver is far from being a clear case.

31　Making constructions of the Law contrary to the true meaning of it was common among that people. Samuel's sons took bribes and perverted judgment. Isaiah complained that they justified the wicked for reward. Zephaniah, contemporary with Jeremiah, on account of the injustice of the civil magistrates declared that those judges were evening wolves, and that the priests did violence to the law [Zeph. 3:3-4].

32　Jeremiah acquaints us that the priests cried, "Peace, peace," when there was no peace [Jer. 6:14; 8:11], by which means the people grew bold in their wickedness—and having committed abominations were not ashamed, but through wrong constructions of the Law they justified themselves and boastingly said: "We are wise, and the law of the Lord is with us" [Jer. 8:8]. These corruptions continued till the days of our Savior, who told the Pharisees: "You have made the commandment of God of none effect through your tradition" [Matt. 15:6].

33   Thus it appears that they corrupted the law of Moses. Nor is it unlikely that among many others this was one; for oppressing the strangers was a heavy charge against the Jews and very often strongly represented by the Lord's faithful prophets.

34   That the liberty of man was by the inspired Lawgiver esteemed precious appears in this: that such who unjustly deprived men of it were to be punished in like manner as if they had murdered them. "He that stealeth a man and selleth him, or if he be found in his hand, shall surely be put to death" [Exod. 21:16]. This part of the Law was so considerable that Paul, the learned Jew, giving a brief account of the uses of the Law, adds this: "It was made for men-stealers" (1 Tim. 1:10).

35   The great men among that people were exceeding oppressive and, it is likely, exerted their whole strength and influence to have the Law construed to suit their turns. The honest servants of the Lord had heavy work with them in regard to their oppression. A few instances follow: "Thus saith the Lord of hosts, the God of Israel: 'Amend your ways and your doings, and I will cause you to dwell in this place. . . . If you thoroughly execute judgment between a man and his neighbor, if you oppress not the stranger, the fatherless, and the widow, and shed not innocent blood in this place, neither walk after other gods to your hurt, then will I cause you to dwell in this place'" (Jer. 7[:3,5-7]). Again, a message was sent not only to the inferior ministers of justice, but also to the chief ruler: "Thus saith the Lord: 'Go down to the house of the king of Judah and speak there this word; . . . execute ye judgment and righteousness and deliver the spoiled out of the hand of the oppressor; and do no wrong. Do no violence to the stranger, the fatherless, and the widows; neither shed innocent blood in this place,'" then adds that in so doing they should prosper. "'But if ye will not hear these words, I swear by myself,' saith the Lord, 'that this house shall become a desolation'" (Jer. 22[:1,3,5]).

36   The king, the princes, and rulers were agreed in oppression before the Babylonish captivity; for whatever courts of justice were retained

among them or however they decided matters between men of estates, it is plain that the cause of the poor was not judged in equity.

37　It appears that the great men among the Jews were fully resolved to have slaves, even of their own brethren (Jer. 34[:11-22]). Notwithstanding the promises and threatenings of the Lord, by the prophet, and their solemn covenant to set them free, confirmed by the imprecation of passing between the parts of a calf cut in twain (intimating by that ceremony that on breach of the covenant it were just for their bodies to be so cut in pieces), yet after all, they held fast to their old custom and called home the servants whom they had set free: "'And ye were now turned, and had done right in my sight in proclaiming liberty every man to his neighbor; and ye had made a covenant before me in the house which is called by my name; but ye turned and polluted my name, and caused every man his servant—whom he had set at liberty at their pleasure—to return, and brought them into subjection, to be unto you for servants and for handmaids.' Therefore, thus saith the Lord: 'Ye have not hearkened unto me in proclaiming liberty every one to his neighbor and every one to his brother. Behold, I proclaim liberty to you,' saith the Lord, 'to the sword, to the pestilence, and to the famine; and I will make you to be removed into all the kingdoms of the earth. The men who transgressed my covenant which they made and passed between the parts of the calf I will give into the hands of their enemies, and their dead bodies shall be for meat unto the fowls of the heaven and the beasts of the earth'" [Jer. 34:15-20].

38　Soon after this their city was taken and burned, the king's sons and the princes slain, and the king, with the chief men of his kingdom, carried captive to Babylon. Ezekiel, prophesying the return of that people to their own land, directs: "Ye shall divide the land by lot for an inheritance unto you and to the strangers that sojourn amongst you. In what tribe the stranger sojourns, there shall ye give him his inheritance, saith the Lord God" [Ezek. 47:22-23]. Nor is this particular direction and the authority with which it is enforced without a tacit implication—that their ancestors had erred in their conduct towards the stranger.

39　Some who keep slaves have doubted as to the equity of the practice; but as they knew men noted for their piety who were in it, this, they say, has made their minds easy.

40　To lean on the example of men in doubtful cases is difficult. For only admit that those men were not faithful and upright to the highest degree, but that in some particular case they erred, and it may follow that this one case was the same about which we are in doubt; and to quiet our minds by their example may be dangerous to ourselves, and continuing in it prove a stumbling block to tender-minded people who succeed us, in like manner as their examples are to us.

41 But supposing charity was their only motive and they, not foreseeing the tendency of paying robbers for their booty, were not justly under the imputation of being partners with a thief (Prov. 29:24), but were really innocent in what they did, are we assured that we keep them with the same views they kept them? If we keep them from no other motive than a real sense of duty, and true charity governs us in all our proceedings toward them, we are so far safe. But if another spirit which inclines our minds to the ways of this world prevail upon us, and we are concerned for our own outward gain more than for their real happiness, it will avail us nothing that some good men have had the care and management of Negroes.

42 Since mankind spread upon the earth, many have been the revolutions attending the several families, and their customs and ways of life different from each other. This diversity of manners, though some are preferable to others, operates not in favor of any so far as to justify them to do violence to innocent men, to bring them from their own to another way of life. The mind, when moved by a principle of true love, may feel a warmth of gratitude to the universal Father and a lively sympathy with those nations where divine light has been less manifest.

43 This desire for their real good may beget a willingness to undergo hardships for their sakes, that the true knowledge of God may be spread among them. But to take them from their own land with views of profit to ourselves by means inconsistent with pure justice is foreign to that principle which seeks the happiness of the whole creation. Forced subjection, on innocent persons of full age, is inconsistent with right reason: on one side, the human mind is not naturally fortified with that firmness in wisdom and goodness necessary to an independent ruler; on the other side, to be subject to the uncontrollable will of a man liable to err, is most painful and afflicting to a conscientious creature.

44 It is our happiness faithfully to serve the Divine Being who made us. His perfection makes our service reasonable; but so long as men are

biased by narrow self-love, so long an absolute power over other men is unfit for them.

45 Men taking on them the government of others may intend to govern reasonably and make their subjects more happy than they would be otherwise. But as absolute command belongs only to him who is perfect, where frail men in their own wills assume such command, it has a direct tendency to vitiate their minds and make them more unfit for government.

46 Placing on men the ignominious title SLAVE, dressing them in uncomely garments, keeping them to servile labor in which they are often dirty, tends gradually to fix a notion in the mind that they are a sort of people below us in nature, and leads us to consider them as such in all our conclusions about them. And, moreover, a person which in our esteem is mean and contemptible, if their language or behavior towards us is unseemly or disrespectful, it excites wrath more powerfully than the like conduct in one we accounted our equal or superior, and where this happens to be the case it disqualifies for candid judgment; for it is unfit for a person to sit as a judge in a case where his own personal resentments are stirred up, and as members of society in a well-framed government we are mutually dependent. Present interest incites to duty and makes each man attentive to the convenience of others; but he whose will is a law to others and can enforce obedience by punishment, he whose wants are supplied without feeling any obligation to make equal returns to his benefactor, his irregular appetites find an open field for motion, and he is in danger of growing hard and inattentive to their convenience who labor for his support, and so loses that disposition in which alone men are fit to govern.

47 The English government has been commended by candid foreigners for the disuse of racks and tortures, so much practiced in some states; but this multiplying slaves now leads to it. For where people exact hard labor of others without a suitable reward and are resolved to continue in that way, severity to such who oppose them becomes the consequence; and several Negro criminals among the English in America have been executed in a lingering, painful way, very terrifying to others.

48 It is a happy case to set out right and persevere in the same way. A wrong beginning leads into many difficulties, for to support one evil, another becomes customary. Two produces more, and the further men proceed in this way the greater their dangers, their doubts and fears, and the more painful and perplexing are their circumstances, so that such who

are true friends to the real and lasting interest of our country and candidly consider the tendency of things cannot but feel some concern on this account.

49   There is that superiority in men over the brute creatures, and some of them so manifestly dependent on men for a living, that for them to serve us in moderation so far as relates to the right use of things looks consonant to the design of our Creator.

50   There is nothing in their frame, nothing relative to the propagating their species, which argues the contrary; but in men there is. The frame of men's bodies and the disposition of their minds are different. Some who are tough and strong and their minds active choose ways of life requiring much labor to support them. Others are soon weary, and though use makes labor more tolerable, yet some are less apt for toil than others and their minds less sprightly. These latter, laboring for their subsistence, commonly choose a life easy to support, being content with a little. When they are weary they may rest, take the most advantageous part of the day for labor, and in all cases proportion one thing to another that their bodies be not oppressed.

51   Now while each is at liberty the latter may be as happy and live as comfortably as the former; but where men of the first sort have the latter under absolute command, not considering the odds in strength and firmness, do sometimes in their eager pursuit lay on burdens grievous to be borne, by degrees grow rigorous, and aspiring to greatness they increase oppression; and the true order of kind Providence is subverted.

52   There are weaknesses sometimes attending us which make little or no alteration in our countenances, nor much lessen our appetite for food, and yet so affect us as to make labor very uneasy. In such case masters intent on putting forward business and jealous of the sincerity of their slaves may disbelieve what they say and grievously afflict them.

53   Action is necessary for all men, and our exhausting frame requires a support which is the fruit of action. The earth must be labored to keep us alive: labor is a proper part of our life; to make one answer the other in some useful motion looks agreeable to the design of our Creator. Motion rightly managed tends to our satisfaction, health, and support.

54   Those who quit all useful business and live wholly on the labor of others have their exercise to seek; some such use less than their health

44

requires; others choose that which by the circumstances attending it proves utterly reverse to true happiness. Thus while some are [in] divers ways distressed for want of an open channel of useful action, those who support them sigh and are exhausted in a stream too powerful for nature, spending their days with too little cessation from labor.

55 Seed sown with the tears of a confined oppressed people, harvest cut down by an overborne discontented reaper, makes bread less sweet to the taste of an honest man, than that which is the produce or just reward of such voluntary action which is one proper part of the business of human creatures.

56 Again, the weak state of the human species in bearing and bringing forth their young, and the helpless condition of their young beyond that of other creatures, clearly show that Perfect Goodness designs a tender care and regard should be exercised toward them, and that no imperfect, arbitrary power should prevent the cordial effects of that sympathy which is in the minds of well-met pairs to each other and toward their offspring.

57 In our species the mutual ties of affection are more rational and durable than in others below us, the care and labor of raising our offspring much greater. The satisfaction arising to us in their innocent company and in their advances from one rational improvement to another is considerable when two are thus joined and their affections sincere. It however happens among slaves that they are often situate in different places, and their seeing each other depends on the will of men liable to human passions and a bias in judgment, who with views of self-interest may keep them apart more than is right. Being absent from each other and often with other company, there is a danger of their affections being alienated, jealousies arising, the happiness otherwise resulting from their offspring frustrated, and the comforts of marriage destroyed. These things being considered closely as happening to a near friend will appear to be hard and painful.

58 He who reverently observes that goodness manifested by our gracious Creator toward the various species of beings in this world, will see that in our frame and constitution is clearly shown that innocent men capable to manage for themselves were not intended to be slaves.

59 A person lately travelling among the Negroes near Senegal has this remark: "Which way soever I turned my eyes on this pleasant spot, I beheld a perfect image of pure nature: an agreeable solitude bounded on

every side by charming landscapes, the rural situation of cottages in the midst of trees, the ease and indolence of the Negroes reclined under the shade of their spreading foliage, the simplicity of their dress and manners—the whole revived in my mind the idea of our first parents, and I seemed to contemplate the world in its primitive state" (M. Adanson, page 55).[4]

60 Some Negroes in these parts who have had an agreeable education have manifested a brightness of understanding equal to many of us. A remark of this kind we find in Bosman, page 328: "The Negroes of Fida," says he, "are so accurately quick in their merchandise accounts that they easily reckon as justly and quickly in their heads only, as we with the assistance of pen and ink, though the sum amounts to several thousands."[5]

61 Through the force of long custom it appears needful to speak in relation to color. Suppose a white child born of parents of the meanest sort who died and left him an infant falls into the hands of a person who endeavors to keep him a slave. Some men would account him an unjust man in doing so, who yet appear easy while many black people of honest lives and good abilities are enslaved in a manner more shocking than the case here supposed. This is owing chiefly to the idea of slavery being connected with the black color and liberty with the white. And where false ideas are twisted into our minds, it is with difficulty we get fairly disentangled.

---

[4] [Michel Adanson, *Voyage to Senegal and River Gambia. Translated from the French, with notes by an English Gentleman who resided in that Country* (London: 1759). Adanson (1727-1806) was a French naturalist of Scottish descent who, between 1748 and 1754, explored and mapped Senegal, collecting its plants and animals, systematizing its meteorological and astronomical phenomenon, and making grammars and dictionaries of its native languages.]

[5] [Willem Bosman (dates unknown) was a Dutch commercial agent or factor trading on the coast of Guinea. In 1705 his book on the international competition in the West African trade, which had been published in Dutch the year before, appeared in London under the fully-explanatory English title *A new and accurate description of the coast of Guinea, divided into the Gold, the Slave, and the Ivory Coasts . . . with a particular account of the rise, progress and present condition of all the European settlements upon that coast; and the just measures for improving the several branches of the Guinea trade. To which is prefix'd, an exact map of the whole coast of Guinea, that was not in the original.* 2nd English translation (London: 1721).]

62 A traveler in cloudy weather misses his way, makes many turns while he is lost, still forms in his mind the bearing and situation of places; and though the ideas are wrong, they fix as fast as if they were right. Finding how things are, we see our mistake. Yet the force of reason with repeated observations on places and things do not soon remove those false notions so fastened upon us, but it will seem in the imagination as if the annual course of the sun was altered; and though by recollection we are assured it is not, yet those ideas do not suddenly leave us.

63 Selfishness being indulged clouds the understanding; and where selfish men for a long time proceed on their way without opposition, the deceivableness of unrighteousness gets so rooted in their intellects that a candid examination of things relating to self-interest is prevented; and in this circumstance some who would not agree to make a slave of a person whose color is like their own, appear easy in making slaves of others of a different color, though their understandings and morals are equal to the generality of men of their own color.

64 The color of a man avails nothing in matters of right and equity. Consider color in relation to treaties. By such, disputes between nations are sometimes settled. And should the Father of us all so dispose things that treaties with black men should sometimes be necessary, how then would it appear among the princes and ambassadors to insist on the prerogative of the white color?

65 Whence is it that men who believe in a righteous Omnipotent Being, to whom all nations stand equally related and are equally accountable, remain so easy in it, but for that the ideas of Negroes and slaves are so interwoven in the mind that they do not discuss this matter with that candor and freedom of thought which the case justly calls for?

66 To come at a right feeling of their condition requires humble serious thinking, for in their present situation they have but little to engage our natural affection in their favor.

67 Had we a son or a daughter involved in the same case in which many of them are, it would alarm us and make us feel their condition without seeking for it. The adversity of an intimate friend will incite our compassion, while others equally good in the like trouble will but little affect us.

68   Again, the man in worldly honor whom we consider as our superior, treating us with kindness and generosity, begets a return of gratitude and friendship toward him. We may receive as great benefits from men a degree lower than ourselves, in the common way of reckoning, and feel ourselves less engaged in favor of them. Such is our condition by nature, and these things, being narrowly watched and examined, will be found to center in self-love.

69   The blacks seem far from being our kinsfolk; and did we find an agreeable disposition and sound understanding in some of them, which appeared as a good foundation for a true friendship between us, the disgrace arising from an open friendship with a person of so vile a stock in the common esteem would naturally tend to hinder it. They have neither honors, riches, outward magnificence nor power, their dress coarse and often ragged, their employ drudgery and much in the dirt. They have little or nothing at command, but must wait upon and work for others to obtain the necessaries of life, so that in their present situation there is not much to engage the friendship or move the affection of selfish men. But such who live in the spirit of true charity, to sympathize with the afflicted in the lowest stations of life is a thing familiar to them.

70   Such is the kindness of our Creator that people applying their minds to sound wisdom may, in general, with moderate exercise, live comfortably where no misapplied power hinders it. We in these parts have cause gratefully to acknowledge it. But men leaving the true use of things, their lives are less calm and have less of real happiness in them.

71   Many are desirous of purchasing and keeping slaves that they may live in some measure conformable to those customs of the times which have in them a tincture of luxury; for when we in the least degree depart from that use of the creatures which the Creator of all things intended for them, there luxury begins.

72   And if we consider this way of life seriously, we shall see there is nothing in it sufficient to induce a wise man to choose it before a plain, simple way of living. If we examine stately buildings and equipage, delicious foods, superfine cloths, silks, and linens; if we consider the splendor of choice metal fastened upon raiment, and the most showy inventions of men; it will yet appear that the humble-minded man who is contented with the true use of houses, food, and garments, and cheerfully exercises himself agreeable to his station in civil society to earn them, acts

more reasonably and discovers more soundness of understanding in his conduct than such who lay heavy burdens on others to support themselves in a luxurious way of living.

73   George Buchanan, in his *History of Scotland*, page 62, tells of some ancient inhabitants of Britain who were derived from a people that "had a way of marking their bodies, as some said, with instruments of iron, with variety of pictures, and with animals of all shapes, and wear no garments—that they should not hide their pictures—and were therefore called Picts."[6] Did we see those people shrink with pain for a considerable time together under the point or edge of this iron instrument and their bodies all bloody with the operation, did we see them sometimes naked, suffering with cold, and refuse to put on garments that those imaginary ensigns of grandeur might not be concealed, it is likely we should pity their folly and fondness for those things. But if we candidly compare their conduct in that case with some conduct among ourselves, will it not appear that our folly is the greatest?

74   In true gospel simplicity free from all wrong use of things, a spirit which breathes peace and good will is cherished; but when we aspire after imaginary grandeur and apply to selfish means to attain our end, this desire in its original is the same with the Picts in cutting figures on their bodies; but the evil consequences attending our proceedings are the greatest.

75   A covetous mind which seeks opportunity to exalt itself is a great enemy to true harmony in a country. Envy and grudging usually accompany this disposition, and it tends to stir up its likeness in others. And where this disposition arises so high as to embolden us to look upon honest, industrious men as our own property during life, and to keep them to hard labor to support us in those customs which have not their foundation in right reason, or to use any means of oppression, a haughty spirit is cherished on one side and the desire of revenge frequently on the other, till the inhabitants of the land are ripe for great commotion and trouble; and thus luxury and oppression have the seeds of war and desolation in them.

---

6 [George Buchanan, *The History of Scotland* 3rd edition, vol. I (London: 1733). Buchanan (1506-1582) was a Scottish historian and humanist scholar (and a teacher of Montaigne at Bordeaux).]

Some Account of the Slave-Trade from the Writings of Persons who have been at the Places where they are First Purchased, viz.

76 Bosman on Guinea, who was a factor for the Dutch about sixteen years in that country (page 339), thus remarks:

> But since I have so often mentioned that commerce, I shall describe how it is managed by our factors. The first business of one of our factors when he comes to Fida is to satisfy the customs of the king and the great men, which amounts to about one hundred pounds in Guinea value, as the goods must sell there, after which we have free license to trade, which is published throughout the whole land by the crier. And yet before we can deal with any person, we are obliged to buy the king's whole stock of slaves at a set price, which is commonly one-third or fourth higher than ordinary, after which we have free leave to deal with all his subjects of what rank soever. But if there happen to be no stock of slaves, the factor must resolve to run the risk of trusting the inhabitants with goods to the value of one or two hundred slaves, which commodities they send into the inland country in order to buy with them slaves at all markets—and that sometimes two hundred miles deep in the country. For you ought to be informed that markets of men are here kept in the same manner as they of beasts are with us.
>
> Most of the slaves which are offered to us are prisoners of war, which are sold by the victors as their booty. When these slaves come to Fida, they are put in prisons all together; and when we treat them, they are all brought out in a large plain where, by our surgeons whose province it is, they are thoroughly examined, even to the smallest member—and that naked, both men and women, without the least distinction or modesty. Those which are approved as good are set on one side. The invalids and maimed being thrown out, the remainder are numbered and it is entered who delivered them. In the meanwhile a burning iron with the arms or name of the company lies in the fire, with which ours are marked on the breast. This is done that we may distinguish

them from the slaves of the English, French, or others. When we have agreed with the owners of the slaves, they are returned to their prisons, where from that time forward they are kept at our charge, cost us two pence a day a slave, which serves to subsist them like our criminals on bread and water; so that, to save charges, we send them on board our ships the first opportunity, before which their masters strip them of all they have on their backs, so that they come on board stark naked—as well women as men—in which condition they are obliged to continue if the master of the ship is not so charitable (which he commonly is) as to bestow something on them to cover their nakedness.

The inhabitants of Popo, as well as those of Coto, depend on plunder and the slave trade, in both which they very much exceed the latter; for being endowed with more courage, they rob more successfully and by that means increase their trade, notwithstanding which, to freight a vessel with slaves requires some months attendance. In the year 1697, in three days time I could get but three slaves; but they assured me that if I would have patience for other three days only, they should be able to deliver me one or two hundred.—Same author, page 310.

We cast anchor at Cape Mizurada, but not one Negro coming on board I went on shore; and being desirous to be informed why they did not come on board, was answered that about two months before, the English had been there with two vessels and had ravaged the country, destroyed all their canoes, plundered their houses, and carried off some of their people for slaves, upon which the remainder fled to the inland country. They tell us they live in peace with all their neighbors and have no notion of any other enemy than the English, of which nation they had taken some then, and publicly declared that they would endeavor to get as many of them as the two mentioned ships had carried off of their natives. These unhappy English were in danger of being sacrificed to the memory of their friends, which some of their nation carried off.—Bosman, page 440.

Extracts from a Collection of Voyages, Vol. 1.

77   The author,[7] a popish missionary, speaking of his departing from the Negro country to Brazil, says:

> I remember the Duke of Bambay (a Negro chief) one day sent me several blacks to be my slaves, which I would not accept of, but sent them back to him. I afterwards told him I came not into his country to make slaves, but rather to deliver those from the slavery of the devil, whom he kept in miserable thralldom. The ship I went aboard was loaded with elephants' teeth and slaves, to the number of 680 men, women, and children. It was a pitiful sight to behold how all these people were bestowed. The men were standing in the hold, fastened one to another with stakes for fear they should rise and kill the whites. The women were between the decks, and those that were with child in the great cabin, the children in the steerage pressed together like herrings in a barrel, which caused an intolerable heat and stench. (page 507).

> It is now time (saith the same author) to speak of a brutish custom these people have amongst them in making slaves, which I take not to be lawful for any person of a good conscience to buy.

He then describes how women betray men into slavery, and adds: "there are others going up into the inland country, and through pretense of jurisdiction seize men upon any trifling offense and sell them for slaves" (page 537).

78   The author of this treatise, conversing with a person of good credit, was informed by him that in his youth while in England he was minded to come to America, and happening on a vessel bound for Guinea and from thence into America, he, with a view to see Africa, went on board her and continued with them in their voyage and so came into this country. Among other circumstances he related these:

---

7   [John Lockman (1698-1771) was an English author and translator who edited a volume of reports from Jesuits in the field to their superiors. The book was titled *The Travels of the Jesuits in Various Parts of the World, Particularly China and the East Indies* 2nd ed. (London: T. Piety, 1762).]

They purchased on the coast about three hundred slaves. Some of them he understood were captives of war, some stolen by other Negroes privately. When they had got many slaves on board but were still on that coast, a plot was laid by an old Negro, notwithstanding the men had irons on their hands and feet, to kill the English and take the vessel, which being discovered the man was hanged and many of the slaves made to shoot at him as he hung up.

Another slave was charged with having a design to kill the English; and the captain spoke to him in relation to the charge brought against him, as he stood on deck, whereupon he immediately threw himself into the sea and was drowned.

Several Negroes confined on board were (he said) so extremely uneasy with their condition that after many endeavors used, they could never make them eat nor drink after they came in the vessel, but in a desperate resolution starved themselves to death, behaving toward the last like madmen.

79 In Randall's *Geography*,[8] printed in 1744, we are informed that "in a time of full peace nothing is more common than for the Negroes of one nation to steal those of another and sell them to the Europeans. It is thought that the English transmit annually near fifty thousand of these unhappy creatures, and the other European nations together about two hundred thousand more."

80 It is through the goodness of God that the reformation from gross idolatry and barbarity has been thus far effected. If we consider our conditions as Christians and the benefits we enjoy and compare them with the condition of those people, and consider that our nation trading with them for their country produce have had an opportunity of imparting useful instructions to them, and remember that but little pains have been taken therein, it must look like an indifference in us. But when we reflect on a custom the most shocking of any among them, and remember that with a view to outward gain we have joined as parties in it, that our concurrence with them in their barbarous proceedings has tended to harden them in cruelty and been a means of increasing calamities in their

---

[8] [Joseph Randall, *A System of Geography: Or, A Dissertation on the Creation and various Phaenomena of the Terraqueous Globe* (London: Joseph Lord, 1744).]

country, we must own that herein we have acted contrary to those worthies whose lives and substance were spent in propagating truth and righteousness among the heathen. When Saul, by the hand of Doeg, slew four score priests at once, he had a jealousy that one of them at least was confederate with David, whom he considered as his enemy. Herod slaying all the male children in Bethlehem of two years old and under was an act of uncommon cruelty, but he supposed there was a male child there within that age who was likely to be king of the Jews, and finding no way to destroy him but by destroying them all, thought this the most effectual means to secure the kingdom to his own family.

81   When the sentence against the Protestants of Marindol, etc., in France, was put in execution, great numbers of people fled to the wilderness, among them were ancient people, women great with child, and others with babes in their arms, who endured calamities grievous to relate; and in the end some perished with hunger, and many were destroyed by fire and sword. But they had this objection against them—that they obstinately persisted in opposition to Holy Mother Church, and being heretics, it was right to work their ruin and extirpation and raze out their memory from among men (Foxe's *Actes and Monuments*, page 646).[9]

82   In favor of those cruelties, every one had what they deemed a plea. These scenes of blood and cruelty among the barbarous inhabitants of Guinea are not less terrible than those now mentioned. They are continued from one age to another, and we make ourselves parties and fellow-helpers in them. Nor do I see that we have any plea in our favor more plausible than the plea of Saul, of Herod, or the French in those slaughters.

83   Many who are parties in this trade by keeping slaves with views of self-interest, were they to go as soldiers in one of these inland expeditions to catch slaves, they must necessarily grow dissatisfied with such employ or cease to profess their religious principles. And though the first and most striking part of the scene is done at a great distance and by other hands, yet every one who is acquainted with the circumstances, and notwithstanding joins in it for the sake of gain only, must in the nature of things be chargeable with the others.

---

[9]   [John Foxe (1517-1587), the English martyrologist, author of *Actes and Monumentes of these latter and perilous days, touching matters of the church* (London: John Day, 1563).]

84   Should we consider ourselves present as spectators when cruel Negroes privately catch innocent children who are employed in the fields, hear their lamentable cries under the most terrifying apprehensions, or should we look upon it as happening in our own families—having our children carried off by savages—we must needs own that such proceedings are contrary to the nature of Christianity. Should we meditate on the wars which are greatly increased by this trade and on that affliction which many thousands live in, through apprehensions of being taken or slain; on the terror and amazement that villages are in when surrounded by these troops of enterprisers; on the great pain and misery of groaning, dying men who get wounded in those skirmishes; we shall necessarily see that it is impossible to be parties in such a trade on the motives of gain and retain our innocence.

85   Should we consider the case of multitudes of those people who in a fruitful soil and hot climate with a little labor raise grain, roots, and pulse to eat, spin and weave cotton, and fasten together the large feathers of fowls to cover their nakedness, many of whom in much simplicity live inoffensive in their cottages and take great comfort in raising up children.

86   Should we contemplate on their circumstances when suddenly attacked and labor to understand their inexpressible anguish of soul who survive the conflict; should we think on inoffensive women who fled at the alarm and at their return saw that village, in which they and their acquaintance were raised up and had pleasantly spent their youthful days, now lying in a gloomy desolation, some shocked at finding the mangled bodies of their near friends among the slain, others bemoaning the absence of a brother, a sister, a child, or a whole family of children, who by cruel men are bound and carried to market, to be sold without the least hopes of seeing them again; add to this the afflicted condition of these poor captives who are separated from family connections and all the comforts arising from friendship and acquaintance, carried among a people of a strange language, to be parted from their fellow captives, put to labor in a manner more servile and wearisome than what they were used to, with many sorrowful circumstances attending their slavery—and we must necessarily see that it belongs not to the followers of Christ to be parties in such a trade on the motives of outward gain.

87   Though there were wars and desolations among the Negroes before the Europeans began to trade there for slaves, yet now the calamities are greatly increased, so many thousands being annually

brought from thence; and we by purchasing them with views of self-interest are become parties with them and accessory to that increase.

88   In this case we are not joining against an enemy who is fomenting discords on our continent and using all possible means to make slaves of us and our children, but against a people who have not injured us.

89   If those who were spoiled and wronged should at length make slaves of their oppressors and continue slavery to their posterity, it would look rigorous to candid men. But to act that part toward a people when neither they nor their fathers have injured us, has something in it extraordinary, and requires our serious consideration.

90   Our children breaking a bone, getting so bruised that a leg or an arm must be taken off, lost for a few hours, so that we despair of their being found again, a friend hurt so that he dies in a day or two—these move us with grief. And did we attend to these scenes in Africa in like manner as if they were transacted in our presence, and sympathize with the Negroes in all their afflictions and miseries as we do with our children or friends, we should be more careful to do nothing in any degree helping forward a trade productive of so many and so great calamities. Great distance makes nothing in our favor. To willingly join with unrighteousness to the injury of men who live some thousand miles off is the same in substance as joining with it to the injury of our neighbors.

91   In the eye of pure justice actions are regarded according to the spirit and disposition they arise from. Some evils are accounted scandalous, and the desire of reputation may keep selfish men from appearing openly in them. But he who is shy on that account and yet by indirect means promotes that evil and shares in the profit of it cannot be innocent.

92   He who with a view to self-interest buys a slave made so by violence, and only on the strength of such purchase holds him a slave, thereby joins hands with those who committed that violence and in the nature of things becomes chargeable with the guilt.

93   Suppose a man wants a slave, and being in Guinea goes and hides by the path where boys pass from one little town to another, and there catches one the day he expects to sail, and taking him on board, brings him home without any aggravating circumstances. Suppose another buys a man taken by them who live by plunder and the slave-trade—they often

steal them privately and often shed much blood in getting them. He who buys the slave thus taken pays those men for their wickedness and makes himself party with them.

94   Whatever nicety of distinction there may be betwixt going in person on expeditions to catch slaves, and buying those with a view to self-interest which others have taken, it is clear and plain to an upright mind that such distinction is in words, not in substance; for the parties are concerned in the same work and have a necessary connection with and dependence on each other. For were there none to purchase slaves, they who live by stealing and selling them would of consequence do less at it.

95   Some would buy a Negro brought from Guinea with a view to self-interest and keep him a slave, who yet would seem to scruple to take arms and join with men employed in taking slaves.

96   Others have civil Negroes who were born in our country, capable and likely to manage well for themselves, whom they keep as slaves without ever trying them with freedom, and take the profit of their labor as a part of their estates, and yet disapprove bringing them from their own country.

97   If those Negroes had come here as merchants with their ivory and gold dust in order to trade with us, and some powerful person had taken their effects to himself and then put them to hard labor and ever after considered them as slaves, the action would be looked upon as unrighteous.

98   Those Negro merchants having children after their being among us, whose endowments and conduct were like other peoples in common, who attaining to mature age and requesting to have their liberty, should be told they were born in slavery and were lawful slaves, and therefore their request denied—the conduct of such persons toward them would be looked upon as unfair and oppressive.

99   In the present case relating to home-born Negroes, whose understandings and behavior are as good as common among other people, if we have any claim to them as slaves, that claim is grounded on their being the children or offspring of slaves who in general were made such through means as unrighteous and attended with more terrible circumstances than the case here supposed, so that when we trace our claim to the bottom, these home-born Negroes having paid for their

education and given reasonable security to those who owned them in case of their becoming chargeable, we have no more equitable right to their service than we should if they were the children of honest merchants who came from Guinea in an English vessel to trade with us.

100 If we claim any right to them as the children of slaves, we build on the foundation laid by them who made slaves of their ancestors, so that of necessity we must either justify the trade or relinquish our right to them as being the children of slaves.

101 Why should it seem right to honest men to make advantage by these people more than by others? Others enjoy freedom, receive wages equal to their work at, or near, such time as they have discharged these equitable obligations they are under to those who educated them. These have made no contract to serve, been no more expensive in raising up than others, and many of them appear as likely to make a right use of freedom as other people. Which way then can an honest man withhold from them that liberty which is the free gift of the Most High to his rational creatures?

102 The upright in heart cannot succeed the wicked in their wickedness, nor is it consonant to the life they live to hold fast an advantage unjustly gained.

103 The Negroes who live by plunder and the slave-trade steal poor innocent children, invade their neighbors' territories, and spill much blood to get these slaves. And can it be possible for an honest man to think that with view to self-interest we may continue slavery to the offspring of these unhappy sufferers, merely because they are the children of slaves—and not have a share of this guilt?

104 It is granted by many that the means used in getting them are unrighteous and that buying them when brought here is wrong; yet as setting them free is attended with some difficulty, they do not comply with it, but seem to be of the opinion that to give them food and raiment and keep them servants without any other wages is the best way to manage them that they know of, and hoping that their children after them will not be cruel to the Negroes, conclude to leave them as slaves to their children.

105 While present outward interest is the chief object of our attention, we shall feel many objections in our minds against renouncing our claim to them as the children of slaves; for being prepossessed with wrong opinions

prevents our seeing things clearly which to indifferent persons are easy to be seen.

106   Suppose a person seventy years past, in low circumstances, bought a Negro man and woman, and that the children of such person are now wealthy and have the children of such slaves. Admit that the first Negro man and his wife did as much business as their master and mistress and that the children of the slaves have done some more than their young masters. Suppose on the whole that the expense of living has been less on the Negroes' side than on the other (all which are no improbable suppositions), it follows that in equity these Negroes have a right to a part of this increase—that should some difficulties arise on their being set free, there is reason for us patiently to labor through them.

107   As the conduct of men varies relating to civil society, so different treatment is justly due to them. Indiscreet men occasion trouble in the world, and it remains to be the care of such who seek the good of mankind to admonish as they find occasion.

108   The slothfulness of some of them in providing for themselves and families, it is likely, would require the notice of their neighbors Nor is it unlikely that some would with justice be made servants, and others punished for their crimes. Pure justice points out to each individual their due. But to deny a people the privilege of human creatures on a supposition that being free many of them would be troublesome to us, is to mix the condition of good and bad men together and treat the whole as the worst of them deserve.

109   If we seriously consider that liberty is the right of innocent men, that the Mighty God is a refuge for the oppressed, that in reality we are indebted to them, that they being set free are still liable to the penalties of our laws and as likely to have punishment for their crimes as other people, this may answer all our objections. And to retain them in perpetual servitude without just cause for it, will produce effects in the event more grievous than setting them free would do when a real love to Truth and equity was the motive to it.

110   Our authority over them stands originally in a purchase made from those who, as to the general, obtained theirs by unrighteousness. Whenever we have recourse to such authority, it tends more or less to obstruct the channels through which the perfect plant in us receives nourishment.

111   There is a principle which is pure, placed in the human mind, which in different places and ages has had different names. It is, however, pure and proceeds from God. It is deep and inward, confined to no forms of religion nor excluded from any, where the heart stands in perfect sincerity. In whomsoever this takes root and grows, of what nation soever, they become brethren in the best sense of the expression. Using ourselves to take ways which appear most easy to us, when inconsistent with that purity which is without beginning, we thereby set up a government of our own and deny obedience to him whose service is true liberty.

112   He that has a servant made so wrongfully, and knows it to be so, when he treats him otherwise than a free man, when he reaps the benefit of his labor without paying him such wages as are reasonably due to free men for the like service (clothes excepted), these things, tho' done in calmness without any show of disorder, do yet deprave the mind in like manner and with as great certainty as prevailing cold congeals water. These steps taken by masters, and their conduct striking the minds of their children while young, leave less room for that which is good to work upon them. The customs of their parents, their neighbors, and the people with whom they converse working upon their minds, and they from thence conceiving ideas of things and modes of conduct, the entrance into their hearts becomes in a great measure shut up against the gentle movings of uncreated Purity.

113   From one age to another the gloom grows thicker and darker, till error gets established by general opinion; that whoever attends to perfect goodness and remains under the melting influence of it finds a path unknown to many, and sees the necessity to lean upon the arm of divine strength and dwell alone, or with a few in the right, committing their cause to him who is a refuge for his people in all their troubles.

114   Where through the agreement of a multitude some channels of justice are stopped, and men may support their characters as just men by being just to a party, there is great danger of contracting an alliance with that spirit which stands in opposition to the God of love and spreads discord, trouble, and vexation among such who give up to the influence of it.

115   Negroes are our fellow creatures and their present condition among us requires our serious consideration. We know not the time when those scales in which mountains are weighed may turn. The parent of mankind is gracious. His care is over his smallest creatures, and a

multitude of men escape not his notice; and though many of them are trodden down and despised, yet he remembers them. He sees their affliction and looks upon the spreading, increasing exaltation of the oppressor. He turns the channels of power, humbles the most haughty people, and gives deliverance to the oppressed at such periods as are consistent with his infinite justice and goodness. And wherever gain is preferred to equity, and wrong things publicly encouraged, to that degree that wickedness takes root and spreads wide among the inhabitants of a country, there is real cause for sorrow to all such whose love to mankind stands on a true principle and wisely consider the end and event of things.

6

A Word of Remembrance & Caution to the Rich &c

Written ca. 1763; 1ˢᵗ printed 1793

Editor's Introduction

1763 has been understood as the year in which this major essay was written. By then Woolman had completed the most extensive journeys he would ever undertake in America. He had traveled as far into the southern colonies as North Carolina in 1746 and again in 1757. He had gone as far up the Atlantic seaboard as New England in 1747 and again in 1760. And he had spent nearly a month visiting beyond the frontier in northeastern Pennsylvania to be among "the natives of this land who dwell far back in the wilderness"[1] in 1763. Indeed, in this essay there is reference to "the natives of North America"[2] as if the memory of that visitation was fresh in the author's mind. In any event, by 1763 Woolman's formative encounters with the American rich as well as with the poor and dispossessed had so deeply settled into his spiritual being that his thoughts on the subject would have reached maturity and been ready for written expression.

There is, however, no direct evidence from Woolman himself when this work was written. He does not refer to its writing in the *Journal*. It was not published, nor does it appear to have been submitted for publication, in his lifetime. And in contrast to his two major essays on enslavement[3] which have no known holographs, there are not only two complete holographs extant for this one essay but the two are significantly different in their texts and in their titles. One of the holographs is entitled "A Plea for the Poor" and it has three final chapters (Chapters 14 to 16), albeit non sequiturs, that are not to be found in the other holograph which is entitled "A Word of Remembrance & Caution to the Rich &c." Additionally, there are one other holograph of Chapter 15 and two

---

[1] *Journal*, p. 122. The journey among the Indians is described in the *Journal* at pp. 123-37.
[2] See herein Chaps. XII pars. 1-5.
[3] "Some Considerations on the Keeping of Negroes" and "Considerations on Keeping Negroes: Part Second," Texts 1 and 5 herein.

longhand copies, not in Woolman's hand, of Chapters 1 to 13 only. Other authorities have resolved the vexing issue of dating this essay by concluding that because the holograph for "A Plea for the Poor" is found within a holograph of the *Journal*, where it is inserted between events in 1763 and 1764, this essay should be dated to the same period.[4] In the end, the only certain date for the essay, under the captioned title, is that of its publication in Dublin in 1793.[5] However, notwithstanding they share the same title it must be noted that even the 1793 text (in its twelve chapters) differs significantly from the following text (in its thirteen chapters).

The following text of "A Word. . . to the Rich" is the editor's modernization of the holograph MS W, which was discovered after "A Plea for the Poor," based on MSS A/*Plea* + M, had been set in type for publication in Moulton.[6]

+++
Text

A Word of Remembrance & Caution to the Rich &c

Chapter I[7]

1   [Wealth desired for its own sake obstructs the increase of virtue, and large possessions in the hands of selfish men have a bad tendency, for by their means too small a number of people are employed in useful things; and some of them are necessitated to labor too hard, while others would want business to earn their bread, were not employments invented, which, having no real usefulness, serve only to please the vain mind.

2   Rents set on lands are often so high that persons of but small substance are straitened in taking farms, and while tenants are healthy and prosperous in business, they often find occasion to labor harder than was intended by our gracious Creator.

3   Oxen and horses are often seen at work when, through heat and too much labor, their eyes and the emotion of their bodies manifest they

---

4   Moulton, p. 285.
5   Smith, Vol. 2, p. 960.
6   Moulton, p. 196.
7   [The chapters were numbered by JW.]

are oppressed. Their loads in wagons are frequently so heavy that when weary with hauling them far, their drivers find occasion in going up hills or through mires to raise their spirits by whipping to get forward. Many poor people are so thronged in their business that it is difficult for them to provide shelter for their cattle against the storms.

4   These things are common when in health, but through sickness and inability to labor, through loss of cattle and miscarriage in business, many are so straitened, so much of their increase goes to pay rent, that they have not wherewith to buy what their case requires. Hence one poor woman, in tending on her]⁸ children, providing for her family and helping the sick, does as much business as would for the time be suitable employment for two or three; and honest persons are often straitened to give their children suitable learning.

5   The money which the wealthy receive from the poor, who do more than a proper share of business in raising it, is frequently paid to other poor people for doing business which is foreign from the true use of things.

6   Men who have large estates and live in the spirit of charity, who carefully inspect the circumstances of those who occupy their estates, and⁹ regardless of the customs of the times regulate their demands agreeable to universal love, these by being righteous on principle, do good to the poor without placing it as an act of bounty. Their example in avoiding superfluities tends to incite others to moderation. Their goodness in not exacting what the laws or customs would support them in tends to open the channel to moderate labor in useful affairs and to discourage those branches of business which have not their foundation in true wisdom.

7   To be busied in that which is but vanity, and serves only to please the unstable mind, tends to an alliance with those who promote that vanity, and is a snare in which many poor tradesmen are entangled. To be employed in things connected with virtue is most agreeable to the character and inclination of an honest man.

---

⁸ [Pages 1 and 2 of MS W are missing. This bracketed passage, which marks the missing holographic text, is taken from the first imprint made by T. M. Bates for R. M. Jackson, Dublin, 1793.]
⁹ [At this point Woolman inserted the word "are" but it renders the sentence awkward. The inserted "are" is not found in MS A/*Plea*.]

8   While industrious frugal people are borne down with poverty and oppressed with too much labor in useful things, the way to apply money without promoting pride and vanity remains open to such who truly sympathize with them in their various difficulties.

Chapter II

1   The Creator of the earth is the owner of it. He gave us being thereon, and our nature requires nourishment which is the produce of it. As he is kind and merciful, we as his creatures, while we live answerable to the design of our creation are so far entitled to a convenient subsistence that no man may justly deprive us of it.

2   By the agreements and contracts of our fathers and predecessors, and by doings and proceedings of our own, some claim a much greater share of this world than others, and while those possessions are faithfully improved to the good of the whole it consists with equity.

3   But he who with a view to self-exaltation causes some with their domestic animals to labor immoderately, and with the moneys arising to him therefrom employs others in the luxuries of life, acts contrary to the gracious design of him who is the true owner of the earth; nor can any possessions, either acquired or derived from ancestors, justify such conduct.

4   Goodness remains to be goodness, and the direction of pure wisdom is obligatory on all reasonable creatures, that laws and customs are no further a standard for our proceeding than as their foundation is on universal righteousness.

5   Though the poor occupy our estates by a bargain, to which they in their poor circumstances agreed, and we ask even less than a punctual fulfilling of their agreement, yet if our views are to lay up riches, or to live in conformity to customs which have not their foundation in the Truth, and our demands are such as requires greater toil or application to business in them than is consistent with pure love, we invade their rights as inhabitants of that world of which a good and gracious God is proprietor, under whom we are tenants.

6   Were all superfluities and the desire of outward greatness laid aside, and the right use of things universally attended to, such a number of people might be employed in things useful that moderate labor with the

blessing of heaven would answer all good purposes relating to people and their animals, and a sufficient number have leisure to attend on the proper affairs of civil society.

Chapter III

1   While our strength and spirits are lively we go cheerfully through business. Either too much or too little action is tiresome, but a right portion is healthful to our bodies and agreeable to an honest mind.

2   Where men have great estates they stand in a place of trust. To have it in their power without difficulty to live in that fashion which occasions much labor, and at the same time confine themselves to that use of things, prescribed by our Redeemer and confirmed by his example and the example of many who lived in the early age of the Christian church, that they may more extensively relieve objects of charity, for men possessed of great estates to live thus, requires close attention to divine love.

3   Our gracious Creator cares and provides for all his creatures. His tender mercies are over all his works, and so far as his love influences our minds, so far we become interested in his workmanship and feel a desire to make use of every opportunity to lessen the distresses of the afflicted, and increase the happiness of the creation. Here we have a prospect of one common interest from which our own is inseparable, that to turn all the treasures we possess into the channel of universal love becomes the business of our lives.

4   Men of large estates whose hearts are thus enlarged are like fathers to the poor, and in looking over their brethren in distressed circumstances and considering their own more easy condition, find a field for humble meditation, and feel the strength of those obligations they are under to be kind and tender-hearted toward them.

5   Poor men eased of their burdens, and released from too close an application to business, are at liberty to hire others to their assistance, to provide well for their domestic animals, and find time to perform those visits among their acquaintance which belongs to a well-guided social life.

6   When these reflect on the opportunity those had to oppress them, and consider the goodness of their conduct, they behold it lovely and consistent with brotherhood. And as the man whose mind is conformed to

universal love has his trust settled in God, and finds a firm foundation to stand on, in any changes or revolutions that happen among men, so also the goodness of his conduct tends to spread a kind, benevolent disposition in the world.

Chapter IV

1   Our blessed Redeemer in directing us how to conduct one towards another appeals to our own feeling: "Whatsoever ye would that other men should do to you, do ye even so to them" [Matt. 7:12].

2   Now where such live in fullness on the labor of others, who have never had experience of hard labor themselves, there is often a danger of their not having a right feeling of the laborer's condition, and therefore of being disqualified to judge candidly in their case, as not knowing what they themselves would desire were they to labor hard from one year to another to raise the necessaries of life and pay large rents beside; that it's good for those who live in fullness to labor for tenderness of heart and improve every opportunity of being acquainted with the hardships and fatigues of those who labor for their living, and think seriously with themselves: Am I influenced with true charity in fixing all my demands? Have I no desire to support myself in expensive customs, because my acquaintance live in those customs? Were I to labor as they do toward supporting them and their children in a station like mine, in such sort as they and their children labor for us, could I not on such a change, before I entered into agreements of rent or interest, name some costly articles now used by me or in my family which have no real use in them, the expense whereof might be lessened? And should I not in such case strongly desire the disuse of those needless expenses, that less answering their way of life the terms might be the easier to me?

3   If a wealthy man on serious reflection finds a witness in his own conscience that there are some expenses which he indulges himself in, that are in conformity to customs which might be omitted consistent with the true design of living, and which was he to change places with those who occupy his estate he would desire to be discontinued by them. Whoever are thus awakened to their feeling, will necessarily find the injunction binding on them: "Do thou even so to them."

4   Divine love imposes no rigorous or unreasonable commands but graciously points out the spirit of brotherhood, and way to happiness, in

the attaining to which it is necessary that we go forth out of all that is selfish.

Chapter V

1   To pass through a series of hardships, and to languish under oppression, brings people to a certain knowledge of these things.

2   To enforce the duty of tenderness to the poor the inspired lawgiver referred the children of Israel to their own past experience: "Ye know the heart of a stranger seeing ye were strangers in the land of Egypt" [Exod. 23:9].

3   He who has been a stranger among unkind people, or under their government who were hard-hearted, knows how it feels; but a person who has never felt the weight of misapplied power, comes not to this knowledge but by an inward tenderness in which the heart is prepared to sympathize with others.

4   We may reflect on the condition of a poor, innocent man who by his labor contributes toward supporting one of his own species more wealthy than himself, on whom the rich man from a desire after wealth and luxuries lays heavy burdens. When this laborer looks over the means of his heavy load, and considers that this great toil and fatigue is laid on him to support that which has no foundation in pure wisdom, we may well suppose that there arises an uneasiness in his mind toward those who might without any inconvenience deal more favorably with him.

5   When he considers that by his industry his fellow creature is benefited, and sees that this man who has much wealth is not satisfied with being supported in a plain way but to gratify a wrong desire and conform to wrong customs increases to an extreme the labors of those who occupy his estate, we may reasonably judge that he will think himself unkindly used.

6   When he considers that the proceedings of the wealthy are agreeable to the customs of the times, and sees no means of redress in this world, how would the inward sighing of an innocent person ascend to the throne of that great, good Being who created us all, and has a constant care over his creatures.

7   By candidly considering these things we may have some sense of the condition of innocent people overloaded by the wealthy. But he who toils one year after another to furnish others with wealth and superfluities, who labors and thinks, and thinks and labors, till by overmuch labor he is wearied and oppressed, such an one understands the meaning of that language: "Ye know the heart of a stranger, seeing ye were strangers in the land of Egypt." [Exod. 23:9].

8   As many at this day, who know not the heart of a stranger, indulge themselves in ways of life which occasion more labor in the world than Infinite Goodness intends for man, and yet are compassionate toward such in distress who come directly under their observation, were these to change circumstances a while with some who labor for them, were they to pass regularly through the means of knowing the heart of a stranger, and come to a feeling knowledge of the straits and hardships which many poor, innocent people pass through in a hidden obscure life, were these who now fare sumptuously every day, to act the other part of the scene till seven times had passed over them, and return again to their former estate, I believe many of them would embrace a way of life less expensive, and lighten the heavy burdens of some who now labor out of their sight, and pass through straits with which they are but little acquainted.

9   To see our fellow creatures under difficulties, to which we are in no degree accessory, tends to awaken tenderness in the minds of all reasonable people, but if we consider the condition of such who are depressed in answering our demands, who labor out of our sight, and are often toiling for us while we pass our time in fullness, if we consider that much less than we demand would supply us with all things really needful, what heart will not relent, or what reasonable man [not] refrain from mitigating that grief which he himself is the cause of, when he may do it without inconvenience?[10]

Chapter VI

1   People much spent with labor often take strong liquor to revive them. The portion of the necessaries of life answerable to a day's work is such that those who support their families by day labor find occasion to labor hard, and many of them think strong drink a necessary part of their

---

[10] [MS W here omits a concluding quotation from Ezek. 34:18 which is found in MS A/*Plea*.]

entertainment.[11] Were there more men usefully employed and fewer who eat bread as a reward for doing that which is not useful, then food and raiment would, on a reasonable estimate, be more in proportion to labor than it is at present.

2   For if four men working eight hours in a day, raise and clean three hundred bushels of grain or twelve hundred pounds of flax in sixty days, then five men working six hours and twenty four minutes in a day would at that rate do the same business in the same time.[12]

3   In proceeding agreeable to sound wisdom, a small portion of daily labor might suffice to keep a proper stream, gently circulating through all the channels of society; and this portion of labor might be so divided and taken in the most advantageous parts of the day, that people would not have that plea for the use of strong liquors which they have at present.

4   The quantity of rum and spirits imported and made in our country is great! Nor can so many thousand hogsheads of this liquor be drank every year in our country without having a powerful effect on our manners.

5   When people are spent with action, and take these liquors not only as a refreshment from past labors, but to support them to go on without nature having sufficient time to recruit by resting, it gradually turns them from that calmness of thought which attends those who steadily apply their hearts to true wisdom.

6   The spirits scattered by too much bodily motion, and again revived by strong drink, that this makes a person unfit for divine meditation, I expect will not be denied; and as multitudes of people are in this practice who do not take so much as to hinder them from managing their outward affairs, this custom is strongly supported; but as through divine goodness I have found that there is a more quiet, calm, and happy way intended for us to walk in, I am engaged to express what I feel in my heart concerning it.

7   As cherishing the spirit of love and meekness belongs to the family of Jesus Christ, so to avoid those things which they know works against it is an indispensable duty.

---

[11] [This sentence is not found in MS A/*Plea*.]
[12] [This sentence, not found in MS A/*Plea*, takes the place of a similar calculation in a later paragraph not found in MS W.]

8   Every degree of luxury of what kind soever, and every demand for money inconsistent with divine order has some connection with unnecessary labor. By too much labor the spirits are exhausted and nature craves help from strong drink; and the frequent use of strong drink works in opposition to the Celestial Influence on the mind. This is plain when men take so much as to suspend the use of their reason; and though there are degrees of this opposition, and a man quite drunk may be furthest removed from that frame of mind in which God is worshipped, yet a person being often near spent with too much action, and revived by spirituous liquors, without being quite drunk, inures himself to that which is a less degree of the same thing, and which by long continuance does necessarily hurt both mind and body.

9   There is in the nature of people some degree of likeness with that food and air to which they from their youth have been accustomed. This frequently appears in such, who by a separation from their native air and usual diet grow weak and unhealthy for want of them. Nor is it reasonable to suppose that so many thousand hogsheads of this fiery liquor can be drank by us every year, and the practice continued from age to age without altering in some degree the natures of men and rendering their minds less apt to receive the pure Truth in the love of it.

10   As many who manifest some regard to piety, do yet in some degree conform to those ways of living, and of collecting wealth which increases labor beyond the bounds fixed by divine wisdom, my desire is that they may so consider the connection of things, as to take heed, lest by exacting of poor men more than is consistent with universal righteousness they promote that by their conduct which in words they speak against.

11   To treasure up wealth for another generation by means of the immoderate labor of such who in some measure depend upon us, is doing evil at present, without knowing but that our wealth thus gathered, may be applied to evil purposes when we are gone.

12   To labor too hard or cause others to do so, that we may live conformable to customs which Christ our Redeemer contradicted by his example in the days of his flesh, and which are contrary to divine order, is to manure a soil for propagating an evil seed in the earth.

13   Such who enter deep into these considerations and live under the weight of them will feel these things so heavy and their ill effects so extensive that the necessity of attending singly to divine wisdom will be

evident, thereby to be directed in the right use of things, in opposition to the customs of the times, and supported to bear patiently the reproaches attending singularity.

14   To conform a little to a wrong way strengthens the hands of such who carry wrong customs to their utmost extent; and the more a person appears to be virtuous and heavenly-minded, the more powerfully does his conformity operate in favor of evil doers. Lay aside the profession of a pious life and people expect little or no instruction from the example. But while we profess, in all cases, to live in constant opposition to that which is contrary to universal righteousness, what expressions are equal to the subject, or what language is sufficient to set forth the strength of those obligations we are under to beware, lest by our example we lead others wrong.

Chapter VII

This kind goes not out but by prayer [Matt. 17:21].

1   In our care for our children should we give way to partiality in things relating to what may be when we are gone, yet after death we cannot look at partiality with pleasure.

2   If by our wealth we make them great without a full persuasion that we could not bestow it better, and thus give them power to deal hardly with others more virtuous than they, it can after death give us no more satisfaction than if by this treasure we had raised these others above our own, and given them power to oppress ours.

3   Did a man possess as much good land as would well suffice for twenty industrious, frugal people, and expect that he was lawful heir to it, and intend to give this great estate to his children; but found on a research into the title that one-half this estate was the undoubted property of a number of poor orphans, who as to virtue and understanding, to him, appeared as hopeful as his own children: this discovery would give him an opportunity to consider whether he was attached to any interest distinct from the interest of those children.

4   Some of us have estates sufficient for our children and for as many more to live upon, did they all employ their time in useful business, and live in that plainness consistent with the character of true disciples of Christ, and have no reason to believe that our children after us will apply

them to benevolent purposes, more than some poor children who we are acquainted with would, if they had them; and yet did we believe that after our decease these estates would go equally between our children, and an equal number of these poor children, it would be likely to give us uneasiness. This may show to a thoughtful person that to be redeemed from all the remains of selfishness, to have a universal regard to our fellow-creatures, and love them, as our heavenly Father loves them, we must constantly attend to the influence of his Spirit.

5   When our hearts are enlarged to contemplate on the nature of this divine love, we behold it harmonious; but if we attentively consider that moving of selfishness which would make us uneasy at the apprehension of that, which is in itself reasonable, and which being separated from all previous conceptions and expectations will appear so, we may see an inconsistency in it, for the subject of such uneasiness is in future, and will not affect our children till we were removed into that state of being where there is no possibility of our taking delight in any thing contrary to the pure principle of universal love.

6   As that natural desire of superiority in us, being given way to, extends to such our favorites who we expect will succeed us, and as the grasping after wealth and power for them adds greatly to the burdens of the poor, and increases the evil of covetousness in this age, I have often desired in secret that in looking toward posterity we may remember the purity of that rest which is prepared for the Lord's people, the impossibility of our taking pleasure in any thing distinguishable from universal righteousness, and how vain and weak a thing it is to give wealth and power to such who appear unlikely to apply it to a general good when we are gone.

7   As Christians all we possess are the gifts of God to us; now in distributing it to others we act as his stewards, and it becomes our station to act agreeable to that divine wisdom which he graciously gives to his servants. If the steward of a great family from a selfish attachment to particulars takes that with which he is entrusted and bestows it lavishly on some, to the injury of others, and to the damage of him who employs him, he disunites himself and becomes unworthy of that office.

8   The true felicity of man in this life, and that which is to come, is in being inwardly united to the fountain of universal love and bliss. When we provide for posterity, and make settlements which will not take effect till

after we are centered in another state of being, if we therein act contrary to universal love and righteousness, such conduct must arise from a false, selfish pleasure in directing a thing to be done wrong, in which it will be impossible for us to take pleasure at the time when our directions are put in execution. For if we after such settlement and when too late for an alteration, attain to that purified state which our Redeemer prayed his Father that his people might attain to, of being united to the Father and the Son, a sincere repentance for all things done in a Will[13] separate from universal love must precede this inward sanctification; and though in such depth of repentance and reconciliation all sins are forgiven, and sorrows removed, that our misdeeds heretofore done could no longer afflict us, yet our partial determinations in favor of such whom we loved in a selfish love could not afford us any pleasure.

9   And if after such selfish settlement our Wills continue to stand in opposition to the fountain of universal light and love, there will be an unpassable gulf between the soul and true felicity, nor can anything heretofore done in this separate Will afford us pleasure.

Chapter VIII

1   To labor for an establishment in divine love, where the mind is disentangled from the power of darkness is the great business of man's life.

2   Collecting of riches, covering the body with fine-wrought, costly apparel, and having magnificent furniture operates against universal love, and tends to feed self, that it belongs not to the children of the light to desire these things.

3   He who sent ravens to feed Elijah in the wilderness [1 Kings 17:4,6], and increased the poor widow's small remains of meal and oil [ibid., v.14], is now as attentive to the necessities of his people as ever, that when he numbers us with his people and says, Ye are my sons and daughters, no greater happiness can be desired by them who know how gracious a Father he is.

---

13   [The word "will" in the holograph has been changed by the editor to "Will" to clarify that the author is still referring to the estate dispositions "we provide for posterity" (second sentence of this paragraph 8) in our Last Wills and Testaments.]

4   The greater part of the necessaries of life are so far perishable that each generation has occasion to labor for them and when we look toward a succeeding age with a mind influenced by universal love we endeavor not to exempt some from those cares which necessarily relate to this life, and give them power to oppress others, but desire they may all be the Lord's children and live in that humility and order becoming his family. Our hearts being thus opened and enlarged we feel content in a use of things as foreign to luxury and grandeur as that which our Redeemer laid down as a pattern.

5   By desiring wealth for the power and distinction it gives, and gathering it on this motive a person may properly be called a rich man, whose mind is moved by a draft distinguishable from the drawings of the Father, and cannot be united to the heavenly society where God is the strength of their life, until he is delivered from this contrary drawing.

6   It is easier, says our Savior, for a camel to go through a needle's eye than for a rich man to enter the kingdom of God [Matt. 19:24; Mark 10:25; Luke 18:25]. Here our Lord uses an instructive similitude, for as a camel considered under that character cannot pass through a needle's eye, so a man who trusts in riches, and holds them for the sake of the power and distinction attending them cannot in that spirit enter the kingdom. Now every part of a camel may be so reduced as to pass through a hole as small as a needle's eye, yet such is the bulk of the creature and the hardness of its bones and teeth that it could not be completed without much labor: so man must cease from that spirit which craves riches, and be reduced into another disposition before he inherits the kingdom, as effectually as a camel must cease from the form of a camel in passing through the eye of a needle.[14]

7   When our Savior said to the rich youth, "Go sell that thou hast and give to the poor" [Matt. 19:21; Mark 10:21; Luke 18:22] though undoubtedly it was his duty to have done so, yet to confine this of selling all as a duty on every true Christian would be to limit the Holy One.

8   Obedient children who are entrusted with much outward substance wait for wisdom to dispose of it agreeable to his will, "in whom the fatherless find mercy" [Hos. 14:3]. It may not be the duty of every one to commit at once their substance to other hands, but rather from time to

---

[14]   [In the margin of this paragraph Woolman has written: "A cable may be reduced so as to pass through a needle's eye, but can a camel?"]

time to look round among the numerous branches of the great family as his stewards who said, "Leave thy fatherless children; I will preserve them alive; and let thy widows trust in me" [Jer. 49:11]. But as disciples of Christ however entrusted with much goods they may not conform to sumptuous or luxurious living. For if possessing great treasure had been a sufficient reason to make a fine show in the world, then Christ our Lord, who had an unfailing storehouse, and in a way surpassing the common operations in nature, supplied thousands of people with food, would not have lived in so much plainness.

9   What we equitably possess is a gift from God to us, but by the Son all things were created. Now he who forms things out of nothing, who creates and, having created does possess, is more truly rich than he who possesses by receiving gifts from another. If depth of knowledge and a high title had been sufficient reasons to make a splendid show, he would have made it. He told the woman of Samaria sundry things relative to her past life, made mention of the decease of Lazarus, and answered the scribe who accounted him a blasphemer, without information, and having the Spirit without measure knew what was in man.

10   The title of Lord he owned, nor was it ever more justly given to any, that in riches, and wisdom, and greatness there was none on earth equal to him, and as he lived in perfect plainness, and simplicity, the greatest in his family cannot by virtue of their station claim a right to live in worldly grandeur without contradicting his doctrine who said: It is enough for the disciple to be as his master [Matt. 10:25].

Chapter IX

1   When our eyes are so single as to discern the selfish spirit clearly, we behold it the greatest of all tyrants.

2   Many thousand innocent people under some of the Roman emperors being confirmed in the Truth of Christ's religion from the powerful effects of his Holy Spirit upon them, and scrupling to conform to heathenish rites, were therefore by various kinds of cruel and lingering torments put to death, as is largely set forth by Eusebius.[15] Now if we single

---

[15]   [ca. 260-339; Bishop of Caesarea; the 'Father of Church History' whose *Ecclesiastical History* in ten books was completed 323/4; attended the Council of Nicaea (325) as a theological adviser to Emperor Constantine.]

out Domitian,[16] Nero,[17] or any other of these persecuting emperors, the man, though terrible in his time, will appear as a tyrant of small consequence compared with the selfish spirit. For though his bounds were large yet a great part of the world were out of his reach; and though he grievously afflicted the bodies of those innocent people, yet the minds of many were divinely supported in their greatest agonies, and being faithful unto death were delivered from his tyranny. His reign though cruel for a time was soon over, and he considered in his greatest pomp appears to have been a slave to the selfish spirit. Thus tyranny as applied to a man, rises up and soon has an end. But if we consider the numerous oppressions in many states, and the calamities occasioned by nation contending with nation in various parts and ages of the world, and remember that selfishness has been the original cause of them all; if we consider that such who are finally possessed with this selfish spirit, not only afflict others, but are afflicted themselves and have no real quietness in this life, nor in futurity, but according to the saying of Christ have their portion in that uneasy condition "where the worm dieth not, and the fire is not quenched" [Isa. 66:24]. Under all these circumstances how terrible does this selfishness appear?

3   If we consider the havoc that is made in this age, and how numbers of people are hurried on, striving to collect treasures to please that mind which wanders from perfect resignedness, and in that wisdom which is foolishness with God are perverting the true use of things, laboring as in the fire, contending with one another, even unto blood, and exerting their power to support ways of living foreign to the life of one wholly crucified to the world; if we consider what great numbers of people are employed in preparing the materials of war, and the labor and toil of armies, set apart for protecting their respective territories from the incursions of others, and the extensive miseries which attend their engagements; while many of those who till the lands, and are employed in other useful things, in supporting themselves, supporting those employed in military affairs, and some who own the soil, have great hardships to encounter, through too much labor; while others in several kingdoms are busied in fetching men to help labor from distant parts of the world, to spend the remainder of their lives in the uncomfortable condition of slaves,

---

[16] [Roman Emperor 81-96 at the end of whose reign a persecution of the Christians and Jews broke out.]
[17] [Roman Emperor 54-68 who began persecution of Christians after the fire of 64 destroyed much of Rome.]

and that self is at the bottom of these proceedings. Amidst all this confusion, and these scenes of sorrow and distress, can we remember the Prince of Peace, remember that we are his disciples, and remember that example of humility and plainness which he set for us without feeling an earnest desire to be disentangled from everything connected with selfish customs, in food, in raiment, in houses, and all things else; that being of Christ's family, and walking as he walked, we may stand in that uprightness wherein man was first made, and have no fellowship with those inventions which men in the fallen wisdom have sought out.[18]

Chapter X

Are not two sparrows sold for a farthing and one of them
shall not fall on the ground without your Father [Matt. 10:29].

1   The way of carrying on wars, common in the world, is so far distinguishable from the purity of Christ's religion that many scruple to join in them. Those who are so redeemed from the love of the world, as to possess nothing in a selfish spirit, their life is hid with Christ in God [Col. 3:3], and these he preserves in resignedness even in times of commotion.

2   As they possess nothing but what pertains to his family, anxious thoughts about wealth or dominion have little or nothing in them to work upon, and they learn contentment in being disposed of according to his will who being omnipotent and always mindful of his children causes all things to work for their good. But where that spirit works which loves riches, and in its working gathers wealth and cleaves to customs which have their root in self-pleasing: this spirit thus separating from universal love, seeks help from that power which stands in the separation, and whatever name it has, it still desires to defend the treasures thus gotten. This is like a chain where the end of one link encloses the end of another. The rising up of a desire to attain wealth is the beginning, this desire being cherished moves to action, and riches thus gotten please self, and while self has a life in them it desires to have them defended.

3   Wealth is attended with power by which bargains and proceedings contrary to universal righteousness are supported, and here oppression carried on with worldly policy, and order clothes itself with the name of justice and becomes like a seed of discord in the soil, and as this spirit which wanders from the pure habitation prevails, so the seeds of war swell,

---

[18] [Then follow three paragraphs in MS A/*Plea* which are not found in MS W.]

and sprout, and grow, and becomes strong till much fruits are ripened. Thus comes the harvest spoken of by the prophet which is a heap in the day of grief, and desperate sorrow [Isa. 17:11].

4   Oh that we who declare against wars, and acknowledge our trust to be in God only, may walk in the light and therein examine our foundation and motives in holding great estates: may we look upon our treasures, and the furniture of our houses, and the garments in which we array ourselves, and try whether the seeds of war have any nourishment in these our possessions or not.

5   Holding treasures in the self-pleasing spirit is a strong plant, the fruit whereof ripens fast. A day of outward distress is coming, and divine love calls to prepare against it![19]

Chapter XI

The heaven, even the heavens, are the Lord's, but the
earth hath he given to the children of men (Ps. 115:16).

1   As servants of God, what land or estate we hold, we hold under him, as his gift, and in applying the profits it is our duty to act consistent with the design of our benefactor.

2   Imperfect men may give, on motives of misguided affection; but Perfect Wisdom and Goodness gives agreeable to his own nature: nor is this gift absolute but conditional, for us to occupy as dutiful children and not otherwise, for he alone is the true proprietor. "The world, saith he, is mine, and the fullness thereof" [Ps. 50:12].

3   The inspired Lawgiver directed that such of the Israelites who sold their inheritance should sell it for a term only, and that they, or their children, should again enjoy it in the Year of Jubilee, settled on every fiftieth year. The land shall not be sold forever, for the land is mine saith the Lord, for ye are strangers and sojourners with me (Lev. 25:23). The design of which was to prevent the rich from oppressing the poor by too much engrossing the land, and our blessed Redeemer said "Till heaven and earth pass, one jot, or one tittle shall in no wise pass from the law, till all be fulfilled" [Matt. 5:18].

---

[19] [Then follow four sentences in MS A/*Plea* which are not found in MS W.]

4   Where divine love takes place in the hearts of any people, and they steadily act on a principle of universal righteousness, there the true intent of the law is fulfilled, though their outward modes of proceeding may be distinguishable from one another. But where men are possessed by that spirit hinted at by the prophet, and looking over their wealth, say in their hearts, "Have we not taken to us horns by our own strength" [Amos 6:13] here they deviate from the divine law, and do not account their possessions so strictly God's, nor the weak and poor entitled to so much of the increase thereof, but that they may indulge their desires in conforming to worldly pomp, and thus where "house is joined to house, and field laid to field, till there is no place" [Isa. 5:8], and the poor are thereby straitened: though this be done by bargain and purchase, yet so far as it stands distinguished from universal love, so far that woe prefixed by the prophet will accompany their proceedings.[20]

5   As he who first formed the earth out of nothing was then the true proprietor of it, so he still remains: and though he has given it to the children of men, so that multitudes of people have had sustenance from it while they continued here, yet he has never aliened it, but his right to give is as good as at the first, nor can any apply the increase of their possessions contrary to universal love, nor dispose of lands in a way which they know tends to exalt some by oppressing others, without being justly chargeable with usurpation.

Chapter XII

1   If we count back one hundred and fifty years and compare the inhabitants of Great Britain with the natives of North America on the like compass of ground, the natives, I suppose, would bear a small proportion to the others.

2   On the discovery of this fertile continent, many of those thick-settled inhabitants coming over, the natives generally treated them kindly at the first, and as those brought iron tools and a variety of things convenient for man's use, these gladly embraced the opportunity of traffic, and encouraged these foreigners to settle. I speak only of improvements made peaceably.

---

[20] [Here two paragraphs have been stricken from the holograph regarding the gifting of land to Abraham and to Jacob, citing Gen. 13:15 and 35:12, respectively.]

3   Thus our gracious Father, who at the same time beholds the situation of all his creatures, has opened a way, from a thick-settled land, and given us some room on this. Now if we attentively consider the turning of God's hand in thus far giving us room on this continent, and that the offspring of those ancient possessors of the country (in whose eyes we appear as newcomers) are yet owners and inhabitants of the land adjoining us, and that their way of life requiring much room has been transmitted to them from their predecessors, and probably settled by the custom of a great many ages—under these considerations we may see the necessity of cultivating the lands already obtained of them, and applying the increase consistent with true wisdom, so as to accommodate the greatest number of people it is capable of, before we have any right to plead, as members of the one great family, the equity of their assigning to us more of their possessions, and living in a way requiring less room.

4   Did we all walk as became the followers of our blessed Savior, were all those fruits of our country retained in it which are sent abroad in return for such strong drink, such costly array, and other luxuries, which we should then have no use for, and the labor and expense of importing and exporting applied to husbandry and useful trades, a much greater number of people than now reside here might with the divine blessing live comfortably on the lands already granted us, by these ancient possessors of the country.

5   If we faithfully serve God who has given us some room on this land, I believe he will make some of us useful among them, both in publishing the doctrines of his Son our Savior, and in pointing out to them the advantages of replenishing the earth and subduing it.

6   Some I expect will be careful for such poor people abroad who earn their bread in preparing and trading in those things which we, as true disciples, living in a plainness like our heavenly pattern should have no use for. But laying aside all superfluities and luxuries, while people are so much thicker settled in some parts than in others, a trade in some serviceable articles may be to mutual advantage, and carried on with much more regularity, and satisfaction to a sincere Christian than the trade now generally is.

7   One person in society continuing to live contrary to true wisdom commonly draws others into connection with him, and where these embrace the way this first has chosen, their proceedings are like a wild

vine, which springing from a single seed, and growing strong, their branches extend, and their little twining holders twist round all herbs, and boughs of trees where they reach, and are so braced and locked in, that without much labor or great strength they are not disentangled. Thus these customs small in their beginning, as they increase they promote business, and traffic, and many depend on them for a living. But as it is evident that all business which has not its foundation in true wisdom is unbecoming a faithful follower of Christ, who loves God not only with all his heart, but with all his strength and ability to labor and act in the world. And as the Lord is able to, and will support those whose hearts are perfect toward him, in a way agreeable to his unerring wisdom, it becomes us to meditate on the privileges of his children, to remember that where the Spirit of the Lord is, there is liberty, and that in joining to customs which we know are wrong, there is a departing from the purity of his government and a certain degree of alienation from him.

8   To lay aside curious, costly attire, and use that only which is plain and serviceable, to cease from all superfluities, and too much strong drink, are agreeable to the doctrines of our blessed Redeemer, and if in the integrity of our hearts we do so, we in some degree contribute toward lessening that business which has its foundation in a wrong spirit, and as some well-inclined people are entangled in such business, and at times desirous of being freed from it, such our ceasing from these things may be made helpful to them; and though for a time their business fail, yet if they humbly ask wisdom of God, and are truly resigned to him, he will not fail them nor forsake them.

9   He who created the earth, and has provided sustenance for millions of people in past ages, is now as attentive to the necessities of his children as ever.

10   To press forward toward perfection is our duty and if herein we lessen some business by which some poor people earn their bread, the Lord who calls to cease from these things, will take care of those whose business fails by it, if they sincerely seek him.

11   If the connections we have with the inhabitants of these provinces and our interest considered as distinct from others engage us to promote plain living, in order to enrich our own country, though a plain life is in itself best, yet by living plain in a selfish spirit we advance not forward in true religion.

12   Divine love which enlarges the heart toward mankind universally is that alone which can rightly stop every corrupt stream and open those channels of business and commerce where nothing runs that is not pure, and so establish our goings, that when in our labor we meditate on the universal love of God, and the harmony of holy angels, this serenity of our minds may never be clouded in remembering that some part of our employment tends to support customs which have their foundation in the self-seeking spirit.

Chapter XIII

1   While our minds are prepossessed in favor of customs distinguishable from perfect purity, we are in danger of not attending with singleness to that light which opens to our view the nature of universal righteousness.

2   In the affairs of a thick-settled country are variety of useful employments besides tilling the earth: that for some men to have no more land than is necessary to build on, and to answer the occasions relative to the family may consist with brotherhood; and from the various gifts which God has bestowed on those employed in husbandry, for some to possess and occupy much more than others may likewise; but where any on the strength of their possessions, demands such rent or interest as necessitates those who hire of them to a closer application to business than our merciful Father designed for us, this puts the wheels of perfect brotherhood out of order, and leads to employments the promoting of which belongs not to the family of Christ, whose example in all parts being a pattern of wisdom, so the plainness and simplicity of his outward appearance may well make us ashamed to adorn our bodies in costly array, or treasure up wealth by the least degree of oppression.

3   The soil yields us support and is profitable for man, and though some possessing a larger share of these profits than others may consist with the harmony of true brotherhood, yet that the poorest people who are honest, so long as they remain inhabitants of the earth, are entitled to a certain portion of these profits, in as clear and absolute a sense as those who inherit much, I believe will be agreed to by those whose hearts are enlarged with universal love.

4   The first people who inhabited the earth were the first who had possession of the soil. The gracious Creator and owner of it gave the fruits thereof for their use. And as one generation passed away, another came

and took possession, and thus through many ages innumerable multitudes of people have been supplied by the fruits of the earth. But our gracious Creator is as absolutely the owner of it as he was when he first formed it out of nothing. And though by claims grounded on prior possession, great inequality appears among men, yet the instructions of the great proprietor of the earth are necessary to be attended to in all our proceedings as possessors or claimers of the profits of the soil.

5   The steps of a good man are ordered by the Lord, and those who are thus guided, whose hearts are enlarged in his love, give directions concerning their possessions agreeable thereto. And that claim which stands on universal righteousness is a good right, but the continuance of that right depends on properly applying the profits thereof.

6   The word *right* is commonly used relative to our possessions. We say a *right* of propriety to such a dividend of a province, or a clear, indisputable *right* to the land within such certain bounds. Thus this word is continued as a remembrancer of the original intent of dividing the land by boundaries, and implies that it was designed to be *equitably* or *rightly* divided, to be divided according to *righteousness*.

7   In this, that is, in *equity* and *righteousness* consists the strength of our claims.

8   If we trace an *unrighteous* claim and find gifts, or grants, to be proved by sufficient seals and witnesses, this gives not the claimant a *right*, for that which is opposite to *righteousness* is wrong, and the nature of it must be changed before it can be *right*.

9   Suppose twenty free men, professed followers of Christ, discovered an island unknown to all other people and that they with their wives, independent of all others, took possession of it, and dividing it equitably made improvements and multiplied.

10   Suppose these first possessors being generally influenced by true love, did with paternal regard look over the increasing condition of the inhabitants, and near the end of their lives gave such directions concerning their respective possessions as best suited the convenience of the whole, and tended to preserve love and harmony, and that their successors in the continued increase of people generally followed their pious examples and pursued means the most effectual to keep oppression out of their island. But [suppose] that one of these first settlers, from a fond attachment to

one of his numerous sons, no more deserving than the rest, gives the chief of his lands to him, and by an instrument sufficiently witnessed strongly expresses his mind and will. Suppose this son being landlord to his brethren and nephews, demands such a portion of the fruits of the earth as may supply him and his family and some others, and that these others thus supplied out of his store, are employed in adorning his buildings with curious engravings, and paintings, preparing carriages to ride in, vessels for his house, delicious meats, fine-wrought apparel and furniture, all suiting that distinction lately arisen between him and the other inhabitants; and that having this absolute disposal of these numerous improvements, his power so increases that in all conferences relative to the public affairs of the island, these plain, honest men, who are zealous for equitable establishments, find great difficulty in proceeding agreeable to their righteous inclination.[21]

11   Suppose he from a fondness for one of his sons joined with a desire to continue this grandeur under his own name confirms chief of his possessions to him, and thus for many ages, on near a twentieth part of this island, there is one great landlord, and the rest poor-oppressed people, to some of whom from the manner of their education, joined with a notion of the greatness of their predecessors, labor is disagreeable, who therefore by artful applications to the weakness, unguardedness, and corruption of others, in striving to get a living out of them increase the difficulties among them: while the inhabitants of the other parts who guard against oppression, and with one consent train up their children in frugality, and useful labor live more harmonious.

12   If we trace the claim of the ninth or tenth of these great landlords down to the first possessor, and find the claim supported throughout by instruments strongly drawn and witnessed, after all we could not admit a belief into our hearts that he had a *right* to so great a portion of land, after such a numerous increase of inhabitants.

13   The first possessor of that twentieth part held no more we suppose than an equitable portion, but when the Lord who first gave these twenty men possession of this island unknown to all others, gave being to numerous people who inhabited this twentieth part, whose natures required the fruits thereof for their sustenance, this great claimer of the

---

[21] [Found in MS A/*Plea* following "inclination" is this phrase: "while he stands in opposition to them."]

soil could not have a *right* to the whole, to dispose of it in gratifying his irregular desires, but they as creatures of the Most High God, possessor of heaven and earth, had a *right* to part of what this great claimer held, though they had no instruments to confirm their *right*.

14   Thus oppression in the extreme appears terrible, but oppression in more refined appearances, remains to be oppression, and where the smallest degree of it is cherished it grows stronger and more extensive, that to labor for a perfect redemption from this spirit of oppression is the great business of the whole family of Christ Jesus in this world.[22]

---

[22]   [Then follow three chapters in MS A/*Plea*, titled "On Schools," "On Masters and Servants," and "To keep Negroes as servants till they are thirty years of age. . .: Reasons Offered," respectively, which are not found in MS W.]

7 A

Ephemera: untitled parable on "a tax demanded for evil ends"

Written 1756; not printed

Editor's Introduction

Woolman created this biblical parable as a stage for presenting the Quakers' profound objections against supporting—through taxes and either direct or indirect militia service—the military defense requirements of Pennsylvania's provincial government in the time of the French and Indian War. In the parable, an unjustifiable war is made by the children of Ham, the youngest of Noah's three sons, led by Nimrod, a mighty man of arms, against Shem, an older son of Noah, "with all his offspring."

The following modernized text is based on the holograph which is in the holdings of HC.[1]

+++

Text

As liberty was given to suppose a tax demanded for evil ends I'll thus state the matter—

1   One hundred years next after the Flood some disorders happened among the children of Ham[2] which alarmed the whole family. They all meet and have a free and open conference [and] at length agree that things of this sort ought to be the constant business of judicious men set apart for that purpose and invested with the authority of the whole. They choose Nimrod[3] as chief in this business and Sheba[4] as the mouth or representative of them all. Sheba or one judged fit for the office to be chosen yearly by the brethren. Those two shall form rules of conduct as they judge reasonable, to which all shall submit. They make an article of this agreement and all subscribe to it, are thereby subjected to the rules so framed and to the penalties annexed to the disobeying them. Nimrod is

---

[1] Special Collection 851.
[2] [The youngest of Noah's three sons. See Gen. 5:32; 6:10; 7:13; 9:18,22; 10:1,6,20.]
[3] [Grandson of Ham, son of Cush, and "a mighty hunter before the LORD". See Gen. 10:8-9; 1 Chron. 1:10; Mic. 5:6.]
[4] [Great-grandson of Ham, son of Raamah, and nephew of Nimrod. See Gen. 10:7; 1 Chron. 1:9.]

ordered to put their laws in execution. The king and representative listen to the petitions of the people, plead the cause of the oppressed and give them relief, search out and supply the wants of the poor and fatherless. They view with the spirit of a parent the situation of their family, abridge the schemes of individuals so far as they interfere with the public good, and give light and encouragement to their honest and industrious children. Their demands for money to support themselves and defray all necessary expenses in government are cheerfully paid and they are beloved and honored by their people. Their station gives them reverence and everyone seeks the ruler's favor. Sheba is chosen again.

2   Their hearts are lifted up because of their beauty and their wisdom corrupted by reason of their brightness. By degrees they grow rich and excessive and the desire thereto increases in proportion.

3   Good old Shem[5] with all his offspring lives compact together at a small distance. Their officers are peace and their exacters righteousness. They abound in good things. Shem in the integrity of his heart reproves Nimrod for his apostatising. Reason is against him, he cannot withstand the attack. To own his error were too low for his haughty spirit, to quit his designs were death. He resolves on another expedient. He watches with an evil eye the ways of Shem and his people and with the most intricate oblique frames devices against them, cries aloud of the injuries he has sustained by their fraud and deceit, and demands ample satisfaction. His demands being groundless are rejected by Shem. He calls Sheba, gathers money from his people, hires men who are jealous for their prince though ignorant of the merits of his cause, leads them into Shem's borders, kills all who oppose them, brings [out] sheep and cattle and much treasures. Exalted with success and insatiable of riches and power [Sheba] sends a message to Shem, "submit to my reasonable demands or take the effect." Shem serves God and trusts in him, and cannot bow to a cruel hunter.

4   Nimrod assembles his people. With sophistical orations inveighs against Shem. Sheba by the intrigues of Nimrod is annually chosen. With the assistance of Sheba he demands four times as much money of the people as is necessary to regulate domestic affairs in order say they to reduce Shem to reason.

---

5 [Another of Noah's three sons. See Gen. 5:32; 6:10; 9:18,23,26,27.]

5   There's a number of Ham's family who love truth and justice, well understand Nimrod's tyranny and sympathize with Shem in his trouble. The question is shall they pay the demand actively or not!

6   It is agreed that to promote virtue and discourage vice, so far as we are capable, is our duty, acting always with that integrity and modesty becoming honest men and good subjects.

7   I'll suppose Nimrod through flattery of vicious people, long gratification of wrong desires together with success, is really clouded in his judgment, or suppose him utterly wicked. If those men of wisdom and honesty whose characters add beauty to his kingdom contribute to his designs cheerfully he has no real help from their honest hearts and better understandings. If from their attachment to virtue they conscientiously refuse to contribute actively, but with meekness and fortitude submit to the penalty, Nimrod on this occasion seeing their conduct, may likely make profitable reflections on his own. However that be, they keep a good conscience and maintain their characters. They may be considered as persons disaffected to government and their little kingdom as divided against itself and yet where honesty, meekness and fortitude [are] united, hard words cannot move it. "There's no good in unity except unity be in goodness."

8   Thus much in regard to an unlimited active payment which as here stated I think differs widely from our present circumstance.

9   In our present troubles though our cause be good, yet in national disputes, the innocent suffering with and perhaps more than the promoters of the mischief, we think mortal man as a minister of justice unequal to the task, and therefore cease from war, submitting the issue to him who is the judge of all the earth.

10   The deep sense of our own unworthiness and the great kindness of our heavenly Father in sealing this testimony to us are sufficient causes of humiliation, yet to his people we may say he has in this point brought us a step beyond many other sects. We [?believe] the increase of this principle would be to his glory and man's felicity.

11   If men in authority who have not attained to this quiet resignation demand money of us to promote war, our cheerful compliance looks a little like denying them that help which I have thought (sometimes in deep humiliation) our gracious Father intends for them through us.

12　To meekly suffer by our lawful rulers seems to me like placing the light on the candlestick and adding our mite to help forward toward that mountain where they shall no more hurt or destroy [Isa. 65:25].

7 B

Ephemera: account of peace mission dream

Written 1764; 1st printed 1971

Editor's Introduction

This fragment, precisely dated by Woolman in its opening, records a dream which he had almost thirteen months to the day after returning home from his memorable and courageous missionary journey to be with the Native Americans at Wyalusing. This dream account is of interest because it reveals so much about the dreamer's concerns and intentions, revelations neither found as sharply delineated in Text 6, which is believed to have been written just after the Wyalusing journey, nor shared with John Pemberton (nor seriously offered to Israel Pemberton, John's brother, the influential Indian peacemaker and Quaker reformer).[1]

The following is a modernization of the holograph, MS R2, which is at Rutgers University.

+++
Text

1   26th day, 7th month, 1764. At night I dreamed I was abroad on a religious visit beyond the sea and had been outward of two months, and that while I was out on the visit the people of the country where I was and those of a neighboring kingdom, having concerns together in affairs abroad, had difference which arose so high that they began to fight; and both parties were preparing for general war. I thought there was no sea between them, but only bounded by a line, and that the man who was chief among the other people lived within a day's journey of where I was.

2   I, being troubled at these things, felt a desire in my mind to go and speak with this chief man and try to prevail on him to stop fighting, that they might enquire more fully into the grounds of their disagreement and endeavor to accommodate their difference without shedding more blood.

---

[1]   See herein Appendix 2, Reformers of the mid-eighteenth century American Quaker Church: Israel Pemberton, Jr. and John Woolman, at pp. 233-34.

91

3   So I set off, having one man with me as a pilot; and after traveling some time in the woods, we came in sight of a few of those people at labor, having guns with them. I being foremost came near them before they saw us, and as soon as they discovered that we were from their enemies' country they took up their guns and were preparing to fire on us, whereupon I hastily approached them, holding up both my arms to let them see that I had no warlike weapons. So I shook hands with them and let them know the cause of our coming, at which they appeared well pleased.

4   In the surprise at our meeting, my pilot held forth a small gun he had with him, which I knew not of before; but they so soon understood our business that none fired, after which I saw my pilot no more. But one of these people offering to conduct me to their chief man, he and I set forward and traveled along a path through woods and swamps near southeast; and on our way my new pilot, who could talk broken English, spoke to me with an agreeable countenance and desired that when I came before their chief I would speak my mind freely, and signified their salutation at meeting was to speak to each other but not shake hands.

5   At length we came to the house of this chief man, whom I thought had the command of the soldiers and was at the head of the affairs of their country, but was not called a king. His house stood by itself, and a good garden with green herbs before the door, in which garden I stood while my pilot went to tell this chief man that I wanted to speak with him.

6   As I stood alone in the garden my mind was exercised on the affair I came upon, and presently my pilot returned, and passing by me said he had forgotten to tell me that I had an invitation to dinner. Soon after him came the chief man, who having been told the cause of my coming looked on me with a friendly countenance, and as I was about to enter on the business I awoke. JOHN WOOLMAN.

7 C

Ephemera:
notes and commentaries on A. Benezet's
A Caution and Warning to Great Britain

Written between 1766 and 1770; not printed

Editor's Introduction

One of the close friends with whom John Woolman shared strong moral and social concerns was Anthony Benezet (1713-1784). Benezet was born in France of Huguenot parents who, shortly after his birth, moved to Holland to escape persecution and thence to London where Anthony became a Quaker. Anthony came to Philadelphia in 1731. His principal work was as an educator but he labored hard at social reform, especially in the anti-enslavement cause. He and Woolman supported each other in their mutual reforming labors. These notes of Woolman were made upon his reading Benezet's *A Caution and Warning to Great Britain*[1] published in 1766. Woolman quotes from the 1766, not the 1767, edition of the Benezet work, and refers to it in a footnote in his own 1770 essay "Considerations on the True Harmony of Mankind & how it is to be maintained" (Text 11 herein). This holograph, MS A/*Notes*, is found in MS A at back-to-front pp. 5-14.

+++
Text

[A]

[JW quoting from Benezet, pp. 17-19]

1   Extracts from a Surgeons manuscript Journal who went on board a vessel from Liverpool to the coast of Guinea

---

[1] Anthony Benezet, *A Caution and Warning to Great Britain and her Colonies, in a short representation of the calamitous state of the Enslaved Negroes in the British Dominions. Collected from various Authors, and submitted to the Serious Consideration of all, more especially of those in power* (Philadelphia: printed by Henry Miller, 1766)

93

2   "Sestro decemb [December] da 29 1724 No trade today though many traders came on board, they inform us that the people are gone to war within land and will bring prisoners enough in two or three days, in hopes of which we stay.

3   "Da 30 No trade yet but our traders came on board and informed us that the people had burnt four towns of their enemies so that tomorrow we expect slaves; yesterday came in a large Londoner.

4   "31 fair weather but no trade yet; we see each night towns burning, but we hear the Sestro men are many of them killed by the inland Negroes, so that we fear this war will be unsuccessful.

5   "Da 2 [January] mo 11 last night we saw prodigious fire break out and this morning see the town of Sestro burnt down to the ground it contained some one hundred houses so that we find their enemies are too hard for them at present and our trade spoiled here, so that we weighed anchor, as did likewise the other vessel to proceed lower down." *Caution and Warning to Great Britain &c page 17.*

6   Extracts from a Surgeons manuscript Journal who went from New York to the Coast of Guinea about the year 1746. "Being on the Coast of Bafalia the commander of the vessel according to custom sent a present to the king, letting him know they wanted a cargo of slaves. The king promised to furnish them with slaves and set out to go to war with his enemies, designing also to surprise some town and take all the people prisoners—sometime after the king sent them word, he had not yet met with the desired success having been twice rebuffed in attempting to break up two towns, but still hoped to procure a number of slaves for them, and at length met his enemies in the field where a battle was fought which lasted three days, during which time four thousand and five hundred men were slain. The person who wrote this account saw the dead bodies as they lay in the field. Think says he what a piteous sight it was to see the widows weeping over their lost husbands and orphans deploring the loss of their fathers &c." *page 18.*

[JW commentary on the capture, passage, and
seasoning of Africans seized into the enslavement trade]

1   In these instances we may behold how from a desire of gain the white people stir up the Negroes to push forward most cruel and lamentable wars.

2　　Their vessels frequently take five or six hundred slaves at one freight, and how moving is this subject if attended to with a compassionate heart. If we consider them as violently separated from their homes and from all their most intimate acquaintance their case appears sorrowful; but to be made slaves to a people whose conduct among them appears cruel, must necessarily fill their minds with apprehension of future distress.

3　　But further, even free passengers would meet with difficulty on a long voyage were their number equal to a freight of slaves; but how much greater is the difficulty of these poor sufferers? For this being a scene of violence, the whites in providing against the Negroes rising, tie the men to posts in the hold, where they are but poorly accommodated as to bodily nourishment.

4　　People not used to the sea are often so sick in rough weather that the operation is frequently as strong as physic, which amongst a freight of slaves slightly attended is likely to make their confinement more grievous.

5　　Through distress of mind, through the breathing of so many in a close place, and want of necessary accommodations to keep the place sweet and clean, mortal distempers frequently break out among them.

6　　In sickness we have need of help from sympathizing friends, but how calamitous is the case of these people when sickness thus breaks out among them.

7　　So grievous are these long voyages to these poor crowded sufferers that it is computed *page 31* that no less than ten thousand die every year on their passage.

8　　Those who survive these hardships and are placed under the command of overseers in the American plantation, the work assigned them is so painful, the diet so unequal to the labor, and chastisement so severe that it is computed *page 31*, that near twenty thousand die every year in what is called the seasoning.

9　　If we sit by a friend in his last sickness, behold his hard labor under the pains of death it frequently moves to sympathy, but if thirty thousand are brought every year to an untimely end it is not less than eighty persons to each day, and should it be our lot to behold that number in their last agonies, in one day how gloomy would that day appear to us— yet if they came to their end without violence or hard treatment, without any provocations to hatred and malice, their deaths would be less affecting. But if we consider them dying in such numbers day after day, for many years! And that these poor creatures under the pains of death are also under the strongest temptations to wrath and that their end comes through insupportable oppression, what heart can refrain from sorrow at so lamentable a breach in the harmony of mankind.

10   He that created us created them, and they also are his offspring, and as his gracious regard is toward his creatures he is begetting in many a tender feeling of the grief and distress of their brothers and sisters whose dying groans ascend to him—and I may say in sundry afflictions which I have met with my mind from time to time has been brought into a tender sympathy with these oppressed people and though it be natural to us to be much more afflicted with an injury committed against ourselves or our children than we are in beholding the like injury committed against strangers, though unoffending and helpless, yet through the tender mercies of my heavenly Father I have learned this, that the more we are redeemed from selfishness, and brought into that love in which there is no respect for persons, the more we are prepared to desire and labor for universal harmony among surfeiting wealth.

[B]

[JW quoting from Benezet, p. 5]

1   In regard to those who survive the seasoning—in an account of European settlements in America printed in London 1757, the author says "The Negroes in our colonies endure a slavery more complete and attended with far worse circumstances than what any people in their condition suffer in any other part of the world, or have suffered in any other period of time.

2   "Proofs of this are not wanting. The prodigious waste which we experience in this unhappy part of our species is a full and melancholy evidence of this truth. The Island of Barbadoes, the Negroes on which do not amount to eighty thousand, notwithstanding all the means which they use to increase them by propagation, and that the climate is in every respect except that of being more wholesome resembling the climate from which they come; notwithstanding all this, Barbadoes lies under a necessity of a yearly recruit of five thousand to keep up the stock at the number I have mentioned.

3 "This prodigious failure which is at least in the same proportion in all our islands shows demonstratively that some uncommon and unsupportable hardship lies upon the Negroes which wears them down in such a surprising manner."

[JW commentary on the hardship,
misery, and death of the enslaved in America]

1 It may not be unfruitful, I trust, to meditate awhile on this subject. In passing through the pains of death, without any aggravating circumstances, there is, we see, a conflict that is very painful; but to be worn out with labor and die with extreme oppression is a death attended with great misery.

2 Did we labor in the heat till our weakly natures called for rest, and received not only a denial at the time of those calls, but chastisement for being dilatory, with what pain of mind should we reflect on this treatment.

3 Now if this were limited to a week or a month the hopes of a change for the better might refresh our drooping spirits; but where there is no prospect but that of continued misery, the thoughts of increasing calamities renders the condition more deplorable.

4 An inward experience of the sanctifying power of Christ, of that faith which works by love to the purifying of the heart, this is felt to be a support under affliction superior to all other; but alas what neglect has there been among the professors of Christianity as to hearty sincere labors for the salvation of these people?

5 Were we wearied already with insupportable labors, pinched as to the necessaries of life, and being ready to faint under our burdens, were forced through cruel whippings to toil with wearied limbs and dejected spirits till nature yielded to prevailing weakness—if under this weakness instead of proper care and attendance we were reproached with insincerity and a feigned sickness, how great as to the outward would be our calamity.

6 If all our friends were not only poor as to the things of this world and unable to supply us with that which might be comfortable, but slaves like ourselves and liable to distress like ours, how would our groans ascend to that almighty and gracious being whose tender mercies are over all his works, and who in his own time will be a refuge for the oppressed.

7 Now if afflictions like these lie year after year on great multitudes of our fellow creatures who have not injured us and thousands of them pine away and die under hardships insupportable to nature, what heart can meditate on their condition without feeling some concern for a reformation.

[C]

[JW quoting from Benezet, pp. 7-9]

1 A particular account of the treatment the slaves received in the West Indies was lately published, which even by those who seek excuses for the trade and endeavor to palliate the cruelty is allowed to be a true though rather too favorable representation of the usage they receive, which is as follows.

2 "The iniquity of the slave trade is greatly aggravated by the inhumanity with which the Negroes are treated in the plantations, as well with respect to food and clothing as from the unreasonable labor which is commonly exacted from them. In Barbadoes and some other of the islands six pints of Indian corn and three herrings are reckoned a full weeks allowance for a working slave. Their allowance for clothing in the islands is seldom more than six yards of ofenbrigs[2] each year, and in the more northern colonies where the piercing westerly winds are long and sensibly felt these poor Africans suffer much for want of sufficient clothing; indeed some have none till they are able to pay for it by their labor.

3 "The time that the Negroes work in the West Indies is from day break till noon, then again from two o'clock till dark, during which time they are attended by overseers who severely scourge those who appear dilatory#[3] and before they are suffered to go to their quarters they have still something to do, as collecting herbage for the houses, gathering fuel for the boilers, &c. so that it is often half past twelve before they can get home when they have scarce time to grind and boil their Indian corn, whereby it often happens that they are called again to labor before they can satisfy their hunger and here no delay nor excuse will avail for if they are

---

[2] [A Dutch brown suiting material.]
[3] # I was told by a person eye witness to the fact that a Negro woman in Carolina was severely whipped for being slack in business in the field, and before the next morning was delivered of a living child. JW

98

not in the field immediately upon the usual notice they must expect to feel the overseers' lash. In crop time which lasts many months they are obliged by turns to work most of the night in the boiling house.

4   "Thus from a desire of making the greatest gain by the labor of slaves they lay a heavy burden on them, and yet feed and clothe them very sparingly, and some scarce feed or clothe them at all, so that the poor creatures are obliged to shift for their living in the best manner they can, which occasions their being often killed in the neighboring land, stealing potatoes or other food to satisfy their hunger, and if they take anything from the plantation they belong to, though under such pressing want, they are corrected severely for taking a little of what they have so hardly labored for." *page 8 &c.*

*[JW commentary on the enslaveds' minimal subsistence;
in Christ there is no peace with oppression]*

1   The sufferings of our blessed Savior who was given as a light to lighten the Gentiles and for salvation to the ends of the earth, has much attended my mind in writing on this lamentable subject.

2   Now a practice which so powerfully operates against the gracious design of his coming—a practice so grievous to many [insert: "& so contrary to the harmony of the great family of mankind,"; strikeout: "for whose salvation he suffered"—in JW's hand].

3   A practice so full of misery and untimely deaths having prevailed and continuing to prevail in these provinces and islands loudly calls upon us seriously to lay this matter to heart; and to such who are concerned for a reformation the call is that we take heed and be aware lest through the desires of the flesh we continue so nearly connected in outward interest with the immediate authors of these cruelties, as to strengthen their hand in oppression, and make them more at ease therein than they would be if their neighbors generally manifested a sorrow equal to the case, and a disapprobation proportionable to such extreme cruelty, attended with the untimely deaths of so many people [insert: "equal objects of the love and mercy of a gracious Creator."; strikeout: "for when the Lamb of God was offered as the [unreadable] on the cross" - in JW's hand].

4   The nature of slave—keeping being like that of an absolute government where one man not perfect in wisdom and goodness gives laws to others; and the evil consequence of this trade being of late years so

evident that many sober people appear dissatisfied with the practice of slave-keeping, and yet a considerable number of these have the charge of Negroes. Now as the lamentable sufferings of these people have by several under a religious exercise of mind been laid before us of late years, what an admonition does it carry with it to be watchful against the snares of a custom so prevalent? That a burden so insupportable having lain on them as a people for several years past and continuing at this day to lie upon them. A burden which if particularity opened would fill many large volumes with matter! with matter not less horrible than the sufferings of the Christians under Nero and the other heathen emperors. Such a burden lying on them as a people how necessary is it that we do not in any way contribute to the increasing of it. And where we make a bargain with them about liberty, and have power to make it on our own terms we may attend to that pure principle of equity which leads to Truth and uprightness, in which our conduct may not only be evidently free from the principles of slave-keeping but may be done in that purity of heart, that may be acceptable to him to whom all men are equally accountable.

5   Who can remember the cruelties exercised toward the poor slaves in many places without feeling an earnest desire, not only to be clear as to any claim standing on a foundation laid in violence but that we may be strengthened to endure every degree of self-denial which in the pure light may be opened to us, as one step toward returning as a nation from a revolt so grievous.

6   Were we, our children, and a number of our nearest friends taken by Mohammedans and carried captive in chains as many poor people have been? Were we made to labor so far beyond our strength and the nourishment given us, that under the weight of oppression several of our company died before our eyes. Suppose these men were so strengthened by custom, that none called them to account for the death of our friends, and that month after month we saw more of our company expire, more insupportable hardships, while we were almost overcome. In this lamentable situation, with what sorrow of heart should we reflect on the darkness of these men's minds, who were thus loading us with misery and bringing innocent blood on themselves.

7   When we saw that this conduct toward us was not the effect of sudden passion, arose not from hatred toward our persons, but understood that these people in aiming at ways of life requiring much labor had deliberately oppressed even unto death many before us; when we beheld a

familiarity and the appearance of friendship subsisting between our oppressors and men highly esteemed for their piety, what disagreeable thoughts would arise in us, respecting that religion in which such lamentable cruelties were thus encouraged? And how would the sound of the Mohammedan religion appear like a sound of confusion and misery? How would our minds in this case be turned toward the pure undefiled religion of Jesus Christ in which oppression has no peace? How should we look with longing desires toward a clear impartial judgment? Toward a land where the channels of equity were kept open for the benefit of all? And, alas, how gloomy would outward greetings as the elements of our oppression in that day appear to us?

7 D

Ephemera: untitled fragment on patience and on trusting in God

Written: date unknown; not printed

Editor's Introduction

This orphan, which has neither date nor context, is part of the John Woolman Collection, a donation made in 1912 to the Historical Society of Pennsylvania by Maj. Samuel Comfort, a grandson of the third-born of Woolman's grandsons.

The holograph is in Woolman's hand (except for the donor's name and the date in the upper right corner of the first page).

+++

Text

Major S. Comfort
11.14.1912

1   Do you imitate his patience and example in staying as he does for the coming of the Lord. Be patient therefore, brothers, to the coming of the day of the Lord. Behold: the husbandman waits for the precious fruit of the earth and has long patience for it until he receives the early and the latter rain [James 5:7]. Be you also patient.

2   When we are running towards a goal remote or what we do not see, we think we do not advance because we do not reach it, and because the place to which we tend is not within our view. But yet every step we take is an abatement of the distance, and provided we do not tire, provided we neither stop nor slacken our pace, provided the despair of ever getting to our intended home does not make us go back, all infallibly reap in our last day's journey the whole benefit of those which we so long looked on as lost and fruitless.

V

1   There are favors reserved for latter times, as in the order of nature there are fruits for latter seasons, and those favors are commonly the most important. We must wait for the moment of receiving them, the choice of which is not in our power, and the disposal of which God has reserved to himself alone. We must work and sow all night long as the apostles are said in the gospel to have done, and we must hope that the last moments will recompense all the toil which we before had looked upon as useless. Our Savior had constrained his apostles notwithstanding their reluctance to enter without him into a ship and to go to the opposite shore of the Galilean Sea. A violent and contrary wind opposed their endeavors and they imagined that their toil was unknown to their master though it was perfectly present to him, as St. Mark observes [6:45-52; also Matt. 14:22-33; John 6:15-21]: he saw them toiling in rowing. Towards the end of the night Jesus at last came to them walking upon the sea, which they so little expected that they were all frightened, and cried out as if he had been a spirit. After he had removed all their fears by talking with them, they willingly received him into their ship. And though they had as yet made but a small part of their passage, the ship was immediately at the land whither they went. The inward and spiritual miracle whereof this history is only a type, is more ordinary and common than we think. We row with all our strength, and make but little way. A violent and [gap in MS] wind happens to resist and overpower all our efforts, we think ourselves alone and without Jesus Christ, nay we imagine he has abandoned us, and we scarce know him again when he offers himself at break of day. But his words at last perfectly restore our peace, and his presence procures us in an instant all the comfort and satisfaction that has been deferred till his coming. The wind ceases, the oars become perfectly useless. We in short are at land without knowing how. But this sudden and unexpected success depends on our having wrought without ceasing to the last instant.

2   Besides these examples which respect the best peoples whom [destroyed in page-fold in MS] informs in what they fell short of perfection, while at the same time he grants it by making them more pure and humble, there are examples of another kind which are fit for such as lie long in a weak, drooping and languishing condition but who for all that do not quit their courage and remain constantly by the pool as the paralytic till he was eight and thirty years old did, without being tired with waiting [John 5:2-9]. Though their expectation seems to be in vain, and nobody appears under any concern for their health or offers to throw them into the pool when it is moved by the angel. It is for such that it was written in one

of the books of wisdom: trust in the Lord and abide in thy labor, for it is an easy thing in the sight of the Lord on the sudden to make a poor man rich. The secret of the Lord is unknown to us, and nothing but the end and term of it make it manifest. One would be apt to think on seeing the happy beginnings of certain persons that their election is undoubted. On the contrary, one would naturally be apt to despair of the salvation of some others, in seeing how far they deviate from it during their first years. But the unaccountable delays of the former, and the miraculous resurrection of the latter, informs us by the event how fallible our conjectures were.

3   Thou hast kept the good wine until now [John 2:10].

7 E

Ephemera: copies of two letters on 'high living' and 'expensive customs'

Written: nd, 1769; neither printed

Editor's Introduction

The holographs for these letter copies are found in MS A at pp. 279-81.

+++
Text

Copy of letters

Beloved friend, Since our last conversation I have felt an increase of brotherly love, and therein a liberty to hint further to you, how at different times for years past things have wrought on my mind respecting high living.

1[1]   In some affecting seasons abroad, as I have sat in meetings with desires to attend singly on the pure gift, I have felt that among my brothers grievously entangled in expensive customs, the Lord had a work for some to do by exampling others in the simplicity as it is in Christ (2 Cor. 11:3), and as I have seen that a view to live high has been a stumbling block, and that what some appeared to aim at was no higher than many of the foremost rank in our Society lived, there has been a labor upon me, that in this respect, the way may be cast up and the stumbling block taken out of the way of the people (Isa. 57:14). And here the inexpressible love of Christ in denying himself and enduring grief for our sakes is often before me as an example for us to follow, in denying ourselves of things pleasant to our natural inclination, that we may example others in the pure Christian life in our age.

2   In regard to thieves I have had many serious thoughts, and often been jealous over myself, lest by withholding from a poor man what our heavenly Father may intend for him through me, I should lay a temptation

---

[1] [The paragraph numbering in this letter is that of JW.]

105

in his way to steal, and have often felt a care that no desire for riches, or outward greatness, may prompt me to get that in my house which may create envy and increase this difficulty.

3   I have sometimes written Wills for people when sick, and expected soon to leave their families, who had but little to divide among their children, and I have so far felt a brotherly sympathy that their cares have become mine in regard to a comfortable living for them; and here expensive customs have often made the prospect less clear. Expensive customs on such occasions have often affected me with sadness.

4   The manner of taking possession of the silver mines southwestward, the conduct of the conquerors toward the natives, and the miserable toil of many of our fellow creatures have often been the subject of my thoughts; and though I sometimes handle silver and gold as a currency, my so doing is at times attended with pensiveness, and a care that my ears may not be stopped against further instruction. I often think on the fruitfulness of the soil where we live, the care that has been taken to agree with the former owners, the natives, and the conveniences this land affords for our use; and on the numerous oppressions there are in many places, and feel care that my cravings may be rightly bounded, and that no wandering desire may lead me to so strengthen the hands of the wicked, as to partake of their sins (1 Tim. 5:22).

5   In conversing at times with some well-disposed friends who have been long pressed with poverty, I have thought that some outward help, more than I believed myself a steward to communicate, might be a blessing to them; and at such times the expenses that might be saved among some of my brothers, without any real inconvenience to them, has often been brought to my mind; nor have I believed myself clear without speaking at times publicly concerning it.

6   My mind is often settled on the immutability of the Divine Being, and the purity of his judgments, and a prospect of outward distress in this part of the world has been open before me, and I have had to behold the blessedness of a state in which the mind is fully subjected to the Divine Teacher, and the confusion and perplexity of such who profess the Truth, and are not faithful to the leadings of it; nor have I ever felt pity move more evidently on my mind than I have felt it toward children who by their education are led on in unnecessary expenses, and exampled in seeking gain in the wisdom of this world to support themselves therein.

+++

9th day 7th month 1769   another

1   My dear friend—In our meeting of ministers and elders, I have several times felt the movings of divine love among us, and to me there appeared a preparation for profitable labors in the meeting; but the time appointed for public meeting drawing near, a shortness for time has been felt. And in yearly meetings for the preservation of good order in the Society, when much business has been before us and weighty matters relating to the testimony of Truth been under consideration, I have sometimes felt that a care in some to get forward soon, has prevented so weighty and deliberate a proceeding as by some has been desired.

2   Sincere-hearted Friends who are concerned to wait for the counsel of Truth are often made helps to each other, and when such from distant parts of our extensive yearly meeting have set their houses in order and thus gathered in one place, I believe it is the will of our heavenly Father that we with a single eye to the leadings of his Holy Spirit should quietly wait on him without hurrying in the business before us.

3   As my mind has been on these things some difficulties have arisen in my way: first, there are through prevailing custom many expenses attending our entertainment in town which if the leadings of Truth were faithfully followed might be lessened.

4   Many under an outward show of a delicate life are entangled in the worldly spirit, laboring to support those expensive customs which they at times feel to be a burden.

5   These expenses arising from a conformity to the spirit of this world have often lain as a heavy burden on my mind, and especially at the time of our solemn meetings; and a life truly conformable to the simplicity that there is in Christ, where we may faithfully serve God without distraction, and have no interruption from that which is against the Truth, I see has been very desirable. And, my dear friend, as the Lord in infinite mercies has called you and me to labor at times in his vineyard, and has, I believe, sometimes appointed to us different offices in his work, our opening our experience one to another in the pure feeling of charity may be profitable.

6   The great shepherd of the sheep, I believe, is preparing some to example the people in a plain simple way of living, and I feel a tender care

that you and I may abide in that where our light may shine clear, and nothing pertaining to us may have any tendency to strengthen those customs which are distinguishable from the Truth as it is in Jesus.

7 F

Ephemera: thoughts on the customary use of silver vessels

Written: 1770; printed: 1922

Editor's Introduction

As the year turned from 1769 to 1770 Woolman was seriously ill with pleurisy and noted in his *Journal* that he recently had been "much weaned from the pleasant things of this life" and that "death would be acceptable" to him.[1] This text comes from that time of illness and the thoughts expressed about silver vessels, being examples of ostentatious personal wealth and superfluities, gave Woolman frequent concern, the more so because a number of his closest friends possessed considerable wealth. To the dying Elizabeth Smith, his wealthy Burlington friend and fellow minister (and the sister of another close and wealthy friend, John Smith, who as the son-in-law of James Logan, William Penn's Secretary for Proprietary Affairs in Pennsylvania, had inherited some of the Logan silver tea service),[2] Woolman wrote:

> Friends from the country and in the city are often at your house, and when they behold among your furniture some things which are not agreeable to the purity of Truth, the minds of some, I believe, at times are in danger of being diverted from so close an attention to the light of life as is necessary for us.[3]

Even in the Memorial to Burlington Monthly Meeting which he wrote after the death in 1771 of his cousin Peter Harvey, Woolman felt a need to say:

> [H]e told me that in his youthful years his mind was much on improvement in outward business, and that being successful, many spoke in praise of his conduct, and in this prosperity he got sundry sorts of superfluities in workmanship about him, and though he had not seen clearly what to do with them, yet he saw

---

[1] See *Journal*, pp. 159-60.
[2] Gummere, p. 114.
[3] Letter from JW to Elizabeth Smith, 4th mo 1772, at Gummere, p. 121.

that at the time of getting these things he went on in the dark, and they were latterly a burden to his mind.[4]

The following text is based on the holograph which is at SC.[5]

+++

Text

20 da: 1 mo: 1770   The customary use of silver vessels about houses has deeply affected my mind of late years and under a living concern I have frequently labored in families and sometimes more publicly, to dissuade from the use of these things in which there is a manifest conformity to outward show and greatness. And this morning my understanding being opened in pure wisdom, I felt a necessity to write that which is the counsel of the Lord to this generation respecting these things.

He that can receive it, let him receive it. There is idolatry committed in the use of these things, and where this is the case, if they are sold, they may be idols to others. The example of Jacob is to be followed by such who would come forth in pure counsel.

His household had idols among them. The Lord called him to a pure worship at Bethel. He prevailed on his household to put away their idols,[6] and he hid them under an oak (Gen. 35:1[-5]).

John Woolman

---

4 MS at HSP: MS A, p. 282.
5 Manuscript 041 in the Safe area.
6 [The idols in the biblical text are "all the strange gods which were in their hand, and all their earrings which were in their ears"; (Gen. 35:4).]

8

Considerations on Pure Wisdom, and Human Policy; on Labor; on Schools; and on the Right Use of the Lord's Outward Gifts

Written by 1768; 1st printed 1768

Editor's Introduction

In 1755 Woolman and twelve other Friends[1] were appointed by PYM as a committee to revise the Queries, adopted in 1743, by which the monthly and preparative meetings were to examine themselves in matters regarding not only the quality of their worship but also the ethics of their communities. These ethical concerns touched on alcoholism and marriage, gossip and entertainment, the education of the young, the care of the poor, and the importation and buying of Negroes. The committee enlarged the Queries, and its proposed revisions were adopted before the 1755 PYM adjourned.

"Considerations on Pure Wisdom, and Human Policy; on Labor; on Schools; and on the Right Use of the Lord's Outward Gifts" was written by 1768 and in it Woolman again explores many of the same concerns of social ethics he would have surveyed with his fellow PYM committee members more than a decade earlier. Here he widely ranges over such general issues as work and education, the wise and restrained use of resources, of finding the 'mean' in all things, and of living so that we keep 'our eye single to the Lord.'[2]

The original holograph, which according to its author in the statement at the head of Text 9 was submitted to the Overseers of the Press, is now missing. The following text is the editor's modernization of this work which was almost certainly printed for the first time in Philadelphia in 1768.[3]

---

[1] Isaac Andrews, William Brown, John Churchman, Caleb Cowpland, John Evans, Samuel Fothergill, Joshua Lord, Joseph Shotwell, Samuel Smith, Jonah Thompson, Nathan Tilton, and Joseph White.

[2] This term, frequently used by Woolman and many of his Quaker contemporaries, is a reference to Matt. 6:22 and Luke 11:34 in the Authorized (King James) Version.

[3] While JW, in his preliminary statement at the beginning of "Serious Considerations on Trade" (Text 9 herein), states that this Text 8 was "printed

111

+++
Text

Considerations on Pure Wisdom, and Human Policy; on Labor; on Schools; and on the Right Use of the Lord's Outward Gifts

The wisdom that is from above is first pure, then peaceable, gentle, and easy to be entreated, full of mercy and good fruits, without partiality, and without hypocrisy (James 3:17).

INTRODUCTION

1   My mind has often been affected with sorrow on account of the prevailing of that spirit which leads from an humble waiting on the inward teaching of Christ, to pursue ways of living attended with unnecessary labor, and which draws forth the minds of many people to seek after outward power, and to strive for riches which frequently introduce oppression and bring forth wars and grievous calamities.

2   It is with reverence that I acknowledge the mercies of our heavenly Father who, in infinite love, did visit me in my youth and wrought a belief in me that through true obedience a state of inward purity may be known in this life, in which we may love mankind in the same love with which our Redeemer loves us, and therein learn resignation to endure hardships for the real good of others.

1758," the preponderant and convincing evidence is that the earliest printing of the work was in 1768 by D. Hall and W. Sellers in Philadelphia. For such evidence see:
•Charles R. Hildeburn, *A Century of Printing: The Issues of the Press in Pennsylvania, 1685-1784*, 2 vols. (Philadelphia: n.p.,1835; reprinted New York: Burt Franklin, 1968), vol. 2, p. 85;
•Joseph Smith, *A Descriptive Catalogue of Friends' Books*, 2 vols. (London: n.p.,1867; reprinted New York: Kraus, 1970), vol. 2, p. 960;
• Charles Evans, *American Bibliography: A Chronological Dictionary of all Books, Pamphlets, and Periodical Literature printed in the United States of America from the Genesis of Printing in 1639 down to and including the year 1820*, 14 vols. (Chicago: Blakely Press, 1903-1959), vol. 4, 11124; and
• Clifford K. Shipton and James E. Mooney, *National Index of American Imprints through 1800: the Short- Title Evans*, 2 vols. (Worcester, Mass.: American Antiquary Society and Barre Publishers, 1969), vol. 2, p. 1013.

3   "While the eye is single, the whole body is full of light" (Matt. 6:22 [; Luke 11:34]). But for want of this, selfish desires, and an imaginary superiority, darken the mind, hence injustice frequently proceeds; and where this is the case, to convince the judgment is the most effectual remedy.

4   Where violent measures are pursued in opposing injustice, the passions and resentments of the injured frequently operate in the prosecution of their designs; and after conflicts productive of very great calamities, the minds of contending parties often remain as little acquainted with the pure principle of divine love as they were before. But where people walk in that pure light in which all their "works are wrought in God" (John 3:21)[; Neh. 6:16], and under oppression persevere in the meek spirit, and abide firm in the cause of Truth, without actively complying with oppressive demands, through those the Lord has often manifested his power, in opening the understandings of others, to the promoting righteousness in the earth.

5   A time, I believe, is coming wherein this divine work will so spread and prevail that "nation shall not lift up sword against nation, nor learn war any more (Isa. 2[:4])." And as we, through the tender mercies of God, do feel that this precious work is begun, I am concerned to encourage my brothers and sisters in a holy care and diligence, that each of us may so live under the sanctifying power of Truth as to be redeemed from all unnecessary cares, that our eye being single to him, no customs, however prevalent, which are contrary to the wisdom from above, may hinder us from faithfully following his holy leadings in whatsoever he may graciously appoint for us.

ON PURE WISDOM, AND HUMAN POLICY

1   To have our trust settled in the Lord and not to seek after nor desire outward treasures any further than his Holy Spirit leads us therein, is a happy state, as says the prophet, "Blessed is the man that trusteth in the Lord, and whose hope the Lord is" [Jer. 17:7].

2   Pure wisdom leads people into lowliness of mind, in which they learn resignation to the divine will and contentment in suffering for his cause, when they cannot keep a clear conscience without suffering.

3　In this pure wisdom the mind is attentive to the root and original spring of motions and desires; and as we know "the Lord to be our refuge" [e.g. Ps. 91:9], and find no safety but in humbly walking before him, we feel an holy engagement that every desire which leads therefrom may be brought to judgment.

4　While we proceed in this precious way and find ardent longings for a full deliverance from everything which defiles, all prospects of gain that are not consistent with the wisdom from above are considered as snares, and an inward concern is felt that we may live under the cross and faithfully attend to that Holy Spirit which is sufficient to preserve out of them.

5　When I have considered that saying of Christ (Matt. 6:19), "Lay not up for yourselves treasures upon earth," his omnipotence has often occurred to my mind.

6　While we believe that he is everywhere present with his people and that perfect goodness, wisdom, and power are united in him, how comfortable is the consideration.

7　Our wants may be great, but his power is greater. We may be oppressed and despised, but he is able to turn our patient sufferings into profit to ourselves and to the advancement of his work on earth. His people who feel the power of his cross to crucify all that is selfish in them, who are engaged in outward concerns from a convincement that it is their duty and resign themselves and their treasures to him, these feel that it is dangerous to give way to that in us which craves riches and greatness in this world.

8　As the heart truly contrite earnestly desires "to know Christ, and the fellowship of his sufferings" (Phil. 3:10), so far as the Lord for gracious ends may lead into them, as such feel that it is their interest to put their trust in God and to seek no gain but that which he by his Holy Spirit leads into, so, on the contrary, they who do not reverently wait for this divine teacher and are not humbly concerned, according to their measure, "to fill up that which is behind of the afflictions of Christ" (Col. 1:24), in patiently suffering for the promoting [of] righteousness in the earth, but have an eye toward the power of men and the outward advantage of wealth, these are often attentive to those employments which appear profitable, even though the gains arise from such trade and business which proceeds from the workings of that spirit which is estranged from the self-denying life of an humble contrite Christian.

9   While I write on this subject I feel my mind tenderly affected toward those honestly disposed people who have been brought up in employments attended with those difficulties.

10   To such I may say, in the feeling of our heavenly Father's love, and number myself with you, O that our eyes may be single to the Lord! May we reverently wait on him for strength to lay aside all unnecessary expense of every kind, and learn contentment in a plain, simple life.

11   May we in lowliness submit to the leadings of his Spirit, and enter upon any outward employ which he graciously points out to us, and then, whatever difficulties arise in consequence of our faithfulness, I trust they will work for our good.

12   Small treasure to a resigned mind is sufficient. How happy is it to be content with a little, to live in humility, and feel that in us which breathes out this language, Abba! Father.

13   If that called the wisdom of this world had no resemblance of true wisdom, the name of wisdom, I suppose, had not been given to it.

14   As wasting outward substance to gratify vain desires on one hand, so slothfulness and neglect on the other, do often involve men and their families in trouble and reduce them to want and distress, to shun both those opposite vices is good in itself and has a resemblance to wisdom. But while people, thus provident, have it principally in view to get riches and power and the friendship of this world, and do not humbly wait for the Spirit of Truth to lead them in purity, these, through an anxious care to obtain the end desired, reach forth for gain in worldly wisdom and in regard to their inward state fall into divers temptations and snares. And though such may think of applying wealth to good purposes and to use their power to prevent oppression, yet wealth and power are often applied otherwise, nor can we depart from the leadings of our holy Shepherd without going into confusion.

15   Great wealth is frequently attended with power which nothing but divine love can qualify the mind to use rightly, and as to the humility and uprightness of our children after us, how great is the uncertainty! If in acquiring wealth we take hold on the wisdom which is from beneath and depart from the leadings of Truth and example our children herein, we have great cause to apprehend that wealth may be a snare to them and prove an injury to others over whom their wealth may give them power.

16   To be redeemed from that wisdom which is from beneath and walk in the light of the Lord is a precious situation. Thus his people are brought to put their trust in him and in this humble confidence in his wisdom, goodness, and power the righteous find a refuge in adversities, superior to the greatest outward helps, and a comfort more certain than any worldly advantages can afford.

ON LABOR

1   Having from my childhood been used to bodily labor for a living, I may express my experience therein.

2   Right exercise affords an innocent pleasure in the time of it, and prepares us to enjoy the sweetness of rest; but from the extremes each way arise inconveniences.

3   Moderate exercise opens the pores, gives the blood a lively circulation, and the better enables us to judge rightly respecting that portion of labor which is the true medium.

4   "The fowls of the air sow not, nor gather into barns, yet our heavenly Father feedeth them" (Matt. 6:26). Nor do I believe that infinite goodness and power would have allotted labor to us had he not seen that labor was proper for us in this life.

5   The original design and true medium of labor is a subject that to me appears worthy of our serious consideration.

6   Idle men are often a burden to themselves, neglect the duty they owe to their families, and become burdensome to others also.

7   As outward labor, directed by the wisdom from above, tends to our health and adds to our happiness in this life, so, on the contrary, entering upon it in a selfish spirit and pursuing it too long or too hard has a contrary effect.

8   I have observed that too much labor not only makes the understanding dull but so intrudes upon the harmony of the body that after ceasing from our toil we have another to pass through before we can be so composed as to enjoy the sweetness of rest.

9   From too much labor in the heat frequently proceeds immoderate sweats which do often, I believe, open the way for disorders and impair our constitutions.

10   When we go beyond the true medium and feel weariness approaching, but think business may suffer if we cease, at such a time spirituous liquors are frequently taken with a view to support nature under these fatigues.

11   I have found that too much labor in the summer heats the blood, that taking strong drink to support the body under such labor increases that heat, and though a person may be so far temperate as not to manifest the least disorder, yet the mind, in such a circumstance, does not retain that calmness and serenity which we should endeavor to live in.

12   Thus toiling in the heat and drinking strong liquor makes men more resolute and less considerate and tends very much to disqualify from successfully following him who is meek and low of heart.

13   As laying out business more than is consistent with pure wisdom is an evil, so this evil frequently leads into more. Too much business leads to hurry. In the hurry and toil too much strong drink is often used, and hereby many proceed to noise and wantonness and some, though more considerate, do often suffer loss as to a true composedness of mind.

14   I feel sincere desires in my heart that no rent nor interest might be laid so high as to be a snare to tenants; that no desires of gain may draw any too far in business; that no cares to support customs which have not their foundation in pure wisdom may have place in our minds; but that we may build on the sure foundation, and feel our holy Shepherd to lead us, who alone is able to preserve us and bring forth from everything which defiles.

15   Having several times in my travels had opportunity to observe the labor and manner of life of great numbers of slaves, it appears to me that the true medium is lamentably neglected by many who assign them their portion of labor.

16   Without saying much at this time concerning buying and selling men for term of life, who have as just a right to liberty as we have, nor about the great miseries and effusion of blood consequent to promoting the slave trade, and to speak as favorably as may be with regard to

continuing those in bondage who are among us, we cannot say there is no partiality in it. For whatever tenderness may be manifested by individuals in their lifetime toward them, yet for people to be transmitted from a man to his posterity in the helpless condition of slaves appears inconsistent with the nature of the gospel spirit. From such proceedings it often follows that persons in the decline of life are deprived of monies equitably due to them and committed to the care and subjected to the absolute power of young, inexperienced men who know but little about the weakness of old age, nor understand the language of declining life.

17   Where parents give their estates to their children and then depend on them for a maintenance, they sometimes meet with great inconveniences; but if the power of possession, thus obtained, does often reverse the obligations of gratitude and filial duty, and makes manifest that youth are often ignorant of the language of old age, how hard is the case of ancient Negroes who, deprived of the wages equitably due to them, are left to young people who have been used to look upon them as their inferiors.

18   For men to behold the fruits of their labors withheld from them and possessed by others, and in old age find themselves destitute of those comfortable accommodations and that tender regard which their time of life requires:

19   When they feel pains and stiffness in their joints and limbs, weakness of appetite, and that a little labor is wearisome, and still behold themselves in the neglected, uncomfortable condition of a slave, and oftentimes to a young unsympathizing man:

20   For men to be thus treated from one generation to another who, besides their own distresses, think on the slavery entailed on their posterity, and are grieved! what disagreeable thoughts must they have of the professed followers of Jesus! And how must their groans ascend to that almighty being who "will be a refuge for the oppressed" (Ps. 9:9).

ON SCHOOLS

Suffer the little children to come unto me, and forbid them not, for of such is the kingdom of God (Mark 10:14).

1   To encourage children to do things with a view to get praise of men to me appears an obstruction to their being inwardly acquainted with the spirit of Truth. For it is the work of the Holy Spirit to direct the mind to

God, that in all our proceedings we may have a single eye to him. To give alms in secret, to fast in secret, and to labor to keep clear of that disposition reproved by our Savior, "But all their works they do for to be seen of men" (Matt. 23:5).

2   That divine light which enlightens all men [John 1:9], I believe, does often shine in the minds of children very early, and to humbly wait for wisdom, that our conduct toward them may tend to forward their acquaintance with it and strengthen them in obedience thereto, appears to me to be a duty on all of us.

3   By cherishing the spirit of pride and the love of praise in them, I believe they may sometimes improve faster in learning than otherwise they would; but to take measures to forward children in learning which naturally tends to divert their minds from true humility appears to me to savor of the wisdom of this world.

4   If tutors are not acquainted with sanctification of Spirit, nor experienced in an humble waiting for the leadings of Truth, but follow the maxims of the wisdom of this world, such children who are under their tuition appear to me to be in danger of imbibing thoughts and apprehensions reverse to that meekness and lowliness of heart which is necessary for all the true followers of Christ.

5   Children at an age for schools are in a time of life which requires the patient attention of pious people, and if we commit them to the tuition of such whose minds we believe are not rightly prepared to "train them up in the nurture and admonition of the Lord" [Eph. 6:4], we are in danger of not acting the part of faithful parents toward them, for our heavenly Father does not require us to do evil that good may come of it. And it is needful that we deeply examine ourselves, lest we get entangled in the wisdom of this world and, through wrong apprehensions, take such methods in education as may prove a great injury to the minds of our children.

6   It is a lovely sight to behold innocent children! and when they are sent to such schools where their tender minds are in imminent danger of being led astray by tutors who do not live a self-denying life or by the conversation of such children who do not live in innocence, it is a case much to be lamented.

7   While a pious tutor has the charge of no more children than he can take due care of and keeps his authority in the Truth, the good spirit in

which he leads and governs works on the minds of such who are not hardened, and his labors not only tend to bring them forward in outward learning but to open their understandings with respect to the true Christian life. But where a person has charge of too many, and his thoughts and time are so much employed in the outward affairs of his school that he does not so weightily attend to the spirit and conduct of each individual as to be enabled to administer rightly to all in due season, through such omission he not only suffers as to the state of his own mind, but the minds of the children are in danger of suffering also.

8   To watch the spirit of children, to nurture them in gospel love and labor to help them against that which would mar the beauty of their minds, is a debt we owe them; and a faithful performance of our duty not only tends to their lasting benefit and our own peace, but also to render their company agreeable to us.

9   Instruction thus administered reaches the pure witness in the minds of such children who are not hardened and begets love in them toward those who thus lead them on. But where too great a number are committed to a tutor, and he, through much cumber, omits a careful attention to the minds of children, there is danger of disorders gradually increasing among them till the effects thereof appear in their conduct, too strong to be easily remedied.

10   A care has lived on my mind that more time might be employed by parents at home and by tutors at school in weightily attending to the spirit and inclinations of children, and that we may so lead, instruct, and govern them in this tender part of life that nothing may be omitted in our power to help them on their way to become the children of our Father who is in heaven.

11   Meditating on the situation of schools in our provinces, my mind has at times been affected with sorrow, and under these exercises it has appeared to me that if those who have large estates were faithful stewards and laid no rent nor interest nor other demand higher than is consistent with universal love, and those in lower circumstances would under a moderate employ shun unnecessary expense, even to the smallest article, and all unite in humbly seeking to the Lord, he would graciously instruct us and strengthen us to relieve the youth from various snares in which many of them are entangled.

TEXT 8

ON THE RIGHT USE OF THE LORD'S OUTWARD GIFTS

1   As our understandings are opened by the pure light, we experience that, through an inward approaching to God, the mind is strengthened in obedience; and that by gratifying those desires which are not of his begetting, those approaches to him are obstructed and the deceivable spirit gains strength.

2   These truths, being as it were engraved upon our hearts, and our everlasting interest in Christ evidently concerned herein, we become fervently engaged that nothing may be nourished which tends to feed pride or self-love in us. Thus, in pure obedience we are not only instructed in our duty to God but also in the affairs which necessarily relate to this life, and the Spirit of Truth which guides into all Truth leavens the mind with a pious concern, that "whatsoever we do in word or deed may be done in his name" (Col. 3:17).

3   Hence, such buildings, furniture, food, and raiment as best answer our necessities and are the least likely to feed that selfish spirit which is our enemy, are the most acceptable to us.

4   In this state the mind is tender and inwardly watchful, that the love of gain draws us not into any business which may weaken our love to our heavenly Father, or bring unnecessary trouble to any of his creatures.

5   Thus the way gradually opens to cease from that spirit which craves riches and things fetched far, which so mixes with the customs of this world and so intrudes upon the true harmony of life that the right medium of labor is very much departed from. And as the minds of people are settled in a steady concern not to hold nor possess any thing but what may be held consistent with the wisdom from above, they consider what they possess as the gift of God, and are inwardly exercised that in all parts of their conduct they may act agreeable to the nature of the peaceable government of Christ.

6   A little supports such a life, and in a state truly resigned to the Lord, the eye is single to see what outward employ he leads into as a means of our subsistence, and a lively care is maintained to hold to that, without launching further.

7   There is a harmony in the several parts of this divine work in the hearts of people; he who leads them to cease from those gainful

employments, carried on in that wisdom which is from beneath, delivers also from the desire after worldly greatness, and reconciles the mind to a life so plain that a little does suffice.

8   Here the real comforts of life are not lessened. Moderate exercise, in the way of true wisdom, is pleasant both to mind and body.

9   Food and raiment sufficient, though in the greatest simplicity, are accepted with content and gratitude.

10   The mutual love subsisting between the faithful followers of Christ is more pure than that friendship which is not seasoned with humility, how specious soever the appearance.

11   Where people depart from pure wisdom in one case it is often an introduction to depart from it in many more, and thus a spirit which seeks for outward greatness and leads into worldly wisdom to attain it and support it, gets possession of the mind.

12   In beholding the customary departure from the true medium of labor and that unnecessary toil which many go through in supporting outward greatness and procuring delicacies:

13   In beholding how the true calmness of life is changed into hurry and that many, by eagerly pursuing outward treasure, are in great danger of withering as to the inward state of the mind:

14   In meditating on the works of this spirit and on the desolations it makes among the professors of Christianity, I may thankfully acknowledge that I often feel pure love beget longings in my heart for the exaltation of the peaceable kingdom of Christ, and an enlargement to labor according to the gift bestowed on me for the promoting an humble, plain, temperate way of living: a life where no unnecessary cares nor expenses may encumber our minds, nor lessen our ability to do good; where no desires after riches or greatness may lead into hard dealing; where no connections with worldly-minded men may abate our love to God, nor weaken a true zeal for righteousness; a life wherein we may diligently labor for resignedness to do and suffer whatever our heavenly Father may allot for us, in reconciling the world to himself.

15   When the prophet Isaiah had uttered his vision and declared that a time was coming wherein "Swords should be beat into ploughshares, and

spears into pruning hooks, and that nation should not lift up sword against nation, nor learn war any more" [Isa. 2:4], he immediately directs the minds of the people to the divine teacher in this remarkable language: "O house of Jacob, come ye and let us walk in the light of the Lord" (Isa. 2:5).

16   To wait for the direction of this light in all temporal as well as spiritual concerns appears necessary, for if in any case we enter lightly into temporal affairs without feeling this Spirit of Truth to open our way therein, and through the love of this world proceed on, and seek for gain by that business or traffic which "is not of the Father, but of the world" (1 John 2:16), we fail in our testimony to the purity and peace of his government, and get into that which is for chastisement.

17   This matter has lain heavy on my mind. It being evident that a life less humble, less simple and plain than that which Christ leads his sheep into, does necessarily require a support which pure wisdom does not provide for. Hence there is no probability of our being "a peculiar people, so zealous of good works" (Titus 2:14) "as to have no fellowship with works of darkness" (Eph. 5:11), while we have wants to supply which have their foundation in custom, and do not come within the meaning of those expressions, "your heavenly Father knoweth that ye have need of all these things" (Matt. 6:32).

18   These things which he beholds necessary for his people he fails not to give them in his own way and time, but as his ways are above our ways and his thoughts above our thoughts, so imaginary wants are different "from these things which he knoweth that we have need of" [Matt. 6:8].

19   As my meditations have been on these things compassion has filled my heart toward my fellow creatures involved in customs, grown up in "the wisdom of this world, which is foolishness with God" (1 Cor. 3:19). And O that the youth may be so thoroughly experienced in an humble walking before the Lord, that they may be his children, and know him to be their refuge, their safe unfailing refuge! through the various dangers attending this uncertain state of being.

20   If those whose minds are redeemed from the love of wealth and who are content with a plain, simple way of living do yet find that to conduct the affairs of a family, without giving countenance to unrighteous proceedings or having fellowship with works of darkness, the most diligent care is necessary:

21   If customs distinguishable from universal righteousness and opposite to the true self-denying life are now prevalent and so mixed with trade and with almost every employ that it is only through humble waiting on the inward guidance of Truth that we may reasonably hope to walk safely and support an uniform testimony to the peaceable government of Christ:

22   If this be the case, how lamentably do they expose themselves to temptations who give way to the love of riches, conform to expensive living, and reach forth for gain to support customs which our holy Shepherd leads not into.

9

Serious Considerations on Trade

Written by 1768; first printed 1922

Editor's Introduction

This short work, more an outline than a finished essay, was meant by Woolman to be one of the chapters in "Considerations on Pure Wisdom, and Human Policy; on Labor; on Schools; and on the Right Use of the Lord's Outward Gifts" (Text 8 hereinbefore). In the introductory paragraph of this text he recounts that it was deferred from publication at the time by the Overseers of the Press. That the author kept it with his papers is evidence he meant it should be preserved. It is generally concerned with just and necessary international trade, support for local economies, and the avoidance of excess, all for the maintenance and promotion of peace.

The work was first published in 1922 in Gummere. The following is the editor's modernization of the holograph found in MS A/*Trade*.

+++

Text

When that small piece entitled Considerations on pure wisdom &c (printed 1758)[1] was laid before the Overseers of the Press the substance of the following twelve distinct paragraphs was formed into one chapter, and proposed by me to have been corrected and printed as a part of that piece, but the said Overseers, though they did not reject this chapter, yet expressed some desire that the publication of it might at least be deferred, with which I felt easy, and therefore they did not attempt to correct it.

Serious Considerations on Trade

1[2]

As it has pleased the Divine Being to people the earth by inhabitants descended from one man; and as Christ commanded his disciples to

---

[1] [This date is JW's error. The first printing almost certainly was in 1768 in Philadelphia by D. Hall and W. Sellers. See Text 8, footnote 3.]
[2] [JW numbered the paragraphs.]

preach the gospel to distant countries, the necessity of sometimes crossing the seas is evident.

2

The inhabitants of the earth have often appeared to me as one great family consisting of various parts, divided by great waters, but united in one common interest, that is in living righteously according to that light and understanding wherewith Christ enlightens every man that comes into the world.

3

While a wilderness is improving by inhabitants come from a plentiful thick-settled country, to employ some of the family in crossing the waters to supply the new settlers with some such necessaries as they can well pay for while they clear fields to raise grain, appears to be consistent with the interest of all.

4

When lands are so improved that with a divine blessing they afford food, raiment, and all those necessaries which pertain to the life of a humble follower of Christ, it behooves the inhabitants to take heed that a custom be not continued longer than the usefulness of it, and that the number of that calling who have been helpful in importing necessaries be not greater than is consistent with pure wisdom.

5

Customs contrary to pure wisdom which tend to change agreeable employ into a toil, and to involve people in many difficulties, it appears to be the duty of the fathers in the family to wait for strength to labor against such customs being introduced or encouraged among the inhabitants, and that all true friends to the family so shake their hands from holding bribes as not to cherish any desire of gain by fetching or selling those things which they believe tend to alienate the minds of people from their truest interest.

6

Where some have gotten large possessions, and by an increase of inhabitants have power to acquire riches if they lease them at such a rate that their tenants are necessitated in procuring their rent to labor harder, or apply themselves to business more closely than is consistent with pure wisdom, whether these monies thus obtained are applied to promote a superfluous trade, or any other purpose in a self-pleasing will, here the true harmony of the family appears to be in danger.

7

Where two branches of the same family are each situate on such a soil that with moderate labor, through the divine blessing, each may be supplied by their own produce with all the necessaries of life, and a large hazardous ocean between them, for the inhabitants of each place to live on the produce of their own land appears most likely for them to shun unnecessary cares and labors.

8

For brothers to visit each other in true love, I believe makes part of that happiness which our heavenly Father intends for us in this life; but where pure wisdom directs not our visits, we may not suppose them truly profitable. And for man to so faithfully attend to the pure light as to be truly acquainted with the state of his own mind, and feel that purifying power which prepares the heart to have fellowship with Christ and with those who are redeemed from the spirit of this world, this knowledge is to us of infinitely greater moment than the knowledge of affairs in distant parts of this great family.

9

By giving way to a desire after delicacies and things fetched far many men appear to be employed unnecessarily, many ships built by much labor are lost, many people brought to an untimely end, much good produce buried in the seas, many people busied in that which serves chiefly to please a wandering desire who might better be employed in those affairs which are of real service and ease the burdens of such poor honest people, who to answer the demands of others are often necessitated to exceed the bounds of healthful agreeable exercise.

10

Blessed are the peacemakers for they shall be called the children of God [Matt. 5:9].

Where one in the family is injured, it appears consistent with true brotherhood that such who know it take due care respecting their own behavior and conduct, lest the love of gain should lead them into any affairs so connected with the proceedings of him who does the injury as to strengthen his hands therein, make him more at ease in a wrong way, or less likely to attend to the righteous principle in his own mind.

11

To be well acquainted with the affairs we are interested in, with the disposition of those with whom we have connections, to have outward concerns within proper bounds, and in all things attend to the wisdom from above, appears most agreeable to that pious disposition in which people desire to shun doubtful disputes about property, to have their proceedings so agreeable to righteousness, that whatsoever they do, they may do all to the glory of God, and give none offence, neither to the Jews, nor to the Gentiles, nor to the Church of Christ.

12

Where men give way to a desire after wealth, and to obtain their ends proceed in that wisdom which is from beneath, how often does discord arise between different branches of the great family? whence great numbers of men are often separated from tilling the earth and useful employ, to defend what contending parties mutually claim as their interest, hence many are cut off in youth! And great troubles and devastations do often attend these contests; and besides those sorrowful circumstances, the food those armies eat, the garments they wear, their wages, vessels to transport them from place to place, and support for the maimed, tend to increase the labor of such who till the earth, and to make some employment necessary which without wars would not; here that healthful agreeable exercise which I believe our gracious Creator intended for us is often changed into hurry and toil. O how precious is the Spirit of peace! how desirable that state in which people feel their hearts humbly resigned to the Lord, and live under a labor of mind to do his will on earth as it is done in heaven! Where they feel content with that true simplicity in which no wandering desires lead on to strife. Where no treasures possessed in a selfish spirit tend to beget ill will in other selfish men. And where true love so seasons their proceedings that the pure witness is reached in such who are well acquainted with them.

10

A First Book for Children

Written ca. 1769; lst printed ca. 1769

Editor's Introduction

As well as being an author, missionary, and entrepreneur, John Woolman was a teacher. He gave formal instruction to children at least for the years from 1765 to 1769, as attested in his *Ledger B 1753* and *Account Book 1769*[1] which contain a number of debtors' entries for "schooling thy" followed either by the name or names of a child or children or by "son" or "daughter." Woolman's interest in educational matters was shown in his 1751 appointment by Burlington Monthly Meeting to a committee with fourteen others to implement a PYM direction for establishing "schools in the country for the training up the youth in useful learning under religious schoolmasters among friends."[2] His matured views on education were the subject of the third chapter of Text 8 herein, "Considerations on Pure Wisdom, and Human Policy; on Labor; on Schools; and on the Right Use of the Lord's Outward Gifts."

Given this background it is not surprising that Woolman's educational concerns led him to write a children's primer or elementary spelling book and reader. Such primers were widely used in educating children in the American colonies, biblical literacy often being a primary end. One of the most broadly circulated was *The New-England Primer*, first printed in Boston as early as 1690 and printed in Philadelphia ca. 1769 simultaneously with Woolman's primer and by the same printer, Joseph Crukshank in Second-street. The contrast between these two primers illustrates the different pedagogies of New England Puritanism and middle-colony Quakerism. While both works set out the alphabet in small and capital letters, and had tables of words of one or more syllables (*The New-England Primer* with words up to six syllables, *A First Book for Children* with words up to four syllables), they revealed their differences in the illustrative reading texts used. Woolman employed aphorisms from the Psalms and from the wisdom literature of the Old

---

[1] MS 2 and MS 3 held at HSP in the John Woolman Collection, Call #737.
[2] Burlington Monthly Meeting Minute Book 1737-1756, p. 214, held at HC.

Testament and, for the longest readings, the parables of the Rich Man and Lazarus and of the Good Samaritan from Luke's account of the gospel. Instead of scripture *The New-England Primer* has lengthy exhortatory and catechetical passages, the longest being "The Shorter Catechism agreed upon by the reverend Assembly of [Presbyterian] Divines at Westminster" completed in 1647 and consisting of 107 questions and answers, to be memorized, on Christian doctrine and belief. The next longest is the account of the death in 1555 of John Rogers, the first Protestant martyr under Mary I of England.

The only known copy of *A First Book for Children* is of the third edition which Joseph Smith dates "about 1774."[3] It is in the Library of Friends House, London.

+++

Text

A
First Book for Children

Much useful reading being sullied and torn by children in schools before they can read, this book is intended to save unnecessary expense.

By J O H N   W O O L M A N.

The third edition enlarged.

A B C D E F G H I J K L M N
O P Q R S T U V W X Y Z
a b c d e f g h i j k l m n
o p q r s t u v w x y z

Note: When the above alphabet is defaced, this leaf may be pasted upon the cover, and the alphabet on the other side made use of.

PHILADELPHIA:
Printed and sold by JOSEPH CRUKSHANK in Second-street; and by BENJAMIN FERRISS, stationer and bookbinder, in Wilmington.

---

3 Smith, p. 960.

A B C D E F G H I J K L M N
O P Q R S T U V W X Y Z
a b c d e f g h i j k l m n
o p q r s t u v w x y z &

ba	be	bi	bo	bu
ca	ce	ci	co	cu
da	de	di	do	du
fa	fe	fi	fo	fu
ga	ge	gi	go	gu
ha	he	hi	ho	hu
ka	ke	ki	ko	ku
la	le	li	lo	lu
ma	me	mi	mo	mu
na	ne	ni	no	nu
pa	pe	pi	po	pu
ra	re	ri	ro	ru
sa	se	si	so	su
ta	te	ti	to	tu
va	ve	vi	vo	
wa	we	wi	wo	
ya	ye	yi	yo	
za	ze	zi	zo	zu
ab	eb	ib	ob	ub
ac	ec	ic	oc	uc
ad	ed	id	od	ud
af	ef	if	of	uf
ag	eg	ig	og	ug
ak	ek	ik	ok	uk
al	el	il	ol	ul
am	em	im	om	um
an	en	in	on	un
ap	ep	ip	op	up
ar	er	ir	or	ur
as	es	is	os	us
at	et	it	ot	ut
ax	ex	ix	ox	ux

bla	ble	bli	blo	blu
bra	bre	bri	bro	bru
cha	che	chi	cho	chu
cla`	cle	cli	clo	clu
dra	dre	dri	dro	dru
fra	fre	fri	fro	fru
gla	gle	gli	glo	glu
han	hen	hin	hon	hun
kna	kne	kni	kno	knu
lad	led	lid	lod	lud
man	men	min	mon	mun
nap	nep	nip	nop	nup
one	old	ore	out	ous
pan	pen	pin	pon	pun
qua	que	qui	quo	quu
ran	ren	rin	ron	run
sam	sem	sim	som	sum
tra	tre	tri	tro	tru
van	ven	vin	von	vun
and	art	are	ale	ape
bad	bed	bid	bit	bin
cat	cap	car	can	cob
bag	cag	fag	nag	rag
beg	leg	big	dig	fig
pig	wig	bog	fog	hog
bug	dug	mug	rug	lug
ham	ram	dim	him	rim
gum	hum	rum	sum	tum
ben	den	hen	pen	ten
din	kin	gin	pin	sin
con	son	ton	hon	von
bun	gun	nun	pun	run
cap	gap	lap	map	tap
dip	hip	lip	nip	rip
fop	hop	lop	mop	sop
bar	far	mar	tar	war
bat	cat	fat	hat	rat
bet	get	let	met	net
bit	fit	hit	nit	pit
dot	got	hot	lot	not

but	cut	hut	nut	rut
rex	sex	vex	fix	six
box	fox	the	for	out
cry	dry	fly	thy	try

The Sun is up my Boy,
Get out of thy Bed,
Go thy way, for the Cow,
Let her eat the Hay.
Now the Sun is set,
And the Cow is put up,
The Boy may go to his Bed.
Go not in the Way of a bad Man;
Do not tell a Lie, my Son.

blab	crab	stab	swab	st	sli
chub	club	grub	snub	ss	ffi
bred	bled	fled	shed	ff	ffl
brag	drag	flag	snag	si	sh
brim	grim	swim	trim	fi	ct
crum	drum	plum	scum	sl	&
bran	clan	plan	span	fl	
chin	grin	shin	thin		
chap	clap	trap	snap		
chip	clip	ship	trip		
chop	crop	drop	shop		
face	lace	mace	race		
mice	nice	rice	vice		
fade	jade	made	wade		
hide	ride	side	tide		
cage	page	rage	sage		
bake	cake	make	rake		
bale	dale	gale	male		
pale	sale	tale	vale		
bile	file	mile	pile		
hole	mole	pole	role		
mule	rule	came	dame		
fame	game	lame	name		

lime	time	come	some
bane	lane	mane	pane
dine	fine	kine	line
pine	wine	bone	hone
back	lack	pack	sack
deck	neck	peck	reck
kick	lick	nick	sick
dock	lock	mock	rock
cold	fold	gold	hold
balk	talk	walk	silk
call	fall	gall	wall
bell	fell	sell	tell
fill	hill	kill	mill
halt	malt	salt	part
belt	felt	melt	pelt
damp	lamp	ramp	vamp
pump	lump	jump	rump
band	hand	land	sand
bend	fend	lend	mend
bind	find	kind	mind
bond	fond	pond	long
king	ring	sing	wing

The Dove doth no harm,
The Lamb doth no harm,
A good boy doth no harm.
The Eye of the Lord is on them that fear him.
He will love them, and do them good.
He will keep their Feet in the Way they go, and
save them from the Paths of Death.

ab—sence[4]	ar—rant	bot—tom
a corn	art ist	bri dle
ac tor	bar ber	bro ther
ad der	bar rel	bow els

---

4 [Here begin lists of multi-syllable words in which Woolman used hyphens to indicate the word divisions both on the first line after a text and at the top of a new page; for all other lines he used blank spaces to indicate the divisions.]

ad—vent	bet—ter	car—rot
af ter	·bit ter	car ter
al so	bor der	cam el
am ber	bo som	can dle
an gel	bri er	cap tain
a ny	bro ken	cap tive
art ful	bru tish	car goe
art less	bra zen	com fort
ar dent	bod kin	com mon
com mit	dra per	en ter
com pile	drug get`	e vent
com pose	drunk ard	ev il
com pute	du ty	ex alt
con cord	ear ly	ex act
con dole	ear nest	ex port
con vert	ea sy	ex pound
dal ly	ed dy	fac tor
dam sel	ef fect	fag got
dam son	ef fort	fal low
dan ger	el bow	fals ly
dark ly	el der	fa mine
dar ling	e lect	fan cy
de base	em bark	farm er
de bate	em pire	fa tal
de fend	en camp	fa ther
de fraud	en dow	fat ness
de lay	en gine	fear ful
din ner	en joy	fea ther
fea ture	ha bit	im pair
fel low	hack ney	im pale
fe male	hal ter	im pend
fen nel	ham mer	im plant
gal lon	han dle	im ply
gal lop	hap pen	im press
gam mon	har den	im print
gan der	har dy	in fant
gar land	har lot	in vite
gar lick	har vest	in ward
gar ment	hel met	joy ful
gar ret	her mit	jour nal

gar—ter	hun—gry	kind—ness
gen tile	hus band	king dom
gin ger	hun ter	kins man
glim mer	hur ry	lad der
glit ter	i dle	la ment
gun ner	i dol	lan tern
gut ter	i mage	lap wing
gui nea	im prove	lat chet
late ly	mal let	mar tyr
law ful	man kind	mo ment
law yer	man ner	mor tal
lim ber	man tle	mar vel
li mit	ma nure	ma son
lin tel	mar ket	mar shal
lof ty	mar row	
ma lice	mar—ry	

The Lark will fly in the Field,
The Cat doth run after the Mouse,
The Chub swims in the Brook,
And the good Boy will love to do good in his place.

na—tive	ne—ver	nur—ture
na ture	new ness	o bey
nap kin	no ble	ob ject
nar row	no tice	ob tain
need ful	num ber	of fend
net tle	nut meg	op press
or der	quar rel	re cord
pad dle	quar ry	re fuge
pad lock	quar ter	re fuse
pain ful	quick en	rem nant
pa late	quick ly	re ward
pam per	qui et	re tail
pa per	qui ver	rich es
par cel	rab bet	rid dle
par ty	rack et	ri ver
pa rent	raf ter	rob ber
part ed	rai ment	rot ten

part—ing	rain—bow	sab—bath
pil grim	ran som	sad dle
pon der	ra sor	sad ness
pro fess	ra ven	sad ly
pro tect	rea dy	saf fron
pro verb	rai son	sai lor
pul let	reap er	scho lar
pur ple	rea son	se cret
pur pose	re bel	sel dom

The Cow gives us Milk,
The Sheep spares us Wool,
The Hen lays Eggs,
The good Boy and the good Girl learn their Books.
Good Boys do well.
Bad Boys go to Ruin.

ser—pent	slum—ber	ten—der
se date	so lid	thank ful
ser vant	sor ry	thun der
ser vice	sted fast	time ly
sha dow	ster ling	tim ber
shil ling	stew ard	tor ment
short ly	suf fer	to tal
sick ness	su gar	tra der
sig net	swift ly	tri al
sil ver	swol len	trump et
sim ple	tem per	tu mult
six ty	tem pest	tun nage
tun nel	un to	west ward
tur key	ut ter	wet shod
tur nip	use ful	whis per
turn er	up per	wil ful
tu tor	up shot	will ing
va cant	up side	win ter
var nish	ut most	wis dom
vel vet	wa fer	wo ful
ven ture	wake ful	wor ship
ves sel	wan der	wor sted
vin tage	wan ton	wor thy

vint—ner	war—rant	yon—der
vi per	wel fare	youth ful
vir gin	wed ding	
un der	west ern	

The Rain makes the Grass grow,
The Air is of great Use to us,
The Sun does us good,
It is the Lord who sends us all good Things. O my Child love the Lord, and strive to be good, that it may be well with thee when thou dies; For when a good Child dies, his Soul goes to Christ above, and lives in Joy forever and ever: But when one that is wicked dies in his Sins, his Soul finds no Rest in the other World.

Walk therefore my Son in the good Way, so shall thy last End be Peace.

ab—so—lute	bla—ma—ble
ac ti on	but ter fly
af ter ward	ca ni ster
al ma nack	ca pa ble
al pha bet	car pen ter
a ni mal	car ri age
ap pe tite	car ri er
be ne fit	cau ti ous
bit ter ness	ce le brate
be wil der	cer tain ly
cer ti fy	ex er cise
com pa ny	fac to ry
clo thi er	fa cul ty
con fi dent	faith ful ly
con tra ry	fal si fy
cu ri ous	fa mi ly
de so late	fa ther less
di a mond	fa vor ite
dig ni fy	fi nal ly
dif fer ence	fi nish er
dif fer ent	fir ma ment
di li gent	fol low er
du ra ble	for ci ble

du—ti—ful	for—mer—ly
eat a ble	for ti tude
e ne my	for tu nate
en mi ty	fu ri ous
e ven ing	ge ne ral
e ve ry	gen tle man
e vi dent	glo ri fy
glo ri ous	hy po crite
glut to ny`	ig no rance
go vern or	im pi ous
gra ci ous	im pu dent
gra du al	in di gence
gra vi ty	in di go
gra zi er	in do lent
gree di ly	in fa my
grid i ron	in fan cy
guar di an	in fi del
hap pi ness	in ju ry
har mo ny	in no cence
heart i ly	in stru ment
hea ven ly	in ti mate
hea vi ness	in ward⁵ly
hi sto ry	i vo ry
hi ther to	ju ni per
hor ri bly	ju sti fy
ho spi tal	kna ve ry
hu mor some	la ti tude
la ven der	mes sen ger
le ga cy	migh ti ly
li a ble	mil li on
li ber al	mi ni stry
li ber ty	mi ra cle
lot te ry	mi se ry
low er most	mock e ry
lu sti ly	mo nu ment
mag ni fy	mov a ble
ma je sty	mul ber ry
ma la dy	mul ti tude

---

5 [The word division is omitted in the original.]

ma—ni—fold	na—ti—on
man ner ly	na tu ral
ma ri gold	no ta bly
mar ri age	nu me ral
mar tyr dom	nur se ry
me di tate	ob li gate
me mo ry	ob sti nate
mer ci ful	ob vi ate
mer ci less	oc cu py

The Lord is good to them that wait for him, to the Soul that seek—eth him.

It is good that a Man both hope, and qui—et—ly wait, for the Help of the Lord.

It is good for a Man that he bear the Yoke in his Youth.

He sit—teth a—lone, and keep—eth Silence, because he hath born it upon him.

He put—teth his Mouth in the Dust, if so be there may be Hope.

of—fer—ing	pa—ren—tage
o ni on	pas sen ger
o pe rate	pas si on
or der ly	pa ti ent
o ri gin	pa tri arch
or na ment	pe ri od
pa ra ble	pi e ty
pi ti ful	re si due
plen ti ful	re so lute
po ver ty	re ve rence
pow er ful	ri ot ous
pre sent ly	rob be ry
pro di gal	sa tis fy
pub li can	sanc ti fy
qua li ty	se cond ly
quan ti ty	sen si ble
quar rel some	sen ti ment
quar ter ly	se pa rate
ra ri ty	se ri ous
ra ti fy	set tle ment

rea—di—ly	se—ven—ty
rec kon ing	six ti eth
re com pence	sla ve ry
re gu lar	slip pe ry
re gu late	so lemn ly
re me dy	sol di er
re pro bate	so li tude
so row ful	ve ni son
so ve reign	vic to ry
spec ta cle	vi ne gar
stur ge on	vi o lence
teach a ble	vir tu ous
te di ous	vi sit or
tem per ate	un der hand
tem po ral	un der most
te ne ment	u ni form
ter ri ble	use ful ness
ter ri fy	ut ter ly
te sta ment	war ri or
te sti fy	wea ri ed
to ward ly	wea ri some
tra vel ler	wick ed ness
trou ble some	wil der ness
trump et er	won der ful
ty ran ny	
va li ant	
va ni ty	

Bless—ed are the pure in the Way, who walk in the Law of the Lord.

Bless—ed are they that keep his Law, and that seek him with all their Heart.

The Lord is an—gry with the Proud, and with them who turn a—side to Lies.

The Earth is full of the Good—ness of the Lord. O that all Men would love him and o—bey him.

con—di—ti—on	di—ver—si—ty
con fes si on	di vi si on
con ten ti on	e lec ti on

con—ver—si—on	e—nor—mi—ty	
cor rec ti on	e qua li ty	
cre a ti on	e ter ni ty	
de fec ti on	ex pe di ent	
de ri si on	ex po si tor	
de vo ti on	ex e cu tor	
dex te ri ty	foun da ti on	
di rec ti on	fru gal i ty	
fu tu ri ty	per pe tu al	
har mo ni ous	no mi na ti on	
hu ma nity	ob li ga ti on	
i do la ter	pre pa ra ti on	
im me di ate	re so lu ti on	
im pe ni tent	re pu ta ti on	
im pu ri ty	re for ma ti on	
in fec ti on		
in firm i ty	One	1	I
in i qui ty	two	2	II
in ven ti on	three	3	III
me lo di ous	four	4	IV
me mo ri al	five	5	V
mi nor i ty	six	6	VI
mo ral i ty	se—ven	7	VII
mor tal i ty	eight	8	VIII
na ti vi ty	nine	9	IX
o be di ent	ten	10	X
o pi ni on	eleven	11	XI
per fec ti on	twelve	12	XII

There was a certain rich Man which was cloth-ed in Purple and fine Lin-en, and far-ed sump-tu-ous[6]ly e-ve-ry Day.

And there was a cer-tain Beg-gar nam-ed La-za-rus, which was laid at his Gate, full of Sores.

And de-sir-ing to be fed with the Crumbs which fell from the rich Man's Ta-ble: More-over the Dogs came and lick-ed his Sores.

And it came to pass that the Beg-gar di-ed, and was car-ri-ed by the An-gels in-to A-bra-ham's Bo-som, the rich Man al-so di-ed, and was bu-ri-ed.

---

6 [The word division is omitted in the original.]

And in Hell he lift up his Eyes be-ing in Tor-ments, and se-eth A-bra-ham a-far off and La-za-rus in his Bo-som.

And he cri-ed, and said, Fa-ther A-bra-ham, have Mer-cy on me, and send La-za-rus, that he may dip the Tip of his Fin-ger in Wa-ter, and cool my Tongue, for I am tor-ment-ed in this Flame.

But A-bra-ham said, Son, re-mem-ber that thou in thy Life time receiv-edst thy good Things, and like-wise La-za-rus e-vil Things, but now he is com-fort-ed, and thou art tor-ment-ed.

And be-side all this, be-tween us and you there is a Gulf fix-ed, so that they which would pass from hence to you can-not; nei-ther can they pass to us, that would come from thence.

Then he said, I pray thee, there-fore, Fa-ther, that thou would-est send him to my Fa-ther's House.

For I have five Bre-thren, that he may te-sti-fy un-to them, lest they al-so come in-to this Place of Tor-ment.

A-bra-ham said un-to him, they have Mo-ses and the Pro-phets; let them hear them.

And he said; nay, Fa-ther A-bra-ham, but if one went un-to them from the Dead, they will re-pent.

And he said un-to him, if they hear not Mo-ses and the Pro-phets, nei-ther will they be per-suad-ed though one rose from the Dead.

◇◇◇◇◇◇◇◇◇◇◇◇◇◇◇

Re-mem-ber now thy Cre-a-tor in the Days of thy Youth, while the e-vil Days come not, and the Years draw nigh, when thou shalt say, I have no Plea-sure in them.

In all thy Ways ac-know-ledge him, and he shall di-rect thy Paths.

Keep thy Heart with all Di-li-gence, for out of it are the Is-sues of Life.

My Son, keep my Words, and lay up my Com-mand-ments with thee.

Fear God, and keep his Com-mand-ments, for this is the whole Du-ty of Man.

What does it pro-fit a Man if he gain the whole World, and lose his own Soul? Or what shall a Man give in Ex-change for his Soul?

Let your Light so shine be-fore Men, that they may see your good Works, and glo-ri-fy your Fa-ther which is in Hea-ven.

Thou shalt love the Lord thy God with all thy Soul, and with all thy Strength, and with all thy Mind.

Take good heed, there-fore un-to your-selves, that ye love the Lord your God.

Love not the World, nei-ther the Things that are in the World: If a-ny Man love the World, the Love of the Fa-ther is not in him.

For all that is in the World, the Lust of the Flesh, the Lust of the Eye, and the Pride of Life, is not of the Fa-ther, but of the World.

And the World pass-eth a-way, and the Lust there-of; but he that doth the Will of God, a-bid-eth for e-ver.

Make me to know my End, and the Mea-sure of my Days, what it is; that I may know how frail I am.

O how great is the Good-ness, which thou hast laid up for them that fear thee, and which thou hast wrought for them that trust in thee, e-ven be-fore the Sons of Men.

Yea, though I walk through the Val-ley of the Sha-dow of Death, I will fear no E-vil, for thou art with me, thy Rod and thy Staff they com-fort me.

Be ye fol-low-ers of them who through Faith and Pa-ti-ence in-her-it the Pro-mi-ses.

God is our Re-fuge and Strength, there-fore will I not fear, though the Earth be re-mov-ed. Be-cause we trust in the liv-ing God, we shall not be a-fraid of e-vil Ti-dings, but in Qui-et-ness, and in Con-fi-dence shall be our Strength; may they say who faith-ful-ly fol-low Christ.

◇◇◇◇◇◇◇◇◇◇◇◇◇◇◇

Behold a certain Lawyer stood up, and tempted our blessed Saviour, saying, Master, what shall I do to inherit eternal Life?

He said unto him, what is written in the Law? How readest thou?

And he answering, said, Thou shalt love the Lord thy God with all thy Heart, and with all thy Soul, and with all thy Strength, and with all thy mind; and thy neighbor as thy self.

And he said unto him, Thou hast answered right, this do, and thou shalt live.

But he, willing to justify himself, said unto Jesus, and who is my neighbor?

And Jesus answering, said, A certain Man went down from Jerusalem, to Jericho, and fell among Thieves, which stripping him of his Raiment, and wounded him, and departed, leaving him half-dead.

And it fell out there came down a certain Priest that Way; and when he saw him he passed by on the other Side.

And likewise a Levite when he was at the Place came and looked on him, and passed by on the other Side.

But a certain Samaritan, as he journeyed, came where he was; and when he saw him, he had compassion on him,

And went to him, and bound up his wounds, pouring in Oil and Wine, and set him on his own Beast and brought him to an Inn, and took Care of him.

And on the Morrow when he departed he took out two Pence, and gave them to the Host, and said unto him, Take care of him, and whatsoever thou spendest more, when I come again, I will repay thee.

Which now of these three thinkest thou, was the Neighbour to him that fell among the Thieves?

And he said, he that shewed Mercy upon him. Then said Jesus unto him, Go and do thou likewise.

Considerations on the True Harmony of Mankind & how it is to be maintained

Written by 1770; 1st printed 1770

Editor's Introduction

In this essay Woolman surveys Christian living in the American colonies at a time when cities were growing larger and the entanglements of business were fostering, even among Friends, an increasingly urban sophistication and worldly spirit. His 1768 essay on broad ethical matters— "Considerations on Pure Wisdom, and Human Policy; on Labor; on Schools; and on the Right Use of the Lord's Outward Gifts"—had consisted of four short 'considerations'. This new set of four 'considerations', in which the reader can feel Woolman's ardent "inward labor" for the restoration of mankind to "a state of true harmony,"[1] enlarges on the earlier biblical citations in support of the Truth as Woolman has experienced it. The enlarged support—through theological and historical references—is reflected in the titles of the four chapters: On serving the Lord in our outward employments; On the example of Christ; On merchandizing; and On divine admonitions.

The term "true harmony," which Woolman used in the title as well as in Chapter I pars. 1 and 15 (and also as "true harmonious walking" in Chapter II par. 9 and Chapter III par. 23), may have been his own invention. Among the biblical writers only St. Paul uses the word "harmony," where it appears (in the Revised Standard Version) twice in *The Epistle to the Romans*: "Live in harmony with one another" and "May the God of steadfastness and encouragement grant you to live in such harmony with one another. . ." (12:16; 15:5). It was also used by the author of *The Epistle to the Colossians* (either Paul or one of his disciples): "And above all these put on love, which binds everything together in perfect harmony" (3:14).

The essay is remarkable for its evidence of Woolman's fully developed theological reflection (for example, his thoughts on 'walking', in Chapter I pars. 16-19 and Chapter III par. 8, written after his three walking

---

[1] Chap. I, par. 1.

missions in Maryland taken in 1766-68); his biblical erudition (as in his extended exposition of Isaiah chapter 33 verses 14-17 in Chapter III pars. 8-11); and in his marking humanity's responsibility for the wise stewardship of nature and of the earth for the benefit of its inhabitants (see Chapter IV).

This writing was "inspected by the Overseers of the Press [Woolman himself having been one since 1756] and by them agreed to be printed."[2] It was published by Joseph Crukshank of Philadelphia in 12th month 1770.[3] The following modernization is based on the holograph, designated MS S1/*True Harmony*, which is archived at SC. The holograph, however, includes neither the title page quotation from Micah nor the opening Introduction, both of which appeared, as follows, in the first imprint:

And the remnant of Jacob shall be in the midst of many people, as the dew from the Lord, as the showers upon the grass, that tarries not for man, nor waits for the sons of men (Mic. 5:7).

INTRODUCTION

As mankind from one parent is divided into many families, and as trading to sea is greatly increased within a few ages past, amid this extended commerce how necessary is it that the professed followers of Christ keep sacred his holy name, and be employed about trade and traffic no further than justice and equity evidently accompanies, that we may give no just cause of offense to any, however distant, or unable to plead their own cause, and may continually keep in view the spreading of the true and saving knowledge of God and his son Jesus Christ among our fellow-creatures, which through his infinite love, some feel to be more precious than any other treasure.

---

[2] JW's own words; see Gummere, p. 440.
[3] Smith, p. 960.

Text

Considerations on the True Harmony of Mankind & how it is to be maintained

Chapter I
On serving the Lord in our outward employments

1   Under the humbling dispensations of the Father of mercies, I have felt an inward labor for the good of my fellow creatures, and a concern that the Holy Spirit, which alone can restore mankind to a state of true harmony, may, with singleness of heart, be waited for and followed.

2   I trust there are many under that visitation, which, if faithfully attended to, will make them quick of understanding in the fear of the Lord, and qualify with firmness to be true patterns of the Christian life, who in living and walking may hold forth an invitation to others, to come out of the entanglements of the spirit of this world.

3   And that which I feel first to express is a care for those who are in circumstances which appear difficult with respect to supporting their families in a way answerable to pure wisdom, that they may not be discouraged, but remember that in humbly obeying the leadings of Christ, he owns us as his friends: "Ye are my friends if ye do whatsoever I command you" [John 15:14]. And to be a friend to Christ, is to be united to him who has all power in heaven and in earth; and though a woman may forget her sucking child [Isa. 49:15], yet will he not forget his faithful ones.

4   The condition of many who dwell in cities has often affected me with a brotherly sympathy, attended with a care that resignation may be labored for, and where the holy leader directs to a country life, or some change of employ, he may be faithfully followed; for under the refining hand of the Lord I have seen that the inhabitants of some cities are greatly increased through some branches of business which his Holy Spirit does not lead into, and that being entangled in these things, tends to bring a cloud over the minds of people convinced of the leadings of this holy leader, and obstructs the coming of the kingdom of Christ on earth as it is in heaven.

5   Now, if we indulge a desire to imitate our neighbors in those things which harmonize not with the true Christian walking, these entanglements

148

may hold fast to us, and some who in an awakening time feel tender scruples with respect to their manner of life, may look on the example of others more noted in the church, who yet may not be refined from every degree of dross, and by looking on these examples, and desiring to support their families in a way pleasant to the natural mind, there may be danger of the worldly wisdom gaining strength in them, and of their departure from that pure feeling of Truth; which if faithfully attended to would teach contentment in the divine will, even in a very low estate.

6   One formerly⁴ speaking on the profitableness of true humility said, "He that troubles not himself with anxious thoughts for more than is necessary, lives little less than the life of angels, while by a mind content with little, he imitates their want of nothing." *Cave's Primitive Christianity*, [part 2,] p.31.⁵

7   "It is not enough," says Tertullian,⁶ "that a Christian be chaste and modest, but he must appear to be so: a virtue of which he should have so great a store, that it should flow from his mind upon his habit, and break from the retirements of his conscience, into the superficies [the purely external aspects] of his life." *Ibid.*, p. 43.

8   "The garments we wear," says Clemens,⁷ "ought to be mean and frugal—that is true simplicity of habit which takes away what is vain and superfluous; that the best and most solid garment, which is the farthest from curiosity." *Ibid.*, p. 49.

9   Though the change from day to night is by a motion so gradual as scarcely to be perceived, yet when night is come we behold it very different from the day, and thus as people become wise in their own eyes, and prudent in their own sight, customs rise up from the spirit of this world, and spread by little and little, till a departure from the simplicity that there is in Christ becomes as distinguishable as light from darkness to such who are crucified to the world.

---

4 [At this place in the MS Woolman inserted "One formerly" and struck "Gregory," a reference to St. Gregory of Nyssa (ca. 330-ca. 395).]

5 [William Cave (1637-1713), *Primitive Christianity: or, the religion of the ancient Christians in the first ages of the gospel.* in 3 parts, 2d ed. (London: printed by J.M. for Richard Chiswell, 1675).]

6 [African Church Father (ca. 160-220), a native of Carthage.]

7 [The reference is to St. Clement of Alexandria (ca. 150-ca. 215), a theologian and teacher of Origen.]

10   Our holy shepherd to encourage his flock in firmness and perseverance reminds them of his love for them: "As the Father hath loved me, so have I loved you, continue ye in my love" [John 15:9]; and in another place graciously points out the danger of departing therefrom by going into unsavory employments. This he represents in the similitude of offence from that useful, active member, the hand; and to fix the instruction the deeper, names the right hand: "If thy right hand offend thee, cut it off, and cast it from thee" [Matt. 5:30]. If you feel offence in your employment, humbly follow him who leads into all Truth, and is a strong and faithful friend to those who are resigned to him.

11   Again he points out those things which appearing pleasant to the natural mind, are not best for us, in the similitude of offence from the eye, "If thy right eye offend thee, pluck it out, and cast it from thee" [Matt. 5:29]. To pluck out the eye, or cut off the hand, is attended with sharp pain; and how precious is the instruction which our Redeemer thus opens to us, that we may not faint under the most painful trials but put our trust in him, even in him who sent an angel to feed Elijah in the wilderness, who fed a multitude with a few barley loaves, and is now as attentive to the wants of his people as ever.

12   The prophet Isaiah represents the unrighteous doings of the Israelites toward the poor, as the fruits of an effeminate life: "As for my people, children are their oppressors, and women rule over them. What mean ye that ye beat my people to pieces, and grind the faces of the poor, saith the Lord God" [Isa. 3:12,15]. Then he mentions the haughtiness of the daughters of Zion, and enumerates many tinkling ornaments as instances of their vanity, to uphold which the poor were so hardly dealt with, that he sets forth their poverty, their leanness, and inability to help themselves, in the similitude of a man maimed by violence, or beaten to pieces, and forced to endure the painful operation of having his face gradually worn away in the manner of grinding.

13   And I may here add, that at times when I have felt true love open my heart toward my fellow creatures, and been engaged in weighty conversation in the cause of righteousness, the instructions I have received, under these exercises, in regard to the true use of the outward gifts of God, have made deep and lasting impressions on my mind.

14   I have beheld how the desire to provide wealth, and uphold a delicate life, has grievously entangled many, and been like snares to their

offspring; and though some have been affected with a sense of their difficulties, and appeared desirous at times to be helped out of them; yet for want of abiding under the humbling power of Truth, they have continued in these entanglements; for in remaining conformable to this world, and giving way to a delicate life, this expensive way of living in parents and in children, has called for a large supply; and in answering this call, the faces of the poor have been ground away, and made thin through hard dealing.

15   There is balm, there is a physician! And O what longings do I feel that we may embrace the means appointed for our healing, know that removed which now ministers cause for the cries of many people, to ascend to heaven against their oppressors, and that we may see true harmony restored.

16   "Behold how good, and how pleasant it is, for brethren to dwell together in unity" [Ps. 133:1]. The nature of this unity is thus opened by the apostle; "if we walk in the light, as Christ is in the light, we shall have fellowship one with another, and the blood of Christ will cleanse us from all sin" [1 John 1:7].

17   The land may be polluted with innocent blood, which like the blood of Abel, may cry to the almighty, but those who walk in the light, as Christ is in the light, they know the Lamb of God who takes away sin.

18   Walking is a phrase frequently used in scripture to represent our journey through life, and appears to comprehend the various affairs and transactions properly relating to our being in this world.[8]

19   Christ being the light dwells always in the light, and if our walking be thus, and in every affair and concern we faithfully follow this divine leader, he preserves from giving just cause for any to quarrel with us. And where this foundation is laid and mutually kept to, by families conversant with each other, the way is open for those comforts in society which our heavenly Father intends as a part of our happiness in this world; and then we may experience the goodness and pleasantness of dwelling together in unity; but where ways of living take place which tend to oppression, and in the pursuit of wealth, people do that to others which they know would not be acceptable to themselves, either in exercising an absolute power over

---

[8] [JW had walked on his three missionary journeys into Maryland in 1766, 1767, and 1768. See Table 1 herein.]

them, or otherwise laying on them inequitable burdens; here a fear lest that measure should be meted to them, which they have measured to others, incites a care to support that by craft and cunning devices which stands not on the firm foundation of righteousness: thus the harmony of society is broken, and from hence commotions and wars do frequently arise in the world.

20　"Come out of Babylon, my people, that ye be not partakers of her sins, and that ye receive not of her plagues" (Rev. 18:4). This Babel or Babylon was built in the spirit of self-exaltation: "Let us build us a city and a tower, whose top may reach heaven, and let us make us a name" (Gen. 11:4). In departing from an humble trust in God, and following a selfish spirit, people have intentions to get the upper hand of their fellow creatures, privately meditate on means to obtain their ends, have a language in their hearts which is hard to understand. In Babel, the language is confounded.

21　This city is represented as a place of business, and those employed in it as merchants of the earth: "The merchants of the earth are waxed rich through the abundance of her delicacies" (Rev. 18:3). And it is remarkable in this call that the language from the Father of mercies, is, "Come out of Babylon, my people!" Thus his tender mercies are toward us in an imperfect state, and, as we faithfully attend to the call, the path of righteousness is more and more opened: cravings which have not their foundation in pure wisdom, more and more cease; and in an inward purity of heart, we experience a restoration of that which was lost at Babel, represented by the inspired prophet in the "returning of a pure language" (Zeph. 3:9).

22　Happy for them who humbly attend to the call, "Come out of Babylon, my people!" For though in going forth we may meet with trials which for a time may be painful, yet as we bow in true humility, and continue in it, an evidence is felt that God only is wise and that in weaning us from all that is selfish he prepares the way to a quiet habitation where all our desires are bounded by his wisdom.

23　And an exercise of spirit attends me, that we who are convinced of the pure leadings of Truth, may bow in the deepest reverence, and so watchfully regard this leader, that many who are grievously entangled in a wilderness of vain customs, may look upon us, and be instructed. And O that such who have plenty of this world's goods, may be faithful in that with which they are entrusted! and example others in the true Christian walking!

24 Our blessed savior speaking on worldly greatness, compares himself to one waiting, and attending on a company at dinner: "Whether is greater, he that sitteth at meat, or he that serveth? Is not he that sitteth at meat? but I am amongst you as he that serveth" (Luke 22:27).

25 Thus in a world greatly disordered, where men aspiring to outward greatness were wont to oppress others to support their designs, he who was of the highest descent, being the Son of God, and greater than any among the greatest families of men, by his example and doctrines foreclosed his followers from claiming any show of outward greatness from any supposed superiority in themselves, or derived from their ancestors.

26 He who was greater than earthly princes was not only meek and low of heart, but his outward appearance was plain and lowly, and free from every stain of the spirit of this world.

27 Such was the example of our blessed Redeemer of whom the beloved disciple said, "He that saith he abideth in him ought also to walk even as he walked" [1 John 2:6].

28 John Bradford,[9] who suffered martyrdom under Queen Mary, wrote a letter to his friends out of prison a short time before he was burnt, in which are these expressions: "Consider your dignity as children of God, and temples of the Holy Ghost, and members of Christ; be ashamed therefore to think, speak, or do anything unseemly for God's children and the members of Christ." *Foxe's Actes and Monuments*, p. 1177.[10]

Chapter II
On the Example of Christ

1 As my mind has been brought into a brotherly feeling with the poor as to the things of this life, who are under trials in regard to getting a living, in a way answerable to the purity of Truth; a labor of heart has attended me, that their way may not be made difficult through a love of

---

9 [Protestant martyr (ca. 1510-1555)]

10 [John Foxe (1516-1587), martyrologist and author of *Actes and Monuments of these latter and perilous days: touching matters of the Church* (London: printed by John Day, 1563), an account of the Protestants martyred during Mary's reign.]

money in those who are tried with plentiful estates, but that these with tenderness of heart may sympathize with them. It was the saying of our blessed Redeemer, "Ye cannot serve God and mammon" [Matt. 6:24; Luke 16:13]. There is a deep feeling of the way of purity, a way in which the wisdom of the world has no part, but is opened by the Spirit of Truth, and is "called the way of holiness" [Isa. 35:8]. A way in which the traveler is employed in watching unto prayer; and the outward gain we get in this journey is considered as a trust committed to us, by him who formed and supports the world; the rightful director of the use and application of the product of it.[11]

2   Except the mind be preserved chaste, there is no safety for us, but in an estrangement from true resignation, the spirit of the world casts up a way, in which gain is many times principally attended to, and in which there is a selfish application of outward treasures.

3   How agreeable to the true harmony of society is that exhortation of the apostle; "Look not every man on his own things, but every man also on the things of others, - Let this mind be in you which was also in Christ Jesus" [Phil. 2:4-5].

4   A person in outward prosperity may have the power of obtaining riches, but the same mind being in him which is in Christ Jesus, he may feel a tenderness of heart towards those of low degree, and instead of setting himself above them, may look upon it as an unmerited favor, that his way through life is more easy than the way of many others; may improve every opportunity of leading forth out of those customs which have entangled the family; employ his time in looking into the wants of the poor members, and hold forth such a perfect example of humiliation, that the pure witness may be reached in many minds, and the way opened for an harmonious walking together.

5   Jesus Christ had no reserve in promoting the happiness of others, he was not deficient in looking for the helpless, who lay in obscurity, nor did he save any thing, to render himself honorable among men which might have been of more use to the weak members in his father's family. Of whose compassion towards us I may now speak a little.

---

[11] [At this place in the holograph JW has stricken out: "Here his cause on earth is dear to us. The heart is open to search into the necessities of the poor members of Christ's flock and in the feeling of pure love an evidence is felt respecting the master whom we serve."]

6   He who was perfectly happy in himself, moved with infinite love, took not upon him the nature of angels but our imperfect natures, and therein wrestled with the temptations which attend us in this life; and being the Son of him who is greater than earthly princes, yet became a companion to poor, sincere-hearted men; and though he gave the clearest evidence that a divine power attended him, yet the most unfavorable constructions were framed by a self-righteous people; those miracles represented as the effect of a diabolical power, and endeavors used to render him hateful, as having his mission from the prince of darkness; nor did their envy cease till they took him like a criminal, and brought him to trial. Though some may affect to carry the appearance of being unmoved at the apprehension of distress, our dear Redeemer, who was perfectly sincere, having the same human nature which we have, and feeling a little before he was apprehended the weight of that work upon him, for which he came into the world, was sorrowful, even unto death, here the human nature struggled to be excused from a cup so bitter; but his prayers centered in resignation, "not my will, but thine be done" [Luke 22:42]. In this conflict so great was his agony that sweat like drops of blood fell from him to the ground.

7   Behold now as foretold by the prophet, he is in a judicial manner numbered with the transgressors. Behold him, as some poor man of no reputation, standing before the high priest and elders, and before Herod and Pilate, where witnesses appear against him; and he, mindful of the most gracious design of his coming, declined to plead in his own defence, but as a sheep that is dumb before his shearer, under many accusations, revilings, and buffetings, remained silent. And though he signified to Peter, that he had access to power sufficient to overthrow all their outward forces, yet, retaining a resignation to suffer for the sins of mankind, he exerted not that power, but permitted them to go on in their malicious designs, and pronounce him to be worthy of death, even him who was perfect in goodness; thus "in his humiliation his judgment was taken away" [Acts 8:33], and he, like some vile criminal, "led as a lamb to the slaughter" [Isa. 53:7]. Under these heavy trials (though poor unstable Pilate was convinced of his innocence) the people generally looked upon him as a deceiver, a blasphemer, and the approaching punishment as a just judgment upon him. "They esteemed him smitten of God and afflicted" [Isa. 53:4]. So great had been the surprise of his disciples at his being taken by armed men, that they forsook him and fled. Thus they hid their faces from him, he was despised, and by their conduct it appeared as though they had esteemed him not.

8   But contrary to that opinion of his being smitten of God and afflicted it was for our sakes that "he was put to grief; he was wounded for our transgressions; he was bruised for our iniquities" [Isa. 53:5]; and under the weight of them manifesting the deepest compassion for the instruments of his misery, labored as their advocate, and in the depths of affliction, with an unconquerable patience, cried out, "Father forgive them, they know not what they do!" [Luke 23:34].

9   Now this mind being in us which was in Christ Jesus, it removes from our hearts the desire of superiority, worldly honor, or greatness; a deep attention is felt to the divine counsellor, and an ardent engagement to promote, as far as we may be enabled, the happiness of mankind universally. This state, where every motion from a selfish spirit yields to pure love, I may with gratitude to the Father of mercies acknowledge, is often opened before me as a pearl to dig after; attended with a living concern, that among the many nations and families on the earth, those who believe in the Messiah, that "he was manifested to destroy the works of the devil" [1 John 3:8], and thus to take away the sins of the world, that the will of our heavenly Father to be done on earth as it is in heaven. Strong are the desires I often feel, that this holy profession may remain unpolluted, and the believers in Christ may so abide in the pure, inward feeling of his Spirit, that the wisdom from above may shine forth in their living, as a light by which others may be instrumentally helped on their way, in the true harmonious walking.

Chapter III
On Merchandizing

1   Where the treasures of pure love are opened, and we obediently follow him who is the light of life, the mind becomes chaste; and a care is felt that the unction from the Holy One may be our leader in every undertaking.

2   In being crucified to the world, broken off from that friendship which is enmity with God, and dead to the customs and fashions which have not their foundation in the Truth, the way is prepared to lowliness in outward living, and to a disentanglement from those snares which attend the love of money; and where the faithful friends of Christ are so situated that merchandize appears to be their duty, they feel a restraint from proceeding farther than he owns their proceeding; being convinced that we are not our own but are bought with a price [1 Cor. 6:19-20], that none of

us may live to ourselves, but to him who died for us (2 Cor. 5:15). Thus they are taught, not only to keep to a moderate advance, and uprightness in their dealings; but to consider the tendency of their proceeding; to do nothing which they know would operate against the cause of universal righteousness, and to keep continually in view the spreading of the peaceable kingdom of Christ among mankind.

3   The prophet Isaiah spoke of the gathered church, in the similitude of a city, where many being employed were all preserved in purity. "They shall call them the holy people, the redeemed of the Lord, and thou shalt be called Sought out, a city not forsaken" (Isa. [62:12]). And the apostle after mentioning the mystery of Christ's sufferings exhorts, "Be ye holy in all manner of conversation" (1 Peter 1:15). There is a conversation necessary in trade; and there is a conversation so foreign from the nature of Christ's kingdom, that it is represented in the similitude of one man pushing another with a warlike weapon; "There is that speaketh like the piercings of a sword" (Prov. 12:18). Now in all our concerns it is necessary that the leading of the Spirit of Christ be humbly waited for, and faithfully followed, as the only means of being preserved chaste as an holy people, who in all things are circumspect (Exod. 23:13), that nothing we do may carry the appearance of approbation of the works of wickedness, make the unrighteous more at ease in unrighteousness, or occasion the injuries committed against the oppressed to be more lightly looked over.

4   Where morality is kept to, and supported by the inhabitants of a country, there is a certain reproach attends those individuals among them, who manifestly deviate therefrom. Thus if a person of good report is charged with stealing goods out of an open shop in the day time, and on a public trial found guilty, and the law in that case put in execution, he therein sustains a loss of reputation; but if he be convicted a second and third time of the like offence his good name would cease among such who knew these things. If his neighbor, reputed an honest man, being charged with buying goods of this thief, at a time when the purchaser knew they were stolen, and on a public trial is found guilty, this purchaser would meet with disesteem; but if he persisted in buying stolen goods knowing them to be such, and was publicly convicted thereof a second and third time, he would no longer be considered as an honest man by them who knew these things; nor would it appear of good report to be found in his company buying his traffic, till some evident tokens of sincere repentance appeared in him. But where iniquity is committed openly, and the authors of it are not brought to justice, nor put to shame, their hands grow strong.

Thus the general corruption of the Jews shortly before their state was broken up by the Chaldeans, is described by their boldness in impiety; for as their leaders were connected in wickedness, they strengthened one another, and grew confident; "Were they ashamed when they had committed abominations? nay, they were not at all ashamed, neither could they blush" (Jer. 6:15): on which account the Lord thus expostulates with them, "What hath my beloved to do in my house, seeing she hath wrought lewdness with many, and the holy flesh is passed from thee, when thou doest evil, then thou rejoicest" (Jer. 11:15).

5   Now the faithful friends of Christ, who hunger and thirst after righteousness, and inwardly breathe that the kingdom of God may come on earth as it is in heaven, he teaches them to be quick of understanding in his fear, and to be very attentive to the means he may appoint for promoting pure righteousness in the earth, and as shame is due to those whose works manifestly operate against the gracious design of his sufferings for us, a care lives on their minds that no wrong customs, however supported, may bias their judgments, but that they may humbly abide under the cross and be preserved in a conduct which may not contribute to strengthen the hands of the wicked in their wickedness, or to remove shame from those to whom it is justly due. The coming of that day is precious in which we experience the truth of this expression, "The Lord our righteousness" (Jer. [2]3:6); and feel him to be made unto us wisdom and sanctification.

6   The example of a righteous man is often looked at with attention. Where righteous men join in business, their company gives encouragement to others; and as one grain of incense deliberately offered to the prince of this world, renders an offering to God in that state unacceptable; and from those esteemed leaders of the people, may be injurious to the weak; it requires deep humility of heart, to follow him faithfully, who alone gives sound wisdom, and the Spirit of true discerning; and O how necessary it is to consider the weight of a holy profession!

7   The conduct of some formerly, gave occasion of complaint against them, "Thou hast defiled thy sanctuaries by the multitude of thine iniquities, by the iniquity of thy traffic" (Ezek. 28:18); and in several places it is charged against Israel that they had polluted the holy name.

8   The prophet Isaiah represents inward sanctification in the similitude of being purged from that which is fuel for fire; and particularly

describes the outward fruits, brought forth by those who dwell in this inward holiness; "they walk righteously, and speak uprightly" [Isa. 33:15]. By *walking* he represents the journey through life as a righteous journey; and by *speaking uprightly* seems to point at that which Moses appears to have had in view, when he thus expressed himself, "Thou shalt not follow a multitude to do evil, nor speak in a cause to decline after many to wrest judgment" (Exod. 23:2).

9   He goes on to show their firmness in equity; representing them as persons superior to all the arts of getting money, which have not righteousness for their foundation; "They despise the gain of oppressions" [Isa. 33:15]; and further shows how careful they are that no prospects of gain may induce them to become partial in judgment respecting an injury; "They shake their hands from holding bribes" [ibid.].

10   Again where any interest is so connected with shedding blood that the cry of innocent blood goes along with it he points out their care, to keep innocent blood from crying against them, in the similitude of a man stopping his ears to prevent a sound from entering into his head, "They stop their ears from hearing of blood" [ibid.]. And where they know that wickedness is committed, he points out their care, that they do not by an unguarded friendship with the authors of it, appear like unconcerned lookers on, but as people so deeply affected with sorrow, that they cannot endure to stand by and behold it, this he represents in the similitude of a man "shutting his eyes from seeing evil. Who among us shall dwell with devouring fire? Who among us shall dwell with everlasting burnings? He that walks righteously and speaks uprightly. He that despises the gain of oppressions, that shakes his hands from holding of bribes, that stops his ears from hearing of blood and shuts his eyes from seeing evil" [Isa. 33:14-15].

11   He proceeds in the spirit of prophecy, to show how the faithful being supported under temptations would be preserved from that defilement that there is in the love of money, that as they who in a reverent waiting on God, feel their strength renewed, are said to "mount upward" [Isa. 40:31], so here their preservation from the snares of unrighteous gain, is represented by the likeness of a man borne up above all crafty, artful means, of getting the advantage of another, "They shall dwell on high" [Isa. 33:16], and points out the stability and firmness of their condition, "His place of defence shall be the munition of rocks" [ibid.]. And that under all the outward appearance of loss, in denying himself of gainful

prospects for righteousness' sake, yet through the care of him who provides for the sparrows, he should have a supply answerable to infinite wisdom, "Bread shall be given him, his waters shall be sure" [ibid.]. And as our Savior mentions the sight of God to be attainable by "the pure in heart" [Matt. 5:8] so here the prophet pointed out how in true sanctification the understanding is opened to behold the peaceable, harmonious nature of his kingdom, "Thine eyes shall see the King in his beauty" [Isa. 33:17]. And that looking beyond all the afflictions which attend the righteous, to a "habitation eternal in the heavens" [2 Cor. 5:1], they with an eye divinely opened "shall behold the land that is very far off" [Isa. 33:17]. "He shall dwell on high, his place of defence shall be the munitions of rocks, bread shall be given him, his waters shall be sure. Thine eyes shall see the King in his beauty; they shall behold the land that is very far off" [Isa. 33:16-17].[12]

12   I often remember, and to me the subject is awful, that the great Judge of all the earth does that which is right, and that he "before whom the nations are as the drop of a bucket" [Isa. 40:15], is "no respecter of persons" [Acts 10:34]. Happy for them, who like the inspired prophet, "in the way of his judgments wait for him" (Isa. 26:8).

13   When we feel him to sit as a refiner with fire, and know a resignedness wrought in us to that which he appoints for us, his blessing in a very low estate is found to be more precious than much outward treasure in those ways of life where the leadings of his Spirit are not followed.

14   The prophet in a sight of a divine work among many people, declared in the name of the Lord, "I will gather all nations and tongues, and they shall come and see my glory" (Isa. 66:18). And again, "from the rising of the sun to the going down of the same, my name shall be great among the Gentiles and in every place incense shall be offered to my name, and a pure offering" (Mal. 1:11).

15   Behold here how the prophets had an inward sense of the spreading of the kingdom of Christ; and how he was spoken of as one who should "take the heathen for his inheritance, and the utmost parts of the earth for his possession" (Ps. 2:8). That "He was given for a light to the Gentiles; and for salvation to the ends of the earth" (Isa. 49:6).

---

[12] [At this place in the holograph JW has stricken out: "There is a tender mercy in my heart with such who by their education and condition in life are under greater difficulties than some others, and I feel pure love in which desires prevail for the health and soundness of the family."]

16   When we meditate on this divine work, as a work of ages; a work that the prophets felt long before Christ appeared visibly on earth, and remember the bitter agonies he endured when he "poured out his soul unto death" [Isa. 53:12], that the heathen nations as well as others might come to the knowledge of the Truth and be saved. When we contemplate on this marvelous work, as that which "the angels desire to look into" (1 Pet. 1:12), and behold people among whom this light has eminently broken forth, and who have received many favors from the bountiful hand of our heavenly Father, not only indifferent with respect to publishing the glad tidings among the Gentiles, as yet sitting in darkness, and entangled with many superstitions; but aspiring after wealth and worldly honors, take hold of means to obtain their ends, tending to stir up wrath and indignation, and to beget an abhorrence in them to the name of Christianity, when these things are weightily attended to, how mournful is the subject!

17   It is worthy of remembrance, that people in different ages, deeply baptized into the nature of that work for which Christ suffered, have joyfully offered up their liberty and lives for the promoting of it in the earth.

18   Polycarp[13] who was reputed a disciple of St. John having attained to a great age, was at length sentenced to die for his religion, and being brought to the fire prayed nearly as follows, "Thou God and Father of our Lord Jesus Christ, by whom I have received the knowledge of thee! O God of the angels and powers, and of every living creature, and of all sorts of just men which live in thy presence, I thank thee! that thou hast graciously vouchsafed this day and this hour to allot me a portion among the number of martyrs, among the people of Christ, unto the resurrection of everlasting life, among whom I shall be received in thy sight this day, as a fruitful and acceptable sacrifice; wherefore for all this I praise thee, I bless thee, I glorify thee, through the everlasting high-priest, Jesus Christ, thy well-beloved Son, to whom with thee and the Holy Ghost be all glory, world without end. Amen."

19   Bishop Latimer[14] when sentence of death by fire was pronounced against him, on account of his firmness in the cause of religion, said, "I thank God most heartily! that he hath prolonged my life to this end, that I

---

[13]   [(ca. 69-ca. 155), Bishop of Smyrna who maintained the apostolic tradition; a saint.]

[14]   [Hugh Latimer (ca. 1485-1555), Bishop of Worcester; a reformer.]

may in this case glorify him by this kind of death." *Foxe's Acts and Mon.* p. 936.[15]

20   William Dewsbury[16] who had suffered much for his religion, in his last sickness, encouraging his friends to faithfulness, made mention, like good old Jacob, of the loving kindness of God to him in the course of his life, and that through the power of divine love, he, for Christ's sake, had joyfully entered prisons. *See introduction to his works.*[17]

21   I mention these, as a few examples, out of many, of the powerful operation of the Spirit of Christ, where people are fully devoted to it, and of the ardent longings in their minds for the spreading of his kingdom among mankind.

22   Now to those in the present age, who truly know Christ, and feel the nature of his peaceable government opened in their understandings, how loud is that call wherewith we are called to faithfulness, that in following this pure light of life, "we as workers together with him" [2 Cor. 6:1], may labor in that great work for which he was offered as a sacrifice on the cross, and his peaceable doctrines shine through us in their real harmony, at a time when the name of Christianity is become hateful to many of the heathen.

23   When Gehazi had obtained treasures, which the prophet under divine direction had refused, and was returned from the business, the prophet troubled at his conduct, queried if it was a time thus to prepare for a specious living. "Is it a time to receive money and garments, men-servants and maid-servants? The leprosy therefore of Naaman shall cleave to thee, and to thy seed forever" (2 Kings 5:26[-27]). And O that we may lay to heart the condition of the present time! and humbly follow his counsel, who alone is able to prepare the way for a true harmonious walking among mankind.

---

[15]   [See footnote 10 above.]
[16]   [(1621-1688), a friend of George Fox and an early Quaker.]
[17]   [William Dewsbury, *The faithful testimony of that antient servant of the Lord, and minister of the everlasting gospel William Dewsbery: in his books, epistles and writings, collected and printed for future service* (London: printed and sold by Andrew Sowle, 1689)]

Chapter IV
On Divine Admonitions

1   Such are the perfections of our heavenly Father, that in all the dispensations of his providence, it is our duty "in every thing to give thanks" [Eph. 5:20]. Though from the first settlement of this part of America, he has not extended his judgments to the degree of famine, yet worms at times have come forth beyond numbering, and laid waste fields of grain and grass where they have appeared. Another kind in great multitudes, working out of sight, in grass ground, have so eaten the roots, that the surface being loosened from the soil beneath might be taken off in great sheets.

2   These kind of devouring creatures appearing seldom, and coming in such multitudes, their generation appears different from most other reptiles, and by the prophet, were called "God's army sent among the people" (Joel 2:25).

3   There have been tempests of hail, which have very much destroyed the grain where they extended. Through long drought in summer, grain in some places has been less than half the usual quantity;[18] and in the continuance thereof I have beheld with attention, from week to week, how dryness from the top of the earth has extended deeper and deeper, while the corn and plants have languished, and with reverence my mind has been turned towards him, who being perfect in goodness, in wisdom and power, does all things right. And after long drought, when the sky has grown dark with a collection of matter, and clouds like lakes of water hung over our heads, from whence the thirsty land has been soaked; I have at times, with awfulness, beheld the vehement operation of lightning, made sometimes to accompany these blessings, as a messenger from him who created all things, to remind us of our duty in a right use of those benefits, and give striking admonitions, that we do not misapply those gifts, in which an almighty power is exerted in bestowing them upon us.

4   When I have considered that many of our fellow creatures suffer much in some places, for want of the necessaries of life, while those who rule over them are too much given to luxury, and divers vanities; and behold the apparent deviation from pure wisdom among us, in the use of

---

18 [Here JW entered the following footnote: "When crops fail I often feel a tender care that the case of poor tenants may be mercifully considered."]

the outward gifts of God; those marks of famine have appeared like humbling admonitions from him, that we might be instructed by gentle chastisements, and might seriously consider our ways, remember that the outward supply of life is a gift from our heavenly Father, and no more venture to use, or apply his gifts, in a way contrary to pure wisdom.

5   Should we continue to reject those merciful admonitions, and use his gifts at home contrary to the gracious design of the giver, or send them abroad in a way of trade which the Spirit of Truth does not lead into, and should he whose eyes are upon all our ways, extend his chastisements so far as to reduce us to much greater distress than has yet been felt by these provinces, with what sorrow of heart might we meditate on that subject, "Hast thou not procured this unto thyself, in that thou hast forsaken the Lord thy God, when he led thee by the way? Thine own wickedness shall correct thee, and thy backsliding shall reprove thee, know therefore and see that it is an evil thing and bitter, that thou hast forsaken the Lord thy God, and that my fear is not in thee, saith the Lord of hosts" (Jer. 2:17,19).

6   My mind has often been affected with sorrow, in beholding a wrong application of the gifts of our heavenly Father; and those expressions concerning the defilement of the earth have been opened to my understanding, "The earth was corrupt before God and the earth was filled with violence" (Gen. 6:11). Again "The earth also is defiled under the inhabitants thereof" (Isa. 24:5).

7   The earth being the work of a divine power may not as such be accounted unclean; but when violence is committed thereon, and the channel of righteousness so obstructed that "in our skirts are found the blood of the souls of poor innocents, not by a secret search, but upon all these" (Jer. 2:34).[19]

8   When blood shed unrighteously remains unatoned for, and the inhabitants are not effectually purged from it, when they do not wash their hands in innocency, as was figured in the law, in the case of one being found slain (Deut. 21:6), but seek for gain arising from scenes of violence and oppression, "here the land is polluted with blood." Moreover when the earth is planted and tilled and fruits brought forth are applied to support unrighteous purposes, here the gracious design of infinite goodness, in

[19] [At this place in the MS JW entered the following footnote: "See a caution and warning to Great Britain and her colonies, page 31," referring to Anthony Benezet's work. See Text 7 C herein.]

these his gifts being perverted, the earth is defiled; and the complaint formerly uttered becomes applicable: "Thou hast made me to serve with thy sins, thou hast wearied me with thine iniquities" (Isa. 43:24).

Conversations on the True Harmony of Mankind & how it may be promoted

Written 3ʳᵈ mo 1772; 1ˢᵗ printed 1837

Editor's Introduction

Woolman in his introductory note dates these dialogues to "3ʳᵈ month: 1772," a time within the final weeks before his departure for England on 1 May. In that note he remarks he has had occasion to open his mind "in true brotherly love to converse freely and largely with some who were entrusted with plentiful estates in regard to an application of the profits of them consistent with pure wisdom."[1] In the two extended conversations recorded here, Woolman himself is undoubtedly the "laboring man," while the "man rich in money" and the "thrifty land-holder" would be from among his 'beloved friends' who were both men of substance and Quaker worthies into whose homes Woolman was readily welcomed. The three Pemberton brothers of Philadelphia and the four Smith brothers (as well as their five sisters) of Burlington immediately come to mind.

In this dialogue *genre*, the author illustrates the themes of the preceding essay, "Considerations on the True Harmony of Mankind" (Text 11), and shows through the discourse of the "laboring man" the onerous burdens then carried by many Americans who were subject to interest rates of seven percent, heavy rents and inadequate wages, and a foreign trade policy driven by the pursuit of gold. In the author's view, if a nation strives not for a society grounded in economic fairness but rather for the creation of personal wealth and the possession of gold, its destiny looks grim indeed. As expressed by the "laboring man":

> With gold men often hire armies and make great preparations for war. . . .The battles of the warrior are not only with confused noise and garments rolled in blood, but commonly contrived in the craft and subtlety of man's wisdom, and if we trust in man, make flesh our arm, and are estranged from that purified state in which the mind relies on God, we are on the way towards an

---

[1] Par. 1.

increase of confusion. . . .Now in the bottom of these devices there is unquietness, for where gold or treasures are gathered, and not in that wisdom which is pure and peaceable, the mind in this state is left naked.[2]

The holograph of MS A/*Conversations* (found on pages 14 to 27 from back to front of MS A) was used in modernizing the following text. It does not appear that Woolman offered the work either to the Overseers of the Press for review or to a printer for publication. It was first printed in 1837 in an edition of Woolman's collected works.[3]

Text

Conversations on the True Harmony of Mankind & how it may be promoted

1   I have at sundry times felt my mind opened in true brotherly love to converse freely and largely with some who were entrusted with plentiful estates in regard to an application of the profits of them consistent with pure wisdom. And of late it has often revived on my mind as a duty to write the substance of what then passed, and as I have attended to this concern I have felt my mind opened to enlarge on some points then spoken to.

3rd mo: 1772   John Woolman

The substance of some conversation between a laboring man and a man rich in money.

2   Laborer speaks thus: I observe you live easy as to bodily labor, and perceive you take interest at seven percent. I find occasion among us laboring men in supporting our families to work harder at times than is agreeable to us. I am now thinking of that Christian exhortation, Love as brethren! and propose to you, my neighbor, whether a way may not be opened for you and your family to live comfortably on a lower interest which if once rightly attained would, I believe, work in favor of us laboring people.

---

[2] Pars. 68, 69, 72.
[3] *A Journal of the life, gospel labours, and Christian experiences of that faithful minister of Jesus Christ, John Woolman,* ed. John Comly (Philadelphia: Chapman, 1837).

3   Rich: If you pay no interest wherein does seven percent affect you?

4   Laborer: I was at work for a husbandman who had bought a plantation and paid interest for a great part of the purchase money. As this neighbor and I were talking of the quantity of grain equitable to pay for a day's work, he told me that so much of the produce of his ground went yearly to pay the interest of the remaining purchase money that he thought he could not afford so much rye for a day's work now as was considered pay for a day's work twenty years ago.

5   Rich: Twenty years ago interest was as high as it is now, and grain, flesh, butter, and cheese were then cheaper.

6   Laborer: Seven percent is higher than interest is in England and than it is in most of the neighboring provinces. This is known to many who pay interest, who look at wealthy interest receivers as men having got an advantage of their brethren; and as the provisions are more and more in demand, partly by an enlargement of towns and villages, and partly by a sea trade, some take hold of opportunities to raise the prices of grain, flesh, butter, and the like, and apprehend that herein they are only laboring to bring the price of their produce toward a balance with seven percent.

7   On a rise of grain, of flesh and the like, I have known tradesmen meet and raise the price of their work, thus a poor laboring man who works by the day for the necessaries of life must not only work more for a bushel of grain, but also for weaving of his cloak, for making of his coat, and for the shoes which he wears. There also arises discouragement hereby to tradesmen in our country in general, for tradesmen raising their wages on a rise of grain, the price of cloth, of shoes, of hats, of scythes, and the like, are all raised.

8   Now if interest was lower, grain lower, and kept more plentiful in our country, wages of hired men might with reason be lower also, hence encouragement would naturally arise to husbandmen to raise more sheep, and flax, and prepare means to employ many poor people among us.

9   Sheep are pleasant company on a plantation, their looks are modest, their voice is soft and agreeable, the slowness of their run exposes them a prey to wild beasts, and they appear to be intended by the great Creator to live under our protection and supply us with matter for warm and useful clothing. Sheep being rightly managed tend to enrich our land,

but by sending abroad great quantities of grain and flour, the fatness of our land is diminished.

10   I have known landholders who paid interest for large sums of money and being intent on paying their debts by raising grain, have by too much tilling so robbed the earth of its natural fatness that the produce thereof has grown light.

11   To till poor land requires near as much labor as to till that which is rich, and as the high interest of money which lies on many husbandmen is often a means of their struggling for present profit, to the impoverishment of their lands, they then on their poor land find greater difficulty to afford poor laborers who work for them equitable pay for tilling the ground.

12   The produce of the earth is a gift from our gracious Creator to the inhabitants, and to impoverish the earth now to support outward greatness appears to be an injury to the succeeding age.

13   Rich: As there has for some years past been a gradual rise of our country produce and we have not raised our interest, if there be any complaint now, it seems as if we are the men to complain.

14   Laborer: My loving friend and neighbor! People, you know, sometimes disagree in attempting to settle accounts (when no fraud is intended on either side) but through want of matters being clearly and fairly stated. Come now, let us patiently hear each other, and endeavor to love as brethren.

15   Some who pay rent for a small house and raise up children, all by days labor, are often taught by very moving instructions. Some keep a cow, and labor hard in the summer to provide hay and grain for her against the winter; but in very cold winters hay is sometimes gone before spring, and grain is so scarce through much sending it and flour abroad that the grain intended for a cow is found necessary to be eaten in the family. I have known grain and hay so scarce that I could not any where near get so much as my family and creatures had need of, being then sparing in feeding our cow she has grown poor. In her pineing condition she has called aloud, I knew her voice, and the sound thereof was the cry of hunger. I have known snowy stormy weather of long continuance. I have seen poor creatures in distress for want of good shelter and plentiful feeding when it did not appear to be in the power of their owners to do much better for them, being straitened in answering the demands of the wealthy. I have seen

small fires in long cold storms and known sufferings for want of fire wood. In wasting away under want, nature has a voice that is very piercing. To these things I have been a witness, and had a feeling sense of them; nor may I easily forget what I have thus learned.

16   Now, my friend, I have beheld that fullness and delicacy in which you and your family live. Those expensive articles from beyond the sea, which serve chiefly to please the desire of the eye, and to please the palate, which I often observe in your family; as in other rich families, these costly things are often revived in my remembrance when those piercing injunctions arising from hunger and want have been before me.

17   Our merchants in paying for these delicacies send a great deal of flour and grain abroad, hence grain is more scarce and dear, which operates against poor laboring people.

18   I have seen in your family that in furnishing the house, in dressing yourselves, and preparations for the table, you might save a good deal if your minds were reconciled to that simplicity mentioned by the apostle, to wit, the simplicity that there is in Christ; and by thus saving you might help poor people several ways. You might abate of your interest money, and that might operate in favor of the poor. Your example in a plain life might encourage other rich families in this simple way of living, who by abating their expenses might the easier abate the rents of their lands, and their tenants having farms on easier terms would have less plea for shortening the wages of the poor in raising the price of grain than they now have.

19   I have felt hardships among poor people and had experience of their difficulties. Now, my friend! were our stations in the world to be changed, were you and your children to labor a few years with your hands, under all the wants and difficulties of the poor, toward supporting us and our families in that expensive way of life in which you and your family now live, you would see that we might have a sufficiency with much less, and on abating our demands might make your labor and the labor of your children much easier, and doubtless in my case, to you such abatements would be desirable.

20   I have read of a heathen king or emperor so affected with that great law of equity laid down by our Redeemer, that he caused it to be fixed up on the wall of his palace: Whatsoever ye would that other men should do to you, do ye even so to them [Matt. 7:12; Luke 6:31]. And as all men by nature are equally entitled to the equity of this law, and under the

obligations of it, there appears on the point of tenderness to the poor, improvement necessary for you, my friend.

21   Rich: If I would abate all those expenses you hint at, I believe some poor people, as hard set to live in the world as those you speak of, would lose some business and be more straitened to live than they are at present.

22   Laborer: I know of no employ in life more innocent in its nature, more healthy, and more acceptable in common to the minds of honest men than husbandry, followed no further than while action is agreeable to the body only as an agreeable employ; but husbandry by the smallness of the number employed in it is often made a toil, and the sweetness thereof changed into hurry and weariness in doing no more than tenants commonly expect from a man, the labor of a day.

23   Rich: I have seen men perform a full day's labor, even in hot weather, and at night appeared cheerful and no signs of weariness on them.

24   Laborer: That may often be seen in strong, hearty men, but sometimes the necessities of poor laboring men induce them to labor when they are weakly, and among poor men, as among others, some are weak by nature, and not of constitutions prepared to go through great labors, and these in doing what is esteemed a day's work in the summer are frequently very weary before night, even when in health; and when weakly, sometimes struggle with labor to a great degree of oppression.

25   Laboring to raise the necessaries of life is in itself an honest labor, and the more men that are employed in honest employments the better. Many of the employments you hint at have been invented to gratify the wandering desires of those, who through means of riches had power to turn money into the channels of vanity, which employments are often distressing to the minds of sincere hearted people who from their childhood have been brought up in them, with intent that thereby they might get a living in the world, with whom I have a brotherly sympathy, and not only desire that their faith fail not, but feel a care that such who have plenty in the things of this life may lay their condition to heart.

26   I feel that it is my duty to love my heavenly Father with all my soul and with all my strength. I feel that pride is opposite to divine love, and if I put forth my strength in any employ which I know is to support pride, I feel it has a tendency to weaken those bands which through the infinite

mercies of God, I have felt at times to bind and unite my soul in a holy fellowship with the Father and with his Son, Jesus Christ. This I have learned through the precious operations of divine love, and ardently desire both for my self and for all who have tasted of it, that nothing may be able to separate us from it.

27   When rich men who have the power of circulating money through channels the most pleasant to them, do not stand upright as in the sight of God, but go forth in a way contrary to pure wisdom it tends to disorder the affairs of society, and where they gather money through the toil of husbandmen and circulate it by trading in superfluities and employing people in vanities, the similitude used by the prophet Ezekiel appears applicable [Ezek. 34:17-22]. He represents rich men as strong cattle who feed on the fat pasture, and then tread down the remainder. And as drinking at a pleasant stream, and then walking in it, till their feet have so stirred up the mud, that the thirsty weak cattle having nothing to drink but dirty water. And this parable of the prophet appears to represent not only the bodily hardships, in outward poverty and want, of such poor people who are pressed down by the power of the wealthy, but may properly be applied to those employments about vanities in which many poor people are entangled.

28   Now if rich men by living in the simplicity of the Truth stop the business of some who labor in gratifying the pride and vanities of peoples' minds and are drinking the dirty waters, if those at the same time abate their interest and the rent of their lands this opens a way for the tenant to be more liberal with the fruits of the ground when put in the balance against the work of poor laboring men.

29   An honest tenant who labors himself and knows what it is to be weary, on agreeing to pay five men full wages for doing that which is now computed a day's work for four, might ease the heavy burdens of weakly laborers and open the way for some now employed in gratifying the vanities of peoples' minds to enter upon useful employ.

30   Men who live on a supply from the interest of their money and do little else but manage it appear to have but a small share of the labor in carrying on the affairs of a province, and where a member of society does but a small share of the business thereof, it appears most agreeable to equity and true brotherly love that he should endeavor to live in such sort as may be most easy to them by whose labor he is chiefly supported.

The substance of some conversation between a thrifty landholder and a laboring man

31   Laboring man speaks as follows: I observe of late years that when I buy a bushel of grain for my family I must do more work to pay for it than I had used to do twenty years past. What is the reason of this change?

32   Landholder: Towns and villages have a gradual increase in these provinces, and the people now employed in husbandry bear, I believe, a less proportion to the whole inhabitants than they did then; this I take to be one reason of the change. But the main cause is that of sending so much grain and flour abroad.

33   Laborer: I believe it is so, but I observe that where land is well cleared and enriched by cattle and sheep, a hundred bushels of rye is raised with less labor now than was necessary when the ground was to clear and the plowing interrupted by many stumps, and as we have great plenty of grain raised in our country, it seems uneasy to me that I must now do more work for a bushel of rye than I did then.

34   Landholder: The price set on labor is high, but as we have now less labor in clearing land than we had then, and as young men who have no land of their own are now more numerous, it appears likely that we may have our labor done for lower wages than we had then. And as our country is now more open, and great quantities of grain are now raised, we are enabled to supply some people beyond the seas with grain and flour, for which in return we get many things convenient from abroad. And this of sending our grain and flour beyond the seas I take to be another cause of the price of grain being higher now than it was thirty years ago.

35   Laborer: Of things which to me appear convenient we through divine favor have plenty in our own land, and in so much sending abroad and fetching from far there is great hazard of men's lives, and the good fruits of the earth brought forth through much labor are often buried in the sea. If our people beforehand in the world would be content in living more on the produce of our own land, and instead of employing so many men on the seas would employ the greater part of them in husbandry and useful trades, and keep grain more plentifully in our country, I believe it would be better for us in general, and laboring people might have grain in proportion to our labor as heretofore, and in the plentiful produce of our country rejoice with the landholders. Among the members of Christ if one of the members rejoice the other members rejoice with it; but while the

landholders have great increase, and therewith gratify themselves and their families with expensive delicacies, and at the same time demand more hard labor of us for a bushel of rye than they did when much less grain was sent abroad, this falls hard on our side, and though a poor laboring man may behold the country in outward prosperity yet feeling the prosperity thereof to be of such a nature that in getting bread for his family he must do more work for a bushel of grain than was required of him in years past, it does not appear that he has a proportionable share in this prosperity.

36   Landholder: There are many people in distant parts who depend on a supply by our grain and flour.

37   Laborer: I believe some trade abroad might be of advantage to us and to some with whom we trade, if that spirit which leads into error has no part in directing this trade.

38   A great stop in trade may not be expected without inconvenience to some but as the right spirit of Truth prevails in our minds we are content with that only which is of real use to us. Thus the love of riches is cast out of our hearts, the desire after costly delicacies is subjected in us, and in true brotherly kindness we are moved to assist the weak members in the family under their difficulties.

39   Our flour is often sent abroad to fruitful places, and were the inhabitants of some of those places to apply themselves more to that of raising a living for themselves out of their own ground and trade less abroad, I believe both we and they, under a divine blessing, might have a sufficient supply, less of the produce of the earth be sunk in the seas, less expense in carrying abroad and fetching from far, and labor be made more easy to the tillers of the ground both here and there.

40   Landholder: We commonly raise more grain in Pennsylvania and New Jersey in a year than is a supply for our inhabitants, and by sending abroad that of which we have no present occasion, we not only get a supply of sundry branches of merchandise from abroad but also get gold among us.

41   Laborer: In rightly laboring for the true prosperity of a country we do nothing at which any one of our inhabitants have just cause to complain, but in putting forward trade beyond the right bounds, grain is made scarce and dear even in a time of plenty, [and] a poor laboring man

must spend more of his strength to get a bushel of rye than was required of him when less was sent abroad. Thus husbandry, one of the most honest, healthful employments, so agreeable and inviting to us, is made a toil, and becomes wearisome by too few being employed in it and too much labor assigned as the work of [a] day.

42 Many branches of business are invented to please the pride and vanity of such who wander from pure wisdom, which branches of business are often uneasy to sincere hearted tradesmen. But husbandry is an employment in itself so necessary, and carried on in the open air, that it appears consistent with pure wisdom to have as many employed in it as the nature of the case will rightly admit of, and that those should not be obliged to work harder for a comfortable living than may be an agreeable employ.

43 Grain of late years is raised, not only in greater plenty than it was formerly, but also with less labor. And that poor laboring men and tradesmen shall be under a necessity to spend more of their strength for a bushel of it than was required of them in years past, is a case that to me does not appear harmonious in society.

44 If gold is brought into our country through means which renders the condition of the poor more difficult, it appears evident that of that gold the country had better be without.

45 I believe the real use of gold among men bears a small proportion to the labor in getting it out of the earth, and carrying it about from place to place.

46 It does not appear to have much use but that of a currency, and if trade extended no further than was consistent with pure wisdom, I believe trade might be carried on without gold.

47 To make an ax or a hoe, iron and steel is worth more to a husbandman than gold of an equal weight.

48 If a man with much gold should travel into those parts of the world where people are all strangers to that high value which is fixed on it, and there endeavor to buy the conveniences of life therewith, to propose in exchange so small a piece of metal for so much of the conveniences of life would doubtless to them be matter of admiration.

49   Gold, where the value fixed thereon is agreed to, appears to be attended with a certain degree of power, and where men get much of this power their hearts are many times in danger of being lifted up above their brethren and of being estranged from that meekness and tender feeling of the state of the poor, which accompanies the faithful followers of Christ.

50   Our blessed Redeemer who is always able to supply our wants, even by miracles when that is consistent with infinite wisdom, he, our gracious Shepherd who well knows our weakness and the danger there is of our hearts being corrupted by that power which attends riches, commanded us, lay not up for yourselves treasures here on earth. And one of his immediate followers warning us of the woeful estate of such who continue in the breach [of] this command said they who will be rich fall into temptation and a snare, and into many foolish and hurtful lusts which drown men in destruction and perdition.

51   Through the desire of money, men are tempted at times to deal hardly with their poor neighbors, and in the possession of riches there is a snare.

52   Through this imaginary greatness the heart is often ensnared with pride, and through plenty of gold the way is more open to gratify the vanity of the desire in delicacies and luxury, and under these gratifications there is often a growing exaltation of mind, an imaginary superiority over such who have a small portion of the things of this life and thus many become estranged from the tender feelings of true brotherly love and charity.

53   In a time of plenty when great quantities of grain and flour are sent to distant parts, a poor man who labors for hire to get bread for his family must now do more labor for a bushel of rye than was required for that quantity thirty years past, which circumstance appears worthy the serious consideration of all such who possess fruitful plantations, or are otherwise entrusted with power, and may justly incite them to beware lest the love of money ensnare their hearts, and lead them on to promote trading beyond the right bounds.

54   They who hold plentiful estates have power over them who have only their hands to labor, and if they misapply this power the joints and bands of society are disordered. Poor laboring men in raising up families find occasion to labor too hard, while other poor men would be idle for want of employ, were not employments provided which serve chiefly to gratify the pride and vanity of people's minds.

55   Where people love money, and their hearts are ensnared with imaginary greatness, the disease frequently spreads from one to another and children indulged in those wants which proceed from this spirit have often wants of the same kind in a much larger degree when they grow up to be men and women, and their parents are often entangled in contriving means to supply them with estates to live answerable to those expensive customs which very early in life have taken root in their minds.

56   In contriving to raise estates on these motives, how often are the minds of parents bewildered, perplexed, and drawn into ways and means to get money, which increase the difficulties of poor people who maintain their families by the labor of their hands?

57   A man may intend to lay up wealth for his children, but may not intend to oppress; yet in this fixed intention to increase his estate the working of his designs may cause the bread of the needy to fail and at the same time their hardships may remain unnoticed by him.

58   This the inspired penman describes in the similitude of a man falling. Now a man falling may go headlong where he had no design to go. Having a will to be rich he may fall, he may fall into the condition of oppressors, though he had no design to oppress. Thus it remains that the love of money is a root from whence spring many evils and they who will be rich fall, they fall into temptations and a snare, and into many foolish and hurtful customs, which strongly operate against the true harmony of society.

59   This of making grain scarce in a plentiful country for the sake of getting a little fine metal as a currency among us, which does not appear to be worth its weight in steel for instruments relating to the common business of getting a living in the world, appears to me to work against the general convenience of poor laboring people and is often a snare to others respecting the inward state of their mind.

60   The members in society to me appear like the members in a man's body, which only move regularly while the motion proceeds from the head. In fits people sometimes have convulsive motions, which though strong, are only manifestations of disorder.

61   While we love God with all our hearts, and love not ourselves in a love different from that which we feel toward mankind universally, so long the way remains open for that Life which is the Light of men to operate in

us, and lead us forward in all the concerns necessary for us. Here we may rejoice in the testimony of our conscience that in simplicity and godly sincerity we have had our conversation among [men].

62   This is a treasure of which through the tender mercies of God I have in a small degree had experience; and when I think on his outward body being dissolved, and look toward ages who may succeed us, this treasure of all others feels the most precious, and what I ardently desire may be possessed by generations to come.

63   If gold comes not rightly into our country we had better be without it. The love of money is the root of evil, and while gold comes among us as an effect of the love of money, in the hearts of the inhabitants of this land branches rising up from this root, like the degenerate plant of a strange vine, will remain to trouble us and interrupt the true harmony of society.

64   The love of Christ, which preserves the faithful in purity of heart, puts men into a motion which works harmoniously and in which their example yields clear and safe instruction. Thus our Redeemer said, Ye are the light of the world [Matt. 5:14].

65   This is the standard which God has commanded to be lifted up to the people, and the possibility of this standard being now lifted up by us, stands in that of a lowly watchful attention to the leadings of him who is the Light of Life. And if we go from this standard, we go into a wilderness of confusion.

66   While we keep to this standard we are content with a little; but in the love of money and outward greatness the wants of one person may require as much labor to supply them as would supply ten whose wants extend no further than those things which our heavenly Father knows that we have need of. And where people are entangled with that spirit in which men receive honor one of another, and seek not the honor which comes from God only, in this state expense arises frequently on expense, and in the increase of outward substance they often find occasion for a greater increase. Thus a man on some new acquaintance with one, whose living in the world is more specious[4] than his own, may feel an inclination to rise up as high as to a level with him, and to attain this may frame new devices to increase his estate, and these devices may cause the bread of the needy to fail though his interest was only to get riches to himself.

---

4 [*Obs.* Outwardly pleasing, showy. Webster's New Collegiate Dictionary.]

67   Now as men have a will to be rich, and in that will follow on in pursuit of devices which work against the convenient living of poor honest people, in this course they decrease as to that of being kind and tenderhearted in seeking after the wants of the weak and helpless. And in that spirit in which men receive honor one from another, their minds are toward outward power to support themselves in that which they possess.

68   With gold men often hire armies and make preparations for war. Now in raising great armies and supporting them, there is much labor becomes necessary, which otherwise would not. And in the long continuation of these things, the yoke lies heavy on many poor people.

69   The battles of the warrior are not only with confused noise and garments rolled in blood, but commonly contrived in the craft and subtlety of man's wisdom, and if we trust in man, make flesh our arm, and are estranged from that purified state in which the mind relies on God, we are on the way towards an increase in confusion and this estate even among much gold and great riches, is less settled and quiet than that of a faithful follower of the lowly Jesus, who is contented with those things which our heavenly Father knows that we have need of.

70   In this state we are dead, and our life is hid with Christ in God [Col. 3:3]. Dead to the love of money. Dead to worldly honor and to that friendship which is at enmity with him, and thus he is felt to be our rock and our safe habitation.

71   In the love of money and outward greatness the mind is perplexed with selfish devices: how to keep! how to defend from the crafty designs of the proud and envious! and from the desperate attempts of the oppressed!

72   Now in the bottom of these devices there is unquietness, for where gold or treasures are gathered, and not in that wisdom which is pure and peaceable, the mind in this state is left naked. The robe of God's righteousness is a covering, which to them who are sanctified in Christ Jesus, is an abundant recompense for the loss of that life, with all its treasures, which stood in the wisdom of this world. Under this robe we feel that all things work together for our good; that we have no cause to promote but the cause of pure universal love, and here all our cares center in a humble trust in him who is omnipotent.

13

1772 An Epistle to the Quarterly and Monthly Meetings of Friends

Written 4th mo 1772; 1st printed 1772

Editor's Introduction

This epistle, Woolman's last, and often referred to as the 'Farewell', expresses his concern with the increasingly worldly spirit among Friends in their churches. The subject matter was fresh in his writings and its importance for him attested by the effort in thought and composition he must have made to complete it on the eve of his departure for England.

The urgency of his concern is heard in paragraph 25 of the text:

[I]f the pure Light of Life is not followed in our proceedings we are in the way of profaning the holy name and of going backward toward that wilderness of sufferings and persecution out of which, through the tender mercies of God, a church in this nation has been gathered. . . [A]nd as the wisdom of this world more and more takes place in conducting the affairs of this visible gathered church and the pure leadings of the Holy Spirit less waited for and followed, so the true suffering seed is more and more oppressed.

The epistle may be divided into three parts:

- In paragraphs 1 through 22 the author addresses the condition of the churches and expresses his concern regarding "a deviation from the purity of our religious principles"¹ and reflects on the need for disciplining the disorderliness and earthly entanglements within the church.
- In paragraphs 23 through 46, he discusses the nature and vocation of what he calls "the visible gathered church"² by which he appears to mean the witnessing, and witnessed, community of Friends

---

¹ Par. 3.
² See pars. 23, 25, 33, 38, 40, 42, and 43.

assembled in divine worship in search of the Truth that will be made manifest in and through their meetings as well as in their public and private lives.

- In paragraphs 47 through 55 he contemplates Christ's peaceable government as well as the principle of peace.

Upon completion the text was submitted to the PYM Meeting for Sufferings, the successor in 1771 to the Overseers of the Press.[3] The minutes of that Meeting for 18th day 6th month 1772 noted:

An Epistle written by our Friend John Woolman directed to the Quarterly and Monthly Meetings of Friends having been read (pursuant to his desire just before he embarked on a religious visit to Friends in Europe) at the last, and again at this meeting, and the subject and general terms thereof being approved, Israel Pemberton, James Pemberton, Anthony Benezet, William Brown, John Reynell & William Horne are appointed to revise it carefully and to treat with a printer for printing it.

At a later meeting the Clerk, John Pemberton, was ordered "to send a share [of the printed copies] to each of the provinces where there are meetings of Friends."[4] Whether Woolman intended for his epistle to be read beyond the monthly meetings in Pennsylvania and New Jersey is not known, but his colleagues in the Meeting for Sufferings ordered it sent to all the American provinces, an appropriate gesture inasmuch as its author had journeyed to, and was personally known in, so many of them.

The holograph, which is in the SC holdings, has been hand-stitched together with, and comes after, the manuscript of "Considerations on the True Harmony of Mankind & how it is to be maintained" (Text 11). It has been designated MS S1/*Farewell* and the following modernization is based upon it.

Text

1772 An Epistle to the Quarterly and Monthly Meetings of Friends

Beloved friends,

1 Feeling at this time a renewed concern that the pure principle of Light and Life, and the righteous fruits thereof, may spread and prevail

---

3 See the Historical Notes with Table 3 herein.
4 Gummere, p. 475.

among mankind, there is an engagement on my heart to labor with my brethren in religious profession, that none of us may be a stumbling block in the way of others, but may so walk that our conduct may reach the pure witness in the hearts of such who are not in profession with us.

2   And, dear friends, while we publicly own that the Holy Spirit is our leader, the profession in itself is weighty, and the weightiness thereof increases in proportion as we are noted among the professors of Truth and active in dealing with such who walk disorderly.

3   Many under our profession, for want of due attention and a perfect resignation to this divine teacher, have in some things manifested a deviation from the purity of our religious principles, and these deviations, having crept in among us by little and little and increased from less to greater, have been so far unnoticed that some living in them have been active in putting discipline in practice with relation to others whose conduct has appeared more dishonorable in the world.

4   Now as my mind has been exercised before the Lord, I have seen that the discipline of the church of Christ stands in that which is pure. That it is the wisdom from above which gives authority to discipline, and that the weightiness thereof stands not in any outward circumstances but in the authority of Christ who is the author of it; and where any walk after the flesh and not according to the purity of Truth, and at the same time are active in putting discipline in practice, a veil is gradually drawn over the purity of discipline and over that holiness of life which Christ leads those into in whom the love of God is verily perfected (1 John 2:5).

5   When we labor in true love with offenders and they remain obstinate, it sometimes is necessary to proceed as far as our Lord directed, let him be to thee as a heathen man or a publican (Matt. 18:17).

6   Now when such are disowned, and they who act therein feel Christ made unto them wisdom and therein are preserved in the meek, restoring Spirit, there is no just cause of offence ministered to any; but when those who are active in dealing with offenders indulge themselves in things which are against the purity of Truth, and yet judge others whose conduct appears more dishonorable than theirs, here the pure authority of discipline ceases as to such offenders, and a temptation is laid in their way to wrangle and contend.

7   Judge not, said our blessed Lord, that ye be not judged [Matt. 7:1; Luke 6:37]. Now this forbidding alludes to man's judgment and points out the necessity of our humbly attending to that sanctifying power under which the faithful experience the Lord to be a spirit of judgment to them (Isa. 28:6). And as we feel his Holy Spirit to mortify the deeds of the body in us, and can say it is no more I that live, but Christ that lives in me [Gal. 2:20], here right judgment is known.

8   And while divine love prevails in our hearts, and self in us is brought under judgment, a preparation is felt to labor in a right manner with offenders; but if we abide not in this love our outward performance in dealing with others and in imitation of worshippers degenerates into formality, for this is the love of God that we keep his commandments (1 John 5:3).

9   How weighty are those instructions of our Redeemer concerning religious duties when he points out that they who pray should be so obedient to the teachings of his Holy Spirit, that humbly confiding in his help they may say, thy name, O Father, be hallowed! thy kingdom come, thy will be done on earth as it is in heaven! [Matt. 6:9-10]. In this awful state of mind people feel that worship which stands in doing the will of God on earth as it is done in heaven and in keeping the holy name sacred.

10   To take a holy profession upon us is awful; nor can we keep this holy name sacred but by humbly abiding under the cross of Christ.

11   Against some who profaned the holy name by their living the apostle laid this heavy complaint, Through you the name of God is blasphemed among the Gentiles (Rom. 2:24 [paraphrasing Isa. 52:5]). Some of our ancestors through many tribulations were gathered into the state of true worshippers and had fellowship in that which is pure; and as one was inwardly moved to kneel down in their assemblies and publicly call on the name of the Lord, those in the harmony of united exercise then present joined in the prayer. I mention this that we of the present age may look unto the rock from whence we were hewn, and remember that to unite in worship is a union in prayer, and that prayer acceptable to the Father is only in a mind truly sanctified, where the sacred name taken on us is kept holy, and the heart resigned to do his will on earth, as it is done in heaven. If ye abide in me, says Christ, and my words abide in you, ye shall ask what ye will and it shall be done unto you [John 15:7]. Now we know not what to pray for as we ought, but as the Holy Spirit does open and direct our minds, and as we faithfully yield to its influences, our

prayers are in the will of our heavenly Father, who fails not to grant that which his own Spirit through his children asks.

12   Thus preservation from sin is known and the fruits of righteousness are brought forth by such who inwardly unite in prayer.

13   How weighty are our solemn meetings when the name of Christ taken upon us is kept holy! How precious is that state in which the children of the Lord are so redeemed from the love of this world that they are accepted and blessed in all that they do! *R. Barclay's Apology, p. 404.*[5]

14   How necessary is it that we who profess these principles, and are outwardly active in supporting them, should faithfully abide in divine strength, that as he who has called us is holy, so we may be holy in all manner of conversation (1 Pet. 1:15).

15   If one professing to be influenced by the Spirit of Christ propose to unite in a labor to promote righteousness in the earth, who in time past has manifestly deviated from equity, then to act consistently the first work is to make restitution so far as he may be enabled, for if he attempts to contribute toward a work intended to promote righteousness while it appears that he neglects or refuses to act righteously himself, his conduct herein has a tendency to entangle the minds of those who are weak in the faith who behold these things, and to draw a veil over the purity of righteousness by carrying an appearance as though that was righteousness which is not.

16   Again, if I propose to assist in supporting those principles wherein that purity of life is held forth, in which customs proceeding from the spirit of this world have no place, and at the same time strengthen others in those customs by my example, then the first step in an orderly proceeding is to cease from those customs myself, and afterwards labor as I may be enabled to promote the like in others.

17   To be convinced of the pure principle of Truth, and diligently exercised in walking answerable thereto, appears necessary before I can consistently recommend this principle to others. I often feel a labor in spirit that we who are active members in [our] Society may experience in

---

5 [Robert Barclay, *An apology for the true Christian divinity, as the same is held forth, and preached, by the people called, in scorn, Quakers* (London?: no pub., 1678)]

ourselves the truth of those expressions of the Holy One—I will be sanctified in them that come nigh me (Lev. 10:3). In this case my mind has been often exercised when alone, year after year, for many years, and in the renewings of divine love, a tender care has been incited in me that we who profess this inward light to be our teacher, may be a family united in that purity of worship which comprehends a holy life and ministers instruction to others.

18   My mind is often [drawn] towards children in the Truth who, having a small share of the things of this life and coming to have families, may be inwardly exercised before the Lord to support them in a way agreeable to the purity of Truth, wherein they may feel his blessing upon them in their labors. The thoughts of such being entangled with customs (contrary to pure wisdom) conveyed to them through our hands, do often very tenderly and movingly affect my heart. While I look towards and think on a succeeding generation,[6] fervent desires are raised in me that we yielding to that Holy Spirit which leads into all Truth, may not do the work of the Lord deceitfully, may not live against the purity of our own principles, but as faithful laborers in our age, may be instrumental in removing stumbling blocks out of the way of such who may succeed us.

19   Such was the love of Christ that he gave himself for the church that he might sanctify and cleanse it, that it should be holy and without blemish, not having spot or wrinkle, or any such thing (Eph. 5:25[-27]). And where any take the name of Christ upon them, and profess to be members of his church and led by his Holy Spirit and yet manifestly deviate from the purity of Truth, such therein act against the gracious design of his giving himself for us [and] minister cause for the continuation of his afflictions, to wit, in his body, the church.

20   Christ suffered afflictions in a body of flesh prepared for him by the Father, but the afflictions of Christ's mystical body are yet unfinished, for those who are baptized into Christ are baptized into his death [Rom. 6:3], and as we humbly abide under his sanctifying power, and are brought forth in newness of life, we feel Christ to live in us, and he being the same yesterday, today, and forever [Heb. 13:8], and always at unity with himself, his Spirit in the hearts of his people leads to an inward exercise for the salvation of mankind, and when under travail of spirit we behold a visited

---

6 [Is JW thinking here of his only child, Mary, and the anticipated birth of her first child? That child, the first of JW's ten grandchildren, none of whom he would know, named John Comfort, was born 20 June 1772, the twelfth day after JW's arrival in England.]

people entangled with the spirit of this world, with its wickedness which is not of the Father but of the world, and therein rendered incapable of being faithful examples to others; under a sense of these things sorrow and heaviness are often experienced, and thus in some measure, is filled up that which remains of the afflictions of Christ [Col. 1:24].

21   Our blessed Savior, speaking concerning gifts offered in divine service said, If thou bring thy gift to the altar, and there remember that thy brother hath aught against thee, leave there thy gift;7 first go and be reconciled to thy brother [Matt. 5:23-24]. Now there is no true unity but in that wherein the Father and the Son are united, nor can there be a perfect reconciliation but in ceasing from that which ministers cause for the continuation of the afflictions of Christ; and if any professing to bring their gift to the altar do remember the customary contradiction which some of their fruits bear to a pure, spiritual worship, here it appears necessary to lay to heart this command: leave thy gift by the altar.

22   Christ graciously calls his people brethren; whosoever shall do the will of God the same is my brother (Mark 3:35). Now if we walk contrary to the Truth as it is in Jesus while we continue to profess it, we offend against Christ, and if under this offence we bring our gift to the altar our Redeemer does not direct us to take back our gift, he does not discourage us from proceeding in a good work, but graciously points out the necessary means by which the gift may be rendered acceptable, leave, says he, thy gift by the altar, first go and be reconciled to thy brother; cease from that which grieves the Holy Spirit, cease from that which is against the Truth as it is in Jesus, and then come and offer thy gift.

23   I feel while I write a tenderness toward such who through divine favor are preserved in a lively feeling of the state of the churches, and who at times may be under discouragements with regard to proceeding in that pure way which Christ by his Holy Spirit leads into. That depth of disorder and weakness which so much prevails being opened, doubtings are apt to arise as to the possibility of proceeding as an assembly of the Lord's people in the pure counsel of Truth; and here I feel a care to express in uprightness that which has been opened in my mind under the power of the cross of Christ relating to a gathered visible church, the members whereof are guided by the Holy Spirit.

---

7 [Here JW has stricken from the holograph: "he says not seek reconciliation before you bring a second gift, but commands a full stop."]

24 This church is called the body of Christ (Col. 1:24). Christ is called the head of the church (Eph. 1:22). The church is called the pillar and ground of the Truth (1 Tim. 3:15). Thus the church has a name that is sacred, and the necessity of keeping this name holy appears evident, for where a number of people unite in a profession of being led by the Spirit of Christ and publish their principles to the world, the acts and proceedings of that people may, in some measure, be considered as that which Christ is the author of.

25 Now while we stand in this station, if the pure Light of Life is not followed in our proceedings we are in the way of profaning the holy name and of going backward toward that wilderness of sufferings and persecution out of which, through the tender mercies of God, a church in this nation has been *in a great measure* gathered. Christ lives in sanctified vessels (Gal. 2:20), and where they behold this holy name profaned, and the pure gospel light eclipsed through the unfaithfulness of such who by their station appear to be standard bearers under the Prince of Peace, these living members in the body of Christ in beholding those things do, in some degree, experience the fellowship of his sufferings; and as the wisdom of this world more and more takes place in conducting the affairs of this visible gathered church and the pure leadings of the Holy Spirit less waited for and followed, so the true suffering seed is more and more oppressed.

26 My mind is often affected with a sense of the condition of sincere-hearted people in some kingdoms where liberty of conscience is not allowed, many of whom being burdened in their minds with prevailing superstition, joined with oppressions, are often under sorrow. And where such have attended to that pure light, which in some degree has opened their understandings, and for their faithfulness to Christ been brought to examination and trial, how heavy are the persecutions which in divers parts of the world are exercised on them?

27 How mighty, as to the outward, is that power by which they are borne down and oppressed!

28 How deeply affecting is the condition of many upright-hearted people taken into the papal inquisition! What lamentable cruelties in deep vaults in a private way are exercised on many of them! And how lingering is that death by a small slow fire, which those have frequently endured who have been faithful to the end!

29   How many tender-spirited Protestants have been sentenced to spend the remainder of their lives in a galley, chained to an oar, under hard-hearted masters, while their young children are placed out for education among strangers and taught principles so contrary to the conscience of the parent that, in dissenting from them, they have hazarded their liberty and all that was dear to them of the things of this world!

30   There have in times past been great persecutions under the English government, and many sincere-hearted people, in different ages, suffered death for the testimony of a good conscience, whose faithfulness in their day has ministered encouragement to others and been a blessing to many who have succeeded them. Thus from age to age the darkness being more and more removed, a channel at length through the tender mercies of God has been opened, for the exercise of the pure gift of the gospel ministry, without interruption from outward power. A work, the like of which is rare, and unknown in many parts of the world.

31   As these things are often fresh in my mind, and this great work of God going on in the world been open before me, that liberty of conscience with which we are favored has not appeared as a light matter.

32   A trust is committed to us, a great and weighty trust, to which a diligent attention is necessary.

33   Wherever the active members in this visible gathered church use themselves to that which is against the purity of our principles, it appears to be a breach of this trust and one step backward toward the wilderness; one step toward undoing what God in infinite love has done, through his faithful servants, in a work of several ages; and appears like laying the foundation for future sufferings.

34   I feel a living invitation in my mind to such who are active in our religious society, that we may lay to heart this matter and consider the station in which we stand.

35   We stand in a place of outward liberty, under the free exercise of our conscience toward God, not obtained but through great and manifold afflictions of those who lived before us. There is gratitude due from us to our heavenly Father. There is justice due to our posterity. Can our hearts endure, or our hands be strong, if we desert a cause so precious, if we turn aside from a work under which so many have patiently labored?

36   May the deep sufferings of Christ be so dear to us that we may never trample under foot the adorable Son of God, nor count the blood of the covenant unholy.

37   May the faithfulness of the martyrs, when the prospect of death by fire was before them, be remembered, and may the patient constant sufferings of upright-hearted servants of God in later ages be revived in our minds; and may we so follow on to know the Lord, that neither the faithful in this age, nor those in ages to come, may ever be brought under sufferings, through our sliding back from the work of reformation in the world.

38   While the active members in the visible gathered church stand upright, and the affairs thereof are carried on under the leadings of the Holy Spirit, though disorders may arise among us and cause many exercises to such who feel the care of the churches upon them, yet, while these continue under the weight of the work and labor in the meekness of wisdom for the help of others, the name of Christ in the visible gathered church may be kept sacred; but while those who are active in the visible gathered church remain and continue in a manifest opposition to the purity of our principles, this, as the prophet Isaiah expresses it, is like as when a standard bearer faints (10:18), and here the way opens to great and prevailing degeneracy and to sufferings for such who, through the power of divine love, are separated to the gospel of Christ and cannot unite with that which stands in opposition to the purity of it.

39   The necessity of an inward stillness has, under these exercises, appeared clear to my mind. In true silence strength is renewed, the mind herein is weaned from all things but as they may be enjoyed in the divine will, and a lowliness in outward living, opposite to worldly honor, becomes truly acceptable to us.

40   In the desire of outward gain the mind is prevented from a perfect attention to the voice of Christ, but in the weaning of the mind from all things but as they may be enjoyed in the divine will, the pure light shines into the soul; and where the fruits of that spirit which is of this world are brought forth by many who profess to be led by the Spirit of Truth, and cloudiness is felt to be gathering over the visible gathered church, the sincere in heart who abide in true stillness, and therein are exercised before the Lord for his name's sake, these have a knowledge of Christ in the fellowship of his sufferings, and inward thankfulness is felt at times that through divine love our own wisdom is cast out, and that forward,

active part subjected in us which would rise up and do something in the visible gathered church without the pure leadings of Christ.

41   While aught remains in us different from a perfect resignation of our wills it is like a seal to a book wherein is written that good and perfect and acceptable will of God concerning us (Rom. 12:2). But when our minds entirely yield to Christ, that silence is known which follows the opening of the last of the seals (Rev. 8:1). In this silence we learn a patient abiding in the divine will, and there feel that we have no cause to promote but that only in which the Light of Life directs us in our proceedings, and that the only way to be useful in the church of Christ is to abide faithfully under the leadings of his Holy Spirit in all cases, that therein being preserved in purity of heart and holiness of conversation, a testimony to the purity of his government may be held forth through us to others.

42   As my mind has been thus exercised I have seen that to be active and busy in the visible gathered church without the leadings of the Holy Spirit is not only unprofitable but tends to increase dimness; and where way is not opened to proceed in the light of Truth, a stop is felt by those who humbly attend to the divine leader, a stop which in relation to good order in the visible gathered church is of the greatest consequence to be observed. Thus Robert Barclay, in his *Treatise on Discipline*,[8] holds forth that the judgment or conclusion of the church or congregation is no further effectual as to the true end and design thereof but as such judgment or conclusion proceeds from the Spirit of God operating on their minds who are sanctified in Christ Jesus.

43   Now in this stop I have learned the necessity of waiting on the Lord in humility, that the works of all may be brought to the light, and those brought to judgment which are wrought in the wisdom of this world; and have seen that, in a mind thoroughly subjected to the power of the cross, there is a savor of life which may be felt and which evidently tends to gather souls to God, while the greatest works in the visible gathered church, brought forth in man's wisdom, remain to be unprofitable.

---

[8]   [Robert Barclay, *A Treatise on Christian Discipline: or, The anarchy of the ranters and other libertines, the hierarchy of the Romanists, and other pretended churches, equally refused and refuted, in a two-fold apology for the church and people of God called in derision Quakers* (Manchester: William Irwin, 1868). According to Smith, Vol. I, p. 179, the work was first printed in 1676 without place or publisher named.]

44   Where people are divinely gathered into a holy fellowship, and faithfully abide under the influence of that Spirit which leads into all Truth, these are they who are the light of the world (Matt. 5:14). Now holding this profession to me has appeared weighty, even weighty beyond what I can fully express, and what our blessed Lord appears to have had in view when he proposed the necessity of counting the cost before we begin to build [Luke 14:28].

45   I trust there are many who at times, under divine visitation, feel an inward inquiry after God and when such, in the simplicity of their hearts, mark the lives of a people who profess to walk by the leadings of his Spirit, of what great concernment is it that our light shine clear, that nothing pertaining to us carry a contradiction to the Truth as it is in Jesus, or be a means of profaning his holy name, and a stumbling block in the way of those sincere inquirers.

46   When such seekers who are wearied with empty forms look toward uniting with us as a people, and behold active members among us in their customary way of living depart from that purity of life which under humbling exercises has been opened before them as the way of the Lord's people, how mournful and discouraging is the prospect! and how strongly does such unfaithfulness operate against the spreading of the peaceable, harmonious principle of Truth among mankind!

47   In entering into that life which is hid with Christ in God [Col. 3:3], we behold the peaceable government of Christ, where the whole family is governed by the same spirit, and doing to others as we would they should do unto us [Matt. 7:12; Luke 6:31] grows up as good fruit from a good tree. The peace, the quietness, and harmonious walking in this government is beheld with humble reverence to him who is the author of it, and in partaking of the Spirit of Christ we partake of that which labors and suffers for the increase of this peaceable government among the inhabitants of the world, and I have felt a labor of long continuance that we who profess this peaceable principle may be faithful standard bearers under the Prince of Peace, and that nothing of a defiling nature tending to discord and wars may remain among us.

48   May each of us query with ourselves: Have the treasures I possess been gathered in that wisdom which is from above, so far as has appeared to me?
        Have none of my fellow creatures an equitable right to any part of that which is called mine?

Have the gifts received by me from others been conveyed in a way free from all unrighteousness, so far as I have seen?

49   The principle of peace, in which our trust is only on the Lord, and our minds weaned from a dependence on the strength of armies, to me has appeared very precious, and I often feel strong desires that we, who profess this principle, may so walk as to give just cause for none of our fellow-creatures to be offended at us; that our lives may evidently manifest that we are redeemed from that spirit in which wars are. Our blessed Savior, in pointing out the danger of so leaning on man as to neglect the leadings of his Holy Spirit, said, "call no man your father upon the earth, for one is your Father which is in heaven" (Matt. 23:9).

50   Where the wisdom from above is faithfully followed, and therein we are entrusted with outward substance, it is a treasure committed to our care in the nature of an inheritance, as an inheritance from him who formed and supports the world. Now in this condition the true enjoyment of the good things of this life is understood, and that blessing felt in which is real safety. This is what our blessed Lord appears to have had in view when he said, blessed are the meek for they shall inherit the earth [Matt. 5:5].

51   Selfish men may hold lands in the selfish spirit, and depending on the outward power of armies be perplexed with secret uneasiness lest the injured should sometime overpower them, or that measure be meted to them which they are measuring to others. Thus, selfish men may possess the earth, but it is the meek who inherit the earth, who enjoy it as an inheritance from their heavenly Father, free from all the defilements and perplexities of unrighteousness.

52   Where proceedings have been in that wisdom which is from beneath, and inequitable gain been gathered by a man, and left as a gift to his children, who being entangled with the worldly spirit have not attained to that clearness in which the channels of righteousness are opened, and [in]justice done to those who remain silent under injuries, here I have seen under humbling exercises that the sins of the fathers are embraced by the children and become their sins, and thus in the days of tribulation the iniquities of the fathers are visited upon these children, who take hold on the unrighteousness of their fathers, and live in that spirit in which those iniquities were committed. To which agrees that prophecy of Moses, concerning a rebellious people, They that are left of you shall pine away in their iniquity in your enemies' lands; and in the iniquities of their fathers

shall they pine away (Lev. 26:39). And our blessed Lord in beholding the hardness of heart in that generation, and feeling in himself that they lived in the same spirit in which the prophets had been persecuted unto death, signified that the blood of all the prophets shed from the foundation of the world should be required of that generation, from the blood of Abel to the blood of Zacharias, who perished between the altar and the temple, verily I say unto you it shall be required of this generation (Luke 11:50-51).

53   Tender compassion fills my heart toward my fellow-creatures estranged from the harmonious government of the Prince of Peace, and a labor attends me that many may be gathered to this peaceable habitation.

54   In being inwardly prepared to suffer adversities for Christ's sake, and weaned from a dependence on the arm of flesh, we feel that there is a rest for the people of God, and that this rest stands in a perfect resignation of ourselves to his will.

55   This condition where all our wants and desires are bounded by pure wisdom and our minds wholly attentive to the inward counsel of Christ has appeared to me as a habitation of safety for the Lord's people in a time of outward commotion and trouble, and desires from the fountain of love are opened in me to invite my fellow creatures to feel for that which gathers the mind into it.[9]

JOHN WOOLMAN

Mount Holly, New Jersey, 4th Month, 1772

---

[9] [The holograph ends here, the final matter presumably being added by the revisers appointed by the PYM Meeting for Sufferings.]

14

[The final essays, written at sea and in England]

Written 1772; 1st printed 1773

Editor's Introduction

Other than the additions he made to the *Journal*, these three essays, called chapters, were the last writings in John Woolman's own hand addressed to the public. They were penned after his departure from America on the religious visit to England. The chapters were titled "On loving our neighbors as ourselves"; "On a sailor's life" (undoubtedly based on Woolman's experience of bunking among the crew members while on the Atlantic voyage); and "On silent worship" (most likely arising from his observation of the practices of the Church of England in Britain).

These writings, which came into print first in London, then later the same year in Dublin, and then the following year in Philadelphia, were prepared for publication after Woolman's death in York, England. Presumably, it was the printers and not the author who had opportunity to control the editing of the three-part work as it originally came before the public. In a second Dublin printing (1776) the work was editorially rearranged into four chapters by moving around blocks of the Woolman text in the first two essays so as to create a new chapter titled "On trading in superfluities" and by inserting it between the first two original, now editorially shortened, chapters. That arrangement was generally kept thereafter in Ireland and Britain but not in America until the Gummere edition in 1920 further rearranged the Woolman text into five chapters by moving paragraphs 43 to 88 from "On loving our neighbors as ourselves" into a new second chapter entitled "On the slave trade."

The first printing of the three essays, collectively titled *Remarks on Sundry Subjects*, was issued in London in 1773 by the Quaker publisher Mary Hinde. Included with the essays in a single volume entitled *Serious Considerations on Various Subjects of Importance* were other Woolman works (Texts 8, 11, and 13 herein, together with some of Woolman's dying expressions). Hinde's imprint was reprinted by Robert Jackson in Dublin the same year. The MS was returned to Philadelphia for inclusion in the

1774 edition of *The Works of John Woolman* printed by Joseph Crukshank.

The original MS is missing and this modernized text is based on the 1773 Hinde printing (which is followed in both the Jackson and Crukshank printings).

+++

Text

Chapter I
On loving our neighbors as ourselves

1   When we love the Lord with all our hearts and his creatures in his love, we are then preserved in tenderness both toward mankind and the animal creation; but if another spirit gets room in our minds and we follow it in our proceedings, we are then in the way of disordering the affairs of society.

2   If a man successful in business expends part of his income in things of no real use while the poor employed by him pass through great difficulties in getting the necessaries of life, this requires his serious attention.

3   If several principal men in business unite in setting the wages of those who work for hire, and therein have regard to a profit to themselves answerable to unnecessary expense in their families, while the wages of the others on a moderate industry will not afford a comfortable living for their families and a proper education for their children, this is like laying a temptation in the way of some to strive for a place higher than they are in, when they have not stock sufficient for it.

4   Now I feel a concern in the spring of pure love that all who have plenty of outward substance may example others in the right use of things, may carefully look into the condition of poor people, and beware of exacting on them with regard to their wages.

5   While hired laborers, by moderate industry, through the divine blessing may live comfortably, raise up families, and give them suitable education, it appears reasonable for them to be content with their wages.

6   If they who have plenty love their fellow creatures in that love which is divine, and in all their proceedings have an equal regard to the

good of mankind universally, their place in society is a place of care, an office requiring attention, and the more we possess the greater is our trust, and with an increase of treasure an increase of care becomes necessary.

7   When our will is subject to the will of God, and in relation to the things of this world we have nothing in view but a comfortable living equally with the rest of our fellow creatures, then outward treasures are no further desirable than as we feel a gift in our minds equal to the trust and strength to act as dutiful children in his service who has formed all mankind and appointed a subsistence for us in this world.

8   A desire for treasures on any other motive appears to be against that command of our blessed Savior, Lay not up for yourselves treasures here on earth (Matt. 6:19).

9   He forbids not laying up in the summer against the wants of winter, nor does he teach us to be slothful in that which properly relates to our being in this world. But in this prohibition he puts in *yourselves*. Lay not up for *yourselves* treasures here on earth.

10   Now in the pure light this language is understood, for in the love of Christ there is no respect of persons; and while we abide in his love [John 15:10], we live not to *ourselves* but to him who died for us [2 Cor. 5:15]. And as we are thus united in Spirit to Christ, we are engaged to labor in promoting that work in the earth for which he suffered.

11   In this state of mind our desires are that every honest member in society may have a portion of treasure and share of trust, answerable to that gift with which our heavenly Father has gifted us.
   In great treasure, there is a great trust.
   A great trust requires great care.
   But the laborious mind wants rest.

12   A pious man is content to do a share of business in society answerable to the gifts with which he is endowed while the channels of business are free from unrighteousness, but is careful lest at any time his heart be overcharged.

13   In the harmonious spirit of society, Christ is all in all (Col. 3:11).

14   Here it is that *Old things are past away, all things are new, all things are of God* (2 Cor. 5:17-18); and the desire for riches is at an end.

15   They of low degree who have small gifts enjoy their help who have large gifts. Those with their small gifts have a small degree of care, while those with their large gifts have a large degree of care. And thus to abide in the love of Christ and enjoy a comfortable living in this world is all that is aimed at by those members in society to whom Christ is made wisdom and righteousness [1 Cor. 1:30].

16   But when they who have much treasure are not faithful stewards of the gifts of God, great difficulties attend it.

17   Now this matter has deeply affected my mind. The Lord through merciful chastisements has given me a feeling of that love in which the harmony of society stands, and a sight of the growth of that seed which brings forth wars and great calamities in the world, and a labor attends me to open it to others.

18   Now to act with integrity according to that strength of mind and body with which our Creator has endowed each of us appears necessary for all; and he who thus stands in the lowest station in society appears to be entitled to as comfortable and convenient a living as he whose gifts of mind are greater and whose cares are more extensive.

19   If some endowed with strong understandings as men abide not in the harmonious state, in which we *love our neighbors as ourselves* [Matt. 19:19], but walk in that spirit in which the children of this world are wise in their generation, these by the strength of contrivance may sometimes gather great treasure, but the wisdom of this world is foolishness with God [1 Cor. 3:19]. And if we gather treasures in worldly wisdom, we lay up treasures for ourselves: and great treasures managed in any other spirit than the Spirit of Truth disorders the affairs of society, for hereby the good gifts of God in this outward creation are turned into the channels of worldly honor, and frequently applied to support luxury, while the wages of poor laborers are such that with moderate industry and frugality they may not live comfortably, raise up families, and give them suitable education, but through the straitness of their condition are often drawn on to labor under weariness, to toil through hardships themselves, and frequently to oppress those useful animals with which we are entrusted.

20   From age to age, throughout all ages, divine love is that alone in which dominion has been, is, and will be rightly conducted.

21   In this the endowments of men are so employed that the friend and the governor are united in one and oppressive customs come to an end.

22   Riches in the hands of individuals in society are attended with some degree of power. And so far as power is put forth separate from pure love so far the government of the Prince of Peace is interrupted. And as we know not that our children after us will dwell in that state in which power is rightly applied, to lay up riches for them appears to be against the nature of his government.

23   The earth through the labor of men under the blessing of him who formed it yields a supply for the inhabitants from generation to generation, and they who walk in the pure light, their minds are prepared to taste and relish not only those blessings which are spiritual, but also feel a sweetness and satisfaction in a right use of the good gifts of God in the visible creation.

24   Here we see that man's happiness stands not in great possessions but in a heart devoted to follow Christ in that use of things where customs contrary to universal love have no power over us.

25   In this state our hearts are prepared to trust in God and our desires for our children and posterity are that they, with the rest of mankind, in ages to come may be of that number of whom he has said, *I will be a Father to them, and they shall be my sons and daughters* (2 Cor. 6:18).

26   When wages in a fruitful land bear so small a proportion to the necessaries of life that poor honest people who have families cannot by a moderate industry attain to a comfortable living and give their children sufficient learning, but must either labor to a degree of oppression or else omit that which appears to be a duty.

27   While this is the case with the poor, there is an inclination in the minds of most people to prepare at least so much treasure for their children that they with care and moderate industry may live free from these hardships which the poor pass through.

28   Now this subject requires our serious consideration. To labor that our children may be put in a way to live comfortably appears in itself to be a duty, so long as these our labors are consistent with universal

righteousness. But if in striving to shun poverty we do not walk in that state where *Christ is our life* [Col. 3:4], then we wander; *He that hath the Son, hath Life* (1 John 5:12). *"This Life is the Light of Men"* (John 1:4). If we walk not in this light we walk in darkness, and *he that walketh in Darkness, knoweth not whither he goeth* (John 12:35).

29   To keep to right means in laboring to attain a right end is necessary. If in striving to shun poverty we strive only in that state where Christ is the light of our life, our labors will stand in the true harmony of society. But if people are confident that the end aimed at is good, and in this confidence pursue it so eagerly as not to wait for the Spirit of Truth to lead them, then they come to loss. *Christ is given to be a leader and commander of the people* (Isa. 55:4). Again: *the Lord shall guide thee continually* (Isa. 58[:11]). Again: *Lord, thou wilt ordain peace for us, for thou also hast wrought all our works in us* (Isa. 26:12).

30   *In the Lord have we righteousness and strength* (Isa. 45:24).

31   In this state our minds are preserved watchful in following the leadings of his Spirit in all our proceedings in this world, and a care is felt for a reformation in general. That our own posterity, with the rest of mankind in succeeding ages, may not be entangled by oppressive customs, transmitted to them through our hands; but if people in the narrowness of natural love are afraid that their children will be oppressed by the rich, and through an eager desire to get treasures depart from the pure leadings of Truth in one case, though it may seem to be a small matter, yet the mind even in that small matter may be emboldened to continue in a way of proceeding without waiting for the divine leader.

32   Thus people may grow expert in business, wise in the wisdom of this world, retain a fair reputation among men, and yet being strangers to the voice of Christ, the safe leader of his flock, the treasures thus gotten may be like snares to the feet of their posterity.

33   Now to keep faithful to the pure Counsellor, and under trying circumstances suffer adversity for righteousness' sake, in this there is a reward.

34   If we being poor are hardly dealt with by those who are rich, and under this difficulty are frugal and industrious, and in true humility open our case to them who oppress us, this may reach the pure witness in their

minds. And though we should remain under difficulties as to the outward, yet if we abide in the love of Christ, all will work for our good.

35   When we feel what it is to suffer in the true suffering state, then we experience the Truth of those expressions, that, *as the sufferings of Christ abound in us, so our consolation aboundeth in Christ* (2 Cor. 1:5).

36   But if poor people who are hardly dealt with do not attain to the true suffering state, do not labor in true love with those who deal hardly with them, but envy their outward greatness, murmur in their hearts because of their own poverty, and strive in the wisdom of this world to get riches for themselves and their children, this is like wandering in the dark.

37   If we who are of a middle station between riches and poverty are affected at times with the oppressions of the poor and feel a tender regard for our posterity after us, O how necessary it is that we wait for the pure counsel of Truth!

38   Many have seen the hardships of the poor, felt an eager desire that their children may be put in a way to escape these hardships. But how few have continued in that pure love which opens our understandings to proceed rightly under these difficulties!

39   How few have faithfully followed that holy Leader who prepares his people to labor for the restoration of true harmony among our fellow creatures!

40   *In the pure gospel spirit we walk by faith and not by sight* (2 Cor. 5:7).

41   In the obedience of faith we die to the narrowness of self-love; and our life being hid with Christ in God [Col. 3:3], our hearts are enlarged toward mankind universally. But in departing from the true Light of Life, many in striving to get treasures have stumbled upon the dark mountains.

42   Now that purity of life which proceeds from faithfulness in following the Spirit of Truth, that state where our minds are devoted to serve God, and all our wants are bounded by his wisdom, this habitation has often been opened before me as a place of retirement for the children of light, where we may stand separated from that which disorders and confuses the affairs of society, and where we may have a testimony of our innocence in the hearts of those who behold us.

43   Through departing from the Truth as it is in Jesus, through introducing ways of life attended with unnecessary expenses, many wants have arisen, the minds of people have been employed in studying to get wealth, and in this pursuit some departing from equity have retained a profession of religion, others have looked at their example and thereby been strengthened to proceed further in the same way. Thus many have encouraged the trade of taking men from Africa and selling them as slaves.

44   It has been computed that near one hundred thousand Negroes have, of late years, been taken annually from that coast by ships employed in the English trade.

45   As I have traveled on religious visits in some parts of America, I have seen many of these people under the command of overseers in a painful servitude.

46   I have beheld them as Gentiles, under people professing Christianity, not only kept ignorant of the holy scriptures but under great provocations to wrath, of whom it may truly be said, *They that rule over them make them to howl, and the holy Name is abundantly blasphemed* (Isa. 52:5). Where children are taught to read the sacred writings, while young and exampled in meekness and humility, it is often helpful to them; nor is this any more than a debt due from us to a succeeding age.

47   But where youth are pinched for want of the necessaries of life, forced to labor hard under the harsh rebukes of rigorous overseers, and many times endure unmerciful whippings, in such an education how great are the disadvantages they lie under! And how forcibly do these things work against the increase of the government of the Prince of Peace!

48   Humphrey Smith [1624-1663], in his works, p. 125,[1] speaking of the tender feelings of the love of God in his heart when he was a child, said, "By the violent wrathful Nature that ruled in others, was my Quietness disturbed, and Anger begotten in me toward them, yet that of God in me was not wholly overcome, but his Love was felt in my Heart, and great was

---

[1] [*A collection of the several writings and faithful testimonies of that suffering servant of God, and patient follower of the Lamb, Humphry Smith, who dyed a prisoner for the testimony of Jesus in Winchester Common-Gaol, the 14th day of the 3rd month, in the year 1663* (London: printed and sold by Andrew Sowle, 1683)]

my Grief when the Earthly-mindedness and wrathful Nature in others so provoked me, that I was estranged from it.

49   "And this I write as a Warning to Parents and others, that in the fear of the living God, you may train up the Youth, and may not be a Means of bringing them into such Alienation."

50   Many are the vanities and luxuries of the present age, and in laboring to support a way of living conformable to the present world the departure from that wisdom that is pure and peaceable has been great.

51   Under the sense of a deep revolt and an overflowing stream of unrighteousness my life has been often a life of mourning, and tender desires are raised in me that the nature of this practice may be laid to heart.

52   I have read some books written by people who were acquainted with the manner of getting slaves in Africa.

53   I have had verbal relations of this nature from several Negroes brought from Africa who have learned to talk English.

54   I have sundry times heard Englishmen speak on this subject who have been in Africa on this business, and from all these accounts it appears evident that great violence is committed and much blood shed in Africa in getting slaves.

55   When three or four hundred slaves are put in the hold of a vessel in a hot climate, their breathing soon affects the air. Were that number of free people to go passengers, with all things proper for their voyage, there would inconvenience arise from their number, but slaves are taken by violence, and frequently endeavor to kill the white people, that they may return to their native land. Hence they are frequently kept under some sort of confinement, by means of which a scent arises in the hold of a ship, and distempers often break out among them, of which many die. Of this tainted air in the hold of ships freighted with slaves, I have had several accounts, some in print and some verbal, and all agree that the scent is grievous. When these people are sold in America and in the Islands, they are made to labor in a manner more servile and constant than that which they were used to at home, that with grief, with different diet from what has been common with them, and with hard labor, some thousands are computed to die every year, in what is called the Seasoning.

56   Thus it appears evident that great numbers of these people are brought every year to an untimely end, many of them being such who never injured us.

57   When the innocent suffer under hard-hearted men, even unto death, and the channels of equity are so obstructed that the cause of the sufferers is not judged in righteousness, *the land is polluted with Blood* (Num. 35:33).

58   When blood has been shed unrighteously, and remains unatoned for, the cry thereof is very piercing.

59   Under the humbling dispensations of divine providence, this cry has deeply affected my heart, and I feel a concern to open, as I may be enabled, that which lies heavy on my mind.

60   When the *iniquity of the house of Israel and of Judah was exceeding great, when the land was defiled with Blood, and the City full of Perverseness* (Ezek. 9:9), some were found sighing and crying for the abominations of the times (Ezek. 9:4), and such who live under a right feeling of our condition as a nation, these, I trust, will be sensible that the Lord at this day does call to mourning, though many are ignorant of it. So powerful are bad customs when they become general, that people growing bold through the examples one of another have often been unmoved at the most serious warnings.

61   Our blessed Savior speaking of the people of the old world, said, They ate, they drank, they married, and were given in Marriage, until the Day that Noah went into the Ark, and the Flood came and destroyed them all (Luke 17:27).

62   The like he spoke concerning the people of Sodom [Luke 17:28-29], who are also represented by the prophet as haughty, luxurious, and oppressive. This was the sin of Sodom, Pride, Fulness of Bread, and Abundance of Idleness were found in her, and in her Daughters; neither did she strengthen the Hands of the Poor and Needy (Ezek. 16:49).

63   Now in a revolt so deep as this, when much blood has been shed unrighteously in carrying on the slave trade and in supporting the practice of keeping slaves, which at this day is unatoned for, and cries from the earth and from the seas against the oppressor!

64   While this practice is continued, and under a great load of guilt there is more unrighteousness committed, the state of things is very moving!

65   There is a love which stands in nature, and a parent beholding his child in misery has a feeling of the affliction; but in divine love, the heart is enlarged towards mankind universally and prepared to sympathize with strangers, though in the lowest stations in life.

66   Of this the prophet appears to have had a feeling, when he said, Have we not all one Father? Hath not one God created us? Why then do we deal treacherously every man with his brother in prophaning the covenant of our fathers (Mal. 2:10)?

67   He who of old heard the groans of the children of Israel under the hard task-masters in Egypt, I trust, has looked down from his holy habitation on the miseries of these deeply oppressed people. Many lives have been shortened through extreme oppression while they labored to support luxury and worldly greatness; and though many people in outward prosperity may think little of those things, yet the gracious Creator has regard to the cries of the innocent, however unnoticed by men.

68   The Lord in the riches of his goodness is leading some into the feeling of the condition of this people, who cannot rest without laboring as their advocate, of which in some measure I have had experience: for, in the movings of his love in my heart, these poor sufferers have been brought near to me.

69   The unoffending aged and infirm made to labor too hard, kept on a diet less comfortable than their weak state required, and exposed to great difficulties under hard-hearted men, to whose sufferings I have often been a witness, and under the heart-melting power of divine love, their misery has felt to me like the misery of my parents.

70   Innocent youth taken by violence from their native land, from their friends and acquaintance, put on board ships with hearts laden with sorrow, exposed to great hardships at sea, placed under people where their lives have been attended with great provocation to anger and revenge.

71   With the condition of these youth my mind has often been affected, as with the afflictions of my children, and in a feeling of the

misery of these people, and of that great offense which is ministered to them, my tears have been often poured out before the Lord.

72   That Holy Spirit which affected my heart when I was a youth, I trust is often felt by the Negroes in their native land, inclining their minds to that which is righteous, and had the professed followers of Christ in all their conduct toward them manifested a disposition answerable to the pure principle in their hearts, how might the holy Name have been honored among the Gentiles, and how might we have rejoiced in the fulfilling of that prophecy, I the Lord love judgment, I hate robbery for burnt-offerings, and I will direct their work in truth, and make an everlasting covenant with them. Their seed shall be known among the Gentiles, and their offspring among the people: All that see them shall acknowledge them, that they are the seed which the Lord hath blessed (Isa. 61:8-9).

73   But in the present state of things how contrary is this practice to that meek Spirit in which our Savior laid down his life for us, that all the ends of the earth might know salvation in his name!

74   How are the sufferings of our blessed Redeemer set at nought and his name blasphemed among the Gentiles through the unrighteous proceedings of his professed followers!

75   My mind has often been affected, even from the days of my youth, under a sense of that marvelous work for which God, in infinite goodness, sent his Son into the world.

76   The opening of that spring of living waters, which the true believers in Christ experience, by which they are redeemed from pride and covetousness and brought into a state of meekness, where their hearts are enlarged in true love toward their fellow creatures universally: this work to me has been precious, and the spreading of the knowledge of the Truth among the Gentiles been very desirable. And the professed followers of Christ joining in customs evidently unrighteous, which manifestly tend to stir up wrath and increase wars and desolations, have often covered my mind with sorrow.

77   If we bring this matter home, and as Job proposed to his friends, *put our soul in their soul's stead* (Job 16:4).
     If we consider ourselves and our children as exposed to the hardships which these people lie under in supporting an imaginary greatness.

Did we in such case behold an increase of luxury and superfluity among our oppressors, and therewith felt an increase of the weight of our burdens, and expected our posterity to groan under oppression after us,

Under all this misery, had we none to plead our cause, nor any hope of relief from man, how would our cries ascend to the God of the spirits of all flesh, who judges the world in righteousness, and in his own time is a refuge for the oppressed!

78   If they who thus afflicted us continued to lay claim to religion and were assisted in their business by others, esteemed pious people, who through a friendship with them strengthened their hands in tyranny:

In such a state when we were hunger-bitten and could not have sufficient nourishment, but saw them in fullness pleasing their taste with things fetched from far:

When we were wearied with labor, denied the liberty to rest, and saw them spending their time at ease; when garments answerable to our necessities were denied us, while we saw them clothed in that which was costly and delicate;

Under such affliction how would these painful feelings rise up as witnesses against their pretended devotion! And if the name of their religion was mentioned in our hearing, how would it sound in our ears like a word which signified self-exaltation and hardness of heart!

79   When a trade is carried on productive of much misery and they who suffer by it are some thousand miles off, the danger is the greater of not laying their sufferings to heart.

80   In procuring slaves on the coast of Africa, many children are stolen privately; wars also are encouraged among the Negroes, but all is at a great distance.

Many groans arise from dying men which we hear not.

Many cries are uttered by widows and fatherless children which reach not our ears.

Many cheeks are wet with tears and faces sad with unutterable grief which we see not.

Cruel tyranny is encouraged. The hands of robbers are strengthened, and thousands reduced to the most abject slavery who never injured us.

81   Were we for the term of one year only to be an eye-witness to what passes in getting these slaves:

Was the blood which is there shed to be sprinkled on our garments:

Were the poor captives bound with thongs, heavy laden with elephants' teeth, to pass before our eyes on their way to the sea:

Were their bitter lamentations day after day to ring in our ears and their mournful cries in the night to hinder us from sleeping:

Were we to hear the sound of the tumult at sea when the slaves on board the ships attempt to kill the English, and behold the issue of these bloody conflicts:

What pious man could be a witness to these things and see a trade carried on in this manner without being deeply affected with sorrow?

82   Through abiding in the love of Christ we feel a tenderness in our hearts toward our fellow creatures entangled in oppressive customs, and a concern so to walk that our conduct may not be a means of strengthening them in error.

83   It was the command of the Lord through Moses, *Thou shalt not suffer sin upon thy brother: thou shalt in any wise rebuke thy brother, and shalt not suffer sin upon him* (Lev. 19:17).
Again: *Keep far from a false matter, and the innocent and righteous slay thou not* (Exod. 23:7).

84   The prophet Isaiah mentions oppression as that which the true church in time of outward quiet should not only be clear of but should be far from it; *Thou shalt be far from oppression* (Isa. 54:14). Now these words, *far from*, appear to have an extensive meaning, and to convey instruction in regard to that of which Solomon speaks, *Though hand join in hand, yet the wicked shall not go unpunished* (Prov. 16:5).

85   It was a complaint against one of old, *When thou sawest* a thief, thou consentedst with him (Ps. 50:18).

86   The prophet Jeremiah represents the degrees of preparation toward idolatrous sacrifice in the similitude of a work carried on by children, men, and women. *The children gather wood, the fathers kindle the fire, and the women knead the dough to bake cakes for the queen of heaven* (Jer. 7:18).

87   It was a complaint of the Lord against Israel, through his prophet Ezekiel, that *they strengthened the hands of the wicked, and made the hearts of the righteous sad* (Ezek. 13:22).

88   Some works of iniquity carried on by the people were represented by the prophet Hosea, in the similitude of ploughing, reaping, and eating the fruit: *You have ploughed wickedness, reaped iniquity, eaten the fruit of lying, because thou didst trust in thy own way, to the multitude of thy mighty men* (Hos. 10:13).

89   I have felt great distress of mind since I came on this island on account of the members of our society being mixed with the world in various sorts of business and traffic carried on in impure channels. Great is the trade to Africa for slaves, and in loading these ships abundance of people are employed in the manufactories.

90   Friends in early time refused, on a religious principle, to make or trade in superfluities, of which we have many large testimonies on record, but for want of faithfulness, some gave way, even some whose example were of note in society, and from thence others took more liberty. Members of our society worked in superfluities, and bought and sold them, and thus dimness of sight came over many. At length Friends got into the use of some superfluities in dress, and in the furniture in their houses, and this has spread from less to more, till superfluity of some kind is common among us.

91   In this declining state many look at the example one of another, and too much neglect the pure feeling of Truth. Of late years a deep exercise has attended my mind, that Friends may dig deep, may carefully cast forth the loose matter, and get down to the rock, the sure foundation, and there hearken to that divine voice which gives a clear and certain sound.

92   And I have felt, in that which does not deceive, that if Friends who have known the Truth keep in that tenderness of heart where all views of outward gain are given up and their trust is only on the Lord, he will graciously lead some to be patterns of deep self-denial in things relating to trade and handicraft labor, and that some who have plenty of the treasures of this world will example in a plain frugal life and pay wages to such whom they may hire more liberally than is now customary in some places.

93   The prophet, speaking of the true church, said *Thy people also shall be all righteous* [Isa. 60:21].

94   Of the depth of this divine work several have spoken:

John Gratton [1641-1712], in his *Journal*, p. 45,[2] said, "The Lord is my Portion, I shall not want. He hath wrought all my Works in me. I am nothing but what I am in him."

95   Gilbert Latey [1626-1705], through the powerful operations of the Spirit of Christ in his soul, was brought to that depth of self-denial, that he could not join with that proud spirit in other people, which inclined them to want vanities and superfluities. This Friend was often among the chief rulers of the nation in times of persecution; and it appears by the testimony of Friends, that his dwelling was so evidently in the pure life of Truth, that in his visits to those great men he found a place in their minds; and that King James the Second, in the times of his troubles, made particular mention in a very respectful manner of what Gilbert once said to him.

The said Gilbert found a concern to write an *Epistle*,[3] in which are these expressions:

Fear the Lord, ye men of all sorts, trades, and callings, and leave off all the evil that is in them, for the Lord is grieved with all the evils used in your employments which you are exercised in.

It is even a grief to see how you are servants to sin, and instruments of Satan.

See his *Works*, p 42, &c.[4]

96   George Fox [1624-1691], in an *Epistle*, writes thus:

---

2 [*A journal of the life of that ancient servant of Christ, John Gratton: giving an account of his exercises when young, and how he came to the knowledge of the truth, and was thereby raised up to preach the gospel; and also of his labours, travels, and sufferings for the same* (London: printed and sold by the assigns of Andrew Sowle, 1720)]

3 [*To all you taylors and brokers, who lyes in wickedness: and to all you tradesmen of what trade, imployment or office soever: This is to you all from the Lord, that you may return from all your evil ways, words and works.* (London: printed for Robert Wilson, 1660)]

4 [No such publication has been found. So also Walter Forrest Altman, "John Woolman's Reading." Publication 23,971, University Microfilms. Ph.D. dissertation, Florida State University, 1957), p. 108, footnote 2.]

Friends, stand in the eternal power of God, witnesses against the pomps and vanities of this world.

Such tradesmen who stand as witnesses in the power of God cannot fulfill the people's minds in these vanities, and therefore they are offended at them.

Let all trust in the Lord, and wait patiently on him. For when Truth first broke forth in London, many tradesmen could not take so much money in their shops for some time, as would buy them bread and water, because they withstood the world's ways, fashions, and customs; yet by their patient waiting on the Lord in their good life and conversation, they answered the Truth in people's hearts, and thus their business increased.

Book of Doctrinals, p. 824[-826].5

97   Now Christ our holy leader graciously continues to open the understandings of his people, and as circumstances alter from age to age, some who are deeply baptized into a feeling of the state of things are led by his Holy Spirit into exercises in some respect different from those which attended the faithful in foregoing ages, and through the constrainings of pure love are engaged to open the feelings they have to others.

98   In faithfully following Christ the heart is weaned from the desire of riches, and we are led into a life so plain and simple that a little suffices, and thus the way opens to deny ourselves, under all the tempting allurements of that gain, which we know is the gain of unrighteousness.

99   The apostle speaking on this subject, asks this question: *What fellowship hath righteousness with unrighteousness* (2 Cor. 6:14)? And again says, *Have no fellowship with the unfruitful works of darkness, but rather reprove them* (Eph. 5:11). Again, *Be not a partaker of other men's sins, keep thyself pure* (1 Tim. 5:22).

100   Where people through the power of Christ are thoroughly settled in a right use of things, free from all unnecessary care and expense, the mind in this true resignation is at liberty from the bands of a narrow self-

---

5 [George Fox, *Gospel truth demonstrated in a collection of doctrinal books given forth by that faithful minister of Jesus Christ, George Fox* (London: Printed and sold by T. Sowle, 1706)]

interest to attend from time to time on the movings of his Spirit upon us, though he leads into that through which our faith is closely tried.

101   The language of Christ is pure, and to the pure in heart this pure language is intelligible; but in the love of money the mind being intent on gain is too full of human contrivance to attend to it.

102   It appears evident that some channels of trade are defiled with unrighteousness, that the minds of many are intent on getting treasures to support a life in which there are many unnecessary expenses.

103   And I feel a living concern attend my mind that under these difficulties we may humbly follow our heavenly shepherd, who graciously regards his flock and is willing and able to supply us both inwardly and outwardly with clean provender that has been winnowed with the shovel and the fan, where we may *sow to ourselves in righteousness, reap in mercy* (Hos. 10:12); and not be defiled with the works of iniquity.

104   Where customs contrary to pure wisdom are transmitted to posterity it appears to be an injury committed against them, and I often feel tender compassion toward a young generation and desires that their difficulties may not be increased through unfaithfulness in us of the present age.

Chapter II
On a sailor's life

1   In the trade to Africa for slaves and in the management of ships going on these voyages many of our lads and young men have a considerable part of their education.

2   Now what pious father beholding his son placed in one of these ships to learn the practice of a mariner could forbear mourning over him?

3   Where youth are exampled in means of getting money, so full of violence and used to exercise such cruelties on their fellow creatures, the disadvantage to them in their education is very great.

4   But I feel it in my mind to write concerning the seafaring life in general.

5   In the trade carried on from the West Indies, and from some part of the Continent, the produce of the labor of slaves is a considerable part.

6   And sailors who are frequently at ports where slaves abound, and converse often with people who oppress without the appearance of remorse, and often with sailors employed in the slave trade, how powerfully do these evil examples spread among the seafaring youth!

7   I have had many opportunities to feel and understand the general state of the seafaring life among us, and my mind has often been sad on account of so many lads and young men being trained up amid so great corruption.

8   Under the humbling power of Christ I have seen that if the leadings of his Holy Spirit were faithfully attended to by his professed followers in general, the heathen nations would be exampled in righteousness. A less number of people would be employed on the seas. The channels of trade would be more free from defilement. Fewer people would be employed in vanities and superfluities.

The inhabitants of cities would be less in number.

Those who have much lands would become fathers to the poor.

More people would be employed in the sweet employment of husbandry, and in the path of pure wisdom, labor would be an agreeable, healthful employment.

9   In the opening of these things in my mind I feel a living concern that we who have felt divine love in our hearts may faithfully abide in it, and like good soldiers endure hardness for Christ's sake.

10   He, our blessed Savior, exhorting his followers to love one another, adds, *As I have loved you* (John 13:34).

He loved Lazarus, yet in his sickness did not heal him but left him to endure the pains of death, that in restoring him to life the people might be confirmed in the true faith.

He loved his disciples, but sent them forth on a message attended with great difficulty among hard-hearted people, some of whom would think that in killing them they did God service.

11   So deep is divine love that in steadfastly abiding in it we are prepared to deny ourselves of all that gain which is contrary to pure wisdom and to follow Christ, even under contempt and through sufferings.

12   While Friends were kept truly humble and walked according to the purity of our principles, the divine witness in many hearts was reached; but when a worldly spirit got entrance, therewith came in luxuries and

superfluities and spread by little and little, even among the foremost rank in society, and from thence others took liberty in that way more abundantly.

13   In the continuation of these things from parents to children there were many wants to supply, even wants unknown to Friends, while they faithfully followed Christ. And in striving to supply these wants, many have exacted on the poor, many have entered on employments in which they often labor in upholding pride and vanity. Many have looked on one another, been strengthened in these things, one by the example of another, and as to the pure divine seeing, dimness has come over many, and the channels of true brotherly love been obstructed.

14   People may have no intention to oppress, yet by entering on expensive ways of life their minds may be so entangled therein and so engaged to support expensive customs as to be estranged from the pure sympathizing Spirit.

15   As I have traveled in England I have had a tender feeling of the condition of poor people, some of whom, though honest and industrious, have nothing to spare toward paying for the schooling of their children.

16   There is a proportion between labor and the necessaries of life, and in true brotherly love the mind is open to feel after the necessities of the poor.

17   Among the poor there are some that are weak through age, and others of a weakly nature who pass through straits in very private life without asking relief from the public.

18   Such who are strong and healthy may do that business which to the weakly may be oppressive; and in performing that in a day which is esteemed a day's labor by weakly persons in the fields and in the shops, and by weakly women who spin and knit in the manufactories, they often pass through weariness; and many sighs I believe are uttered in secret unheard by some who might ease their burdens.

19   Labor in the right medium is healthy, but in too much of it there is a painful weariness; and the hardships of the poor are sometimes increased through want of more agreeable nourishment, more plentiful fuel for the fire, and warmer clothing in winter than their wages will answer.

20   When I have beheld plenty in some houses to a degree of luxury, the condition of poor children brought up without learning, and the condition of the weakly and aged who strive to live by their labor, have often revived in my mind as cases of which some who live in fullness need to be put in remembrance.

21   There are few, if any, who could behold their fellow creatures lie long in distress and forbear to help them when they could do it without any inconvenience; but customs requiring much labor to support them do often lie heavy on the poor, while they who live in these customs are so entangled in a multitude of unnecessary concerns that they think but little of the hardships which the poor people go through.

Chapter III
On silent worship

1   Worship in silence has often been refreshing to my mind, and a care attends me that a young generation may feel the nature of this worship.

2   Great expense arises in relation to that which is called divine worship.

3   A considerable part of this expense is applied toward outward greatness, and many poor people in raising of tithe, labor in supporting customs contrary to the simplicity that there is in Christ, toward whom my mind has often been moved with pity.

4   In pure silent worship we dwell under the holy anointing and feel Christ to be our Shepherd.

5   Here the best of teachers ministers to the several conditions of his flock, and the soul receives immediately from the divine fountain that with which it is nourished.

6   As I have traveled at times where those of other societies have attended our meetings and have perceived how little some of them knew of the nature of silent worship, I have felt tender desires in my heart that we who often sit silent in our meetings may live answerable to the nature of an inward fellowship with God, that no stumbling-block through us may be laid in their way.

7   Such is the load of unnecessary expense which lies on that which is called divine service in many places, and so much are the minds of many people employed in outward forms and ceremonies, that the opening of an inward silent worship in this nation to me has appeared to be a precious opening.

8   Within the last four hundred years many pious people have been deeply exercised in soul on account of the superstition which prevailed among the professed followers of Christ, and in support of their testimony against oppressive idolatry some in several ages have finished their course in the flames.

9   It appears by the history of the Reformation that, through the faithfulness of the martyrs, the understandings of many have been opened and the minds of people, from age to age, been more and more prepared for a real spiritual worship.

10   My mind is often affected with a sense of the condition of those people who, in different ages, have been meek and patient, following Christ through great afflictions. And while I behold the several steps of Reformation, and that clearness to which through divine goodness it has been brought by our ancestors, I feel tender desires that we who sometimes meet in silence may never by our conduct lay stumbling-blocks in the way of others and hinder the progress of the Reformation in the world.

11   It was a complaint against some who were called the Lord's people that they brought polluted bread to his altar, and said the table of the Lord was contemptible.

12   In real silent worship the soul feeds on that which is divine; but we cannot partake of the table of the Lord and that table which is prepared by the god of this world.

13   If Christ is our shepherd and feeds us and we are faithful in following him, our lives will have an inviting language and the table of the Lord will not be polluted.

Appendix 1

A Guide to the Manuscripts of John Woolman's Literary Works, Personal Business Records, and Epistles from PYM to other yearly meetings

A –SYMBOLS FOR THE MANUSCRIPTS

1 – The Literary Works[1]

MS A/*Journal*	*Journal* [at front pp. 2-147, 194-224]
MS A/*Plea*	"A Plea for the Poor" [at front pp. 148-93]
MS A/*Trade*	"Serious Considerations on Trade" [at back pp. 1-4]
MS A/*Notes*	Notes and commentaries on Benezet's *A Caution and Warning to Great Britain* [at back pp. 5-14]
MS A/*Conversations*	"Conversations on the True Harmony of Mankind" [at back pp. 15-27]
MS B	*Journal*
MS C	*Journal*
MS H1	John Woolman's memorial concerning his brother Abner
MS M	"A Plea for the Poor" (chap. 15)
MS P	*Journal* (chap. 9)
MS R1	*Journal* (part of chap. 9)
MS R2	Account of peace mission dream
MS R3	*Journal* (part of chap. 9)
MS S	*Journal* (chaps. 11, 12)
MS S1/*True Harmony*	"Considerations on the True Harmony of Mankind"
MS S1/*Farewell*	"An Epistle to the Quarterly and Monthly Meeting of Friends"
MS T1	*Journal* (1st part of chap. 11)
MS T2	*Journal* (2nd part of chap. 11)

---

[1] This list is a revision of that found in Moulton at pp. 283-87.

MS W   "A Word of Remembrance & Caution to the Rich
                        &c."

2 – The Personal Business Records[2]

MS 1A   Tailoring & day labor book (1743–46)
MS 1B   Book of Executorship (1746–65)
MS 2   Ledger B 1753
MS 3   Account Book 1769

3 – Epistles from PYM to other yearly meetings

Woolman's seven holographs, many in the form of early drafts, for the
epistles that he wrote on behalf of PYM to other American yearly meetings,
are held in the PYM Miscellaneous Records deposited at HC. The box and
call number for each is noted at the respective appendix text herein. The
same holographs can also be examined on microfilm at SC.

    The texts of Woolman's three epistles to London Yearly Meeting
are found in fair copies entered in PYM Minute Book (1747–1779),
deposited at HC, at the page numbers given for each with its appendix text
herein. The Minute Book is also available on film at SC.

B – MANUSCRIPTS OF THE LITERARY WORKS[3]

Work   **Manuscript**

Journal   A/*Journal*, B, C,
                                                      P, R1, R3, S, T1, T2
Account of peace mission dream   R2
"Considerations on True Harmony of Mankind"   S1/*True Harmony*
"Conversations on the True Harmony of Mankind"   A/*Conversations*
"An Epistle to the Quarterly and Monthly Meetings of S1/*Farewell*
    Friends"
John Woolman's memorial concerning his brother Abner H1
Notes and commentaries on Benezet's *A Caution*   A/*Notes*
    and Warning to Great Britain

---

2   All are located at HSP in the John Woolman Papers 1652–1830, Collection
737.

3   There are no known JW manuscripts for Texts 1, 2, 4, 5, 8, 10, and 14 herein.

APPENDIX 1

"A Plea for the Poor"   A/ *Plea*, M
"Serious Considerations on Trade"   A/*Trade*
"A Word of Remembrance & Caution to the Rich &c."   W

C – LOCATION OF THE MANUSCRIPTS

Location   **Manuscript**
In the United States:

Haverford College, Haverford, PA   H1, W
    Quaker Collection, Magill Library

Historical Society of Pennsylvania, Philadelphia, PA   A,[4] 1A, 1B, 2, 3

Rutgers University, New Brunswick, NJ   R1, R2, R3

Swarthmore College, Swarthmore, PA   B, C, M, P, S, S1[5]
    Friends Historical Library

In Europe:

Friends Library, London, England   T2

Mount School, York, England   T1

---

[4] MS A contains: *Journal*, "A Plea for the Poor," "Serious Considerations on Trade," Notes and commentaries on Benezet's *A Caution and Warning to Great Britain*, and "Conversations on the True Harmony of Mankind."

[5] MS S1 contains: "Considerations on the True Harmony of Mankind" and "An Epistle to the Quarterly and Monthly Meeting of Friends."

Appendix 2

Reformers of the mid-eighteenth century American Quaker Church: Israel Pemberton, Jr. and John Woolman

In addition to being nurtured as a man of spiritual letters within his family home, John Woolman's life from the beginning was built on the corporate religious strength that had sustained his forefathers in their coming out of distress in England to the promise of toleration—and economic opportunity—in West New Jersey.[1] That strength was the Christian faith lived according to the principles and discipline of the Society of Friends. It was within the official church structures of the Philadelphia Yearly Meeting of the Society of Friends, the body having general oversight of Quakers in Pennsylvania, East and West New Jersey, "and the adjacent Provinces," that Woolman performed prodigious services, and for which he ministered, traveled, and wrote so selflessly. His writings grew out of those services, and the services themselves arose out of his participation in the many Quaker meetings to which he belonged and in which he was encouraged and collegially supported by men who were leaders in those meetings and who held the positions of authority in PYM itself.[2]

In Woolman's time and with the support of his pen, a major effort was undertaken to reform the American Quaker church.[3] While many men and women labored to bring about the reform, none labored with more energy, financial resources, and commanding authority than Israel Pemberton, Jr. (1715-1779). The fundamental changes in American Quakerism that took place in the middle decades of the eighteenth century occurred during his years of PYM leadership—the same years in which

---

[1] See James Proud, "A Note on John Woolman's Paternal Ancestors," *Quaker History* Vol. 96, No. 2 (2007): 28-53.

[2] As well as worshipping in the Rancocas Meeting for Worship in his early years and in the Mount Holly Preparative Meeting as an adult, Woolman rendered diligent service to the Burlington Monthly Meeting and the Burlington Quarterly Meeting, to the Burlington Quarterly Meeting of Ministers and Elders and the PYM Meeting of Ministers and Elders, and to PYM.

[3] For an important study of this reform see Jack D. Marietta, *The Reformation of American Quakerism, 1748-1783* (Philadelphia, PA: University of Pennsylvania Press, 1984).

Woolman made written witness in the affairs of Truth. That written witness, embodied in the works gathered together in this volume, attest and record Pemberton's and the other reformers' agenda of change regarding the issues of emancipation, peace, poverty, education, justice for Native Americans, and church discipline.[4]

The Pemberton Family and PYM

When Pemberton's paternal ancestors arrived from England they quickly established a leading influence in PYM. The grandfather, Phineas Pemberton (1649-1702), had been employed in Lancashire. When he came to Pennsylvania in 1683 he acquired an estate of five hundred acres on the Delaware River in Bucks County, named it Grove Place, and made it the family seat for his generations. Phineas represented Bucks Quarterly Meeting in PYM beginning in 1688 and served as Clerk of PYM from 1696 to 1701.

The Minute Book of PYM, which records the years from 1681 to 1746 (the entries from 1681 to 1710 being fair copies from the original, incomplete volume which is still preserved), is prefaced by "An Epistle, being a short testimony of the Lord's goodness to us in the settlement of ourselves in these parts of the world and an account of the first setting up of our Yearly Meeting." It was composed by Phineas Pemberton who instructed his son, Israel Pemberton, Sr. (1684/5-1754), to enter the epistle into the minute book to be purchased for that purpose. It was left to the second of Israel's sons, James Pemberton (1723-1809), to make the written entry. In this "Pemberton Epistle" is a clarion call to the need for preserving a church reformed in the way of Truth:

> Therefore for your encouragement in his work was I drawn forth to salute you in this short epistle in the beginning of this book, desiring that you may lay hold of Truth, and steadfastly walk in the way thereof, confirming of your forefathers' testimony to the glory of the Lord who called them, whereby you may obtain the

---

4 Although the Quaker reform movement, which gathered strength between 1750 and 1759 during Pemberton's years as Clerk of PYM, coincided with the later years of the First Great Awakening, which excited American protestantism from the 1730s to the 1770s, it abstained from the revivalistic piety and evangelistic fervor of the Awakening as it tried to resolve the moral and ethical issues raised for Friends by slave-owning, war-making, and poverty. George Whitefield (1714-1770), an important leader of the Great Awakening who preached not only in Pennsylvania but throughout the American colonies, was a contemporary of Pemberton (1715-1779) and Woolman (1720-1772).

like blessings they have; but if you trample under foot their testimony and sufferings, and grow careless, slothful and negligent in his work and service, it will prove heavy, and too heavy to be borne in the day of account.

Israel Pemberton, Sr. was born at Grove Place and became a successful merchant in Philadelphia. He was a member of the Provincial Assembly from 1718 to 1736/7. His service to PYM included representing Philadelphia Quarterly Meeting from 1726 (the year after Woolman's father Samuel began representing Burlington Quarterly Meeting in PYM) and lasted until at least 1736.

Israel, Jr. was a civic and business leader in Philadelphia, and built his personal wealth as an international trader and merchant. He was widely known as the "King of the Quakers." While the Historical Society of Pennsylvania has a voluminous deposit of the Pemberton family's business records and personal correspondence, including letters from Woolman to Israel, Jr. as well as letters about Woolman, a more thorough study of this man who laid such a template of reform on PYM is needed.[5]

The two brothers of Israel, Jr.—James, the penman of the "Pemberton Epistle," and John (1727-1795)—were both younger. Each of them exercised significant reforming influence within PYM and its instrumentalities, and each was an important friend of Woolman. James Pemberton served in the Provincial Assembly of Pennsylvania until 1756 when he and the other anti-war Quakers in that body withdrew from the government as the militia appropriations were being voted upon. He was made Clerk of the Meeting for Sufferings at its inception in 1756. Then he served PYM as Clerk from 1761 to 1766, again from 1768 to 1776, and again from 1778 to 1781. In the greater community he helped found the Pennsylvania Hospital and was Benjamin Franklin's successor as President of the Pennsylvania Abolition Society.

John Pemberton, like Woolman, was a recognized Quaker minister. He began his ministry in England in 1751 as he accompanied John Churchman (1705-1775) on a four-year mission abroad. It was to John Pemberton as Clerk of the Meeting for Sufferings that Woolman

---

5 See Theodore Thayer, *Israel Pemberton: King of the Quakers* (Philadelphia: HSP, 1943).

entrusted the holograph of the *Journal*[6] "together with some other manuscripts" before departing for England. Pemberton also died while on a mission in Europe and is buried in Pyrmont, Germany.

Of Missions and Meetings,
Epistles and Queries, and the Overseers of the Press:

A Chronology of the Pemberton-Woolman Reform Years

The pyramidal structure of the meetings composing Philadelphia Yearly Meeting, in Pemberton's and Woolman's time as in our own, is well described in the authoritative guide to its records. [7] Adjunct to the ordered structure of the meetings, extending from the local base to the regional apex, were the voluminous records kept in the minute books continuously maintained in the separate meetings. By virtue of that monumental achievement, our age can look into the various Quaker business meetings attended by the reformers and find, in the present-tense, the members wrestling over many issues, including those of discipline, worship and order, finance and property, slavery and poverty, peace and war, and read the communications from PYM to its subordinate units and between PYM and London Yearly Meeting. What follows is a brief chronological examination of meeting records, together with the few surviving letters between Woolman and Pemberton,[8] during their joint years of service in which can be observed how these two collaborators became involved in the work of the meetings and then labored together in the reform movement. [9] (N.B.: In this chronology Israel Pemberton, Jr. is identified as IP, and John Woolman is identified as JW.)

1740
• IP first elected a representative to PYM from Philadelphia QM.
• JW's father, Samuel Woolman (1690-1750), a representative from Burlington QM.

---

6 His own spiritual autobiography was titled *The Life and Times of John Pemberton, a minister of the Gospel of Christ.* It was edited by William Hodgson and published in London by Charles Gilpin in 1844.

7 *Guide to the Records of Philadelphia Yearly Meeting,* compiled by Jack Eckert (Haverford College, Records Committee of Philadelphia Yearly Meeting, Swarthmore College, 1989), pp. vii-xiii.

8 There is but one side to their exchange since only letters received by Pemberton from Woolman appear to have been preserved.

9 The minute books consulted herein are described, and their locations cited, in the Guide, where a brief description of the particular meeting will also be found.

1742
- IP named by PYM to group preparing the first set of Queries.
- JW begins his recorded official service in the Society of Friends with an appointment by Burlington MM to attend Burlington QM, together with his father. JW again so appointed in 1743 and frequently for many years thereafter.

1743
- PYM adopts the twelve Queries recommended by group appointed previous year and directs they be read and answered in the monthly and preparative meetings of PYM.
- IP named one of seven new Overseers of the Press.
- IP given first appointment to assist an author (John Reynell) in writing an annual epistle from PYM to another American yearly meeting (Rhode Island).
- JW's recorded ministry commences, as noted in 5th month minutes of Burlington MM:

> Whereas our friends Peter Andrews, John Woolman and Josiah White have had at times a concern on their minds to appear in public by way of exhortation to religious duties, whose appearances are generally well received; wherefore a motion was made here, that they might be recommended to sit in the Meeting of Ministers and Elders. . .

JW now authorized to travel as a minister in the wider Quaker world in America and abroad. (The missionary journeys that he undertook, with the names of his companions, are summarized in Table 1 herein.)
- JW undertook his first mission, in 9th month, by accepting invitation to accompany an experienced minister and Burlington resident, "my esteemed friend"[10] Abraham Farrington (1691 ca.-1758), on a visit to Brunswick, Amboy, Woodbridge, Rahway, and Plainfield, all in East Jersey. It was, for JW, his apprenticeship journey.

> [M]y beloved companion was frequently strengthened to hold forth the Word of Life amongst them. As for me, I was frequently silent through the meetings, and when I spake, it was with much care that I might speak only what Truth opened. My mind was often tender and I learned some profitable lessons. We were out about two weeks.

---

[10] *Journal*, p. 34.

1746

• JW makes first of two missionary journeys into the slaveholding southern colonies in 3ʳᵈ to 6ᵗʰ months and upon return writes "Some Considerations on the Keeping of Negroes" (Text 1 herein).

• JW in 9ᵗʰ month attends PYM [11] for first time as a representative from Burlington QM and is named to assist IP in writing PYM Epistle to Virginia YM. Every year thereafter through 1771 JW was named either to assist or to write the PYM epistle to another American yearly meeting or to the yearly meeting in London. (JW's annual appointments to the epistle committees, with the names of the other committee members, are shown in Table 2 herein.)

• N.B.: JW's stunning appointment to the Virginia Epistle committee with IP, and to other epistle committees thereafter for every year through 1771, was the first of the three important responsibilities JW received within PYM that were either under the influence or within the control of IP. Significantly, they were responsibilities earlier placed upon IP. Besides the epistle committees, the others were the appointments to the committee revising the Queries (in 1755) and to the Overseers of the Press (in 1756). (IP first shared in writing an epistle to an American yearly meeting in 1743; he was appointed to the first Queries committee in 1742; and he was named an Overseer of the Press in 1743.)

1747

• JW makes first of two missionary journeys into Long Island, Connecticut, Rhode Island, and Massachusetts in 3ʳᵈ to 7ᵗʰ months. His companion was Peter Andrews, a near neighbor, who had been simultaneously recorded as a Minister with JW.

• JW appointed to assist in writing the PYM Epistle to Rhode Island YM.

1750

• IP made Clerk (presiding officer) of PYM. The minutes noted:

> Our esteemed friend John Kinsey who was Clerk of this Meeting many years being lately deceased and the Meeting now desiring Israel Pemberton, Jr. to succeed him in that service, he being present, after some consideration consented thereto.

• N.B.: IP holds office of Clerk for next ten years. Kinsey had simultaneously been the Speaker of the Provincial Assembly of Pennsylvania, but with his death the sixty-eight-year custom of electing the

---

[11] During Woolman's years of service, PYM began its meetings each year on the third 1ˢᵗ day of the 9ᵗʰ month.

same person to be PYM Clerk as well as Assembly Speaker was ended and another Quaker, Isaac Norris II, became Speaker.

• PYM, on the request of Philadelphia QM, raised reform concerns about both education and alcoholism:

> Philadelphia Quarterly Meeting adds that their representatives are desired to propose to the consideration of this Meeting some method to encourage the settling of schools in the country under the care of Friends and likewise to recommend that some further methods be taken to prevent the growing practice of giving and taking drams and other strong liquors at vendues[12] and funerals.

1751

• JW (4th mo) appointed in Burlington MM to committee for considering PYM's proposal to establish "schools in the country for the training up the youth in useful learning under religious schoolmasters among friends."

1752

• PYM appoints six new Overseers of the Press, including the abolitionist and educator Anthony Benezet (1713-1784). (The names of the Overseers of the Press between 1743 and 1771, together with historical notes on the Overseers' responsibilities and JW's submissions of his writings for their approval, are set forth in Table 3 herein.)

1754

• In 1st month Philadelphia MM hears Benezet's proposal "of making that rule of our discipline respecting the importation of Negroes, or the purchasing of them after imported, more public, together with some reasons to discourage that practice"; a drafting committee worked on such a statement until 7th month when "after maturely considering the same" PMM referred its "Epistle of Advice and Caution [sic] against Purchasing of Negroes" to Philadelphia QM.

• In 8th month PQM's minutes note that PMM's proposed Epistle was presented for revision and concurrence before publication and that PQM's representatives to PYM were to lay before PYM

> a paper relating to the purchasing of Negroes which hath been under the solid consideration of this meeting, and we think something of the kind published by order of the Yearly Meeting may be of general service.

---

[12] Public sales by auction.

• In 9th month PYM received the proposed "Epistle of Caution against the purchasing of Negroes and of Advice to those who have them in their families," appointed a committee to review and make necessary alterations and amendments, and the next day approved and ordered it printed and distributed among the quarterly and monthly meetings. Later in the year it was printed in Philadelphia by James Chattin under the title "An Epistle of Caution and Advice, Concerning the Buying and Keeping of Slaves."
• Benezet and JW appointed by PYM to write its Epistle to Virginia YM.
• JW's "Some Considerations on the Keeping of Negroes" (Text 1 herein), by order of the Overseers of the Press, was also printed in Philadelphia by James Chattin.

1755

• PYM General Spring Meeting of Ministers and Elders issues the Epistle written for it by JW (Text 2 herein) addressed to Friends on the Continent of America regarding problems arising out of French and Indian War now entering its second year.
• PYM appoints standing committee to correspond with London's YM and Meeting for Sufferings for assistance in present "occasions of difficulty," which committee, with one other concerned with visiting the monthly and quarterly meetings, met in 12th month, at a time when "[t]he calamities of war were now increasing."[13] From that conference came "An Epistle of Tender Love and Caution," signed by JW and twenty others, including Benezet and John Pemberton. The Epistle apparently was the committee's corporate—and collegially written—statement, although the tone and voice of JW is heard.
• PYM, looking to its long-term spiritual health, appoints committee of thirteen members (including such active ministers as JW, John Churchman, William Brown, and Samuel Fothergill) to examine its Queries first adopted in 1743. The 1743 queries were a set of twelve self-examination questions that the preparative and monthly meetings within PYM were to consider and answer quarterly "so that the members of such meetings may, by this means, be from time to time reminded of their duty."[14] But by 1755, the sixth year of IP's clerkship, PYM was undergoing significant changes and facing unprecedented challenges. The recent testimonies against slavery and against war demanded a living discipline among Friends who were often seen as lax in their personal lives. The reformers' purpose was expressed in the Minutes:

---

[13] *Journal*, p. 84; see also pp. 77, 85-86.
[14] Michener, p. 255.

. . .[M]any useful observations [were] made to incite the Elders, Overseers and all others active in the Discipline to be zealously concerned for the cause of Truth and honestly to labor to repair the breaches too obvious in many places that there may be some well grounded hopes of the primitive beauty and purity of the Church being gradually restored.

The twelve questions for self-examination of 1743 became in the 1755 formulation (i) thirteen questions, with an admonition, requiring answers for submission by the local meetings to their respective Quarterly Meetings, and (ii) four additional queries regarding official and statistical matters to be reported by the MMs and QMs to PYM. In addition, the Meeting of Ministers and Elders of PYM proposed, and had approved, its own set of nine Queries, including the question whether Ministers serve "in the ability God only gives and [are] thereby kept from burdening the living."

1756

• IP hosted a dinner for friendly Indian leaders and leading Quakers to promote peace.[15]
• JW traveled alone on a missionary visit to Long Island in 5th month. Later in the year he wrote, with the assistance of John Scarborough, the PYM Epistle to Long Island YM. It was his first PYM appointment as principal author of an epistle.
• JW appointed to Overseers of the Press together with seven others, including James and John Pemberton; John Churchman and his brother-in-law William Brown, both recorded ministers; and William Logan, the son of William Penn's Secretary of Proprietary Affairs in Pennsylvania.
• PYM creates Meeting for Sufferings to provide relief and assistance to those Friends in want and danger at time of French and Indian War. JW and thirty-two others signed letter to PYM for its establishment; James Pemberton serves as Clerk.

1757

• JW began second major missionary journey in 7th month into southern slaveholding colonies of Maryland, Virginia, and North Carolina. The experience formed the background for writing "Considerations on Keeping Negroes: Part Second" (Text 5 herein), which was not completed until 1761. Later in the year he wrote, with the assistance of Aaron Ashbridge, the

---

[15] Gummere, p. 80.

PYM Epistle to Virginia YM, and in the next year wrote, with the assistance of Samuel Smith, the PYM Epistle to North Carolina YM.

• JW subscribed to the Articles of, and promised a contribution of six pounds to, the New-Jersey Association for Helping the Indians,[16] which undertook to purchase "about 2000 acres of the best land that can be got nigh or adjoining to the Barrens in the Counties of Monmouth, Burlington or Gloucester in New-Jersey" as a settlement for the "Native Indians of New-Jersey." The originator of this plan and the draftsman of the Articles, which were dated 16 April 1757, was JW's friend and contemporary Samuel Smith, the author of New Jersey's colonial history.[17]

• IP a principal organizer of the Friendly Association for Regaining and Preserving Peace with the Indians by Pacific Measures.[18]

• The concluding minute of PYM read:

> Israel Pemberton having served this Meeting for a considerable time as Clerk and signified both at the last and this Meeting that it will be a satisfaction to him that this Meeting should consider whether it may not be proper annually to nominate a Clerk to serve the Meeting in the manner as is done in the Yearly Meeting of London or in such other manner as may be more suitable to our circumstances.

The issue of whether to continue IP as Clerk or to hold an annual election was laid over to next year's PYM for the representatives to consider before proceeding to any business.

1758

• The continuance of IP as Clerk was taken up by PYM as its first concern. The members decided to continue IP as Clerk, and JW, in a rare and recorded role of open and political leadership, reported:

> The Representatives [of the several Quarterly Meetings] after being called over retired into the Chamber and after sometime returned and John Woolman on their behalf informed the Meeting that pursuant to the minute of last year having considered the proposal of choosing a Clerk annually, they agree it will not suit the circumstances of this Meeting and that they

---

[16]   HC Special Collections 975B.

[17]   Samuel Smith [1720-1776], *The History of the Colony of Nova Caesaria, or New Jersey* (Burlington: N.J., printed and sold by J. Parker, 1765; reprinted Trenton: Wm. S. Sharp, 1877), pp. v, vi.

[18]   Marietta, p. 188.

desire Israel Pemberton to continue to act as Clerk this year which he consents to.

• PYM appoints a committee of JW, John Churchman (1705-1775), Daniel Stanton (1708-1770), and John Scarborough for jointly or severally visiting Quakers who continue to buy or keep slaves.

1759
• JW and his colleagues reported to PYM on their visits to Quaker owners of enslaved persons.
• JW wrote PYM Epistle to QMs & MMs regarding peace (Text 4 herein).

1760
• JW undertook his second missionary journey into Long Island and New England between 4ᵗʰ and 8ᵗʰ months. Later that year he writes the PYM Epistle to Rhode Island YM, assisted by Isaac Andrews, his fellow minister from Burlington MM and the companion on the first southern mission.

1761
• In three letters JW sought IP's guidance before and after submitting "Considerations on Keeping Negroes: Part Second" (Text 5 herein) to the Overseers of the Press:

Beloved Friend
The piece J[ohn] Churchman took home he perused, but being taken poorly, made no mark in writing on it. My brother Asher being at their last Monthly Meeting, and I writing to J.C. about it, he sent it, and George, I expect by his agreement, sent a letter to me referring it to me carefully to review and transcribe it. Since which I have spent some time therein, and am now come to town in order that if way should open for Friends to meet again upon it, I may be near in case they should want to speak with me. I am a little cautious of being much at your house on account of the small pox, but would gladly meet you at such house as you think suitable, to have a little conversation with you.
I have not yet offered it to any of the Committee. I lodge at Reuben Haines', and am mostly there.

| da mo | I remain your loving friend, |
| 17: 11: 1761 | John Woolman |

[Addressed] For Israel Pemberton, when he comes home.

[Marked by IP] From John Woolman, about his treatise.[19]

Beloved Friend

As I expect to go out of town (if well) in the morning, and it's likely may not see you, I thought it best to acquaint you that I remain well satisfied with what you proposed relating to the preface, and though I have looked over the piece with some care and done according to the best of my understanding, I have all along been apprehensive that if it be made public there was a further labor for some other person necessary, and if you can feel liberty from your other concerns, and freedom to spend some time in a deliberate reviewing and correcting of it, and make such alterations or additions as you believe may be useful, the prospect of it is agreeable to me.

In true brotherly love I remain your friend

John Woolman

Same evening, after we met;

The Committee gave it to Anthony [Benezet]

with a message with it to you.

[Marked by IP] From John Woolman, about his treatise. 1761[20]

da   mo

9:   2:   1762

Beloved Friend

Since I saw you I have been thoughtful in case some of the first part should be printed, whether it would not be best to have them, or a part of them, stitched separate; as they have been plenty in and about these parts I expect some would choose to have one of the Second Part who of choice would not take both together. It has been a query with me if the First Part be printed, whether a less number would not be sufficient of them than the Second. Having thus hinted what I had thought, I am free to leave it with friends, either to omit printing them, or to print as many as to you may appear best.

With love to you and family I remain your loving friend,

John Woolman

Enclosed are some alterations proposed to be

made in First Part if printed

For Israel Pemberton, in Philadelphia

---

19 HSP Collection 484A: Pemberton Family Papers 1641-1880, Vol. XV, p. 74.
20 *Ibid.*, p. 111.

[Marked by IP] 9 2mo 1762. From John Woolman, about his treatise.[21]

1762

• At a time when IP was being subjected to political pressure, JW sent him this letter of comfort:

	da	mo	
Mount Holly;	20	6	1762

Beloved Friend:

As true love moves on our minds we find them turned at times toward certain places and particular persons, and yet unable to give any reason why they are turned that way any more than another— and such is my case at present.

My mind of late has been with you more than usual, and I seem at liberty to open to you the manner in which I have looked toward you.

In those small affairs of life which have fallen to my lot to be concerned in, I have at times found that which has appeared difficult to manage as a Christian, and looking at your situation amid many affairs, and at the family you have the care of, I have felt, as I believe, some degree of your burden.

I have had in view the purity of the heavenly family. The most gracious and most tender visitations of Christ to our souls drawing them from the mixture and entanglements, that they may attain true liberty, and have seemed in company with you, looking for and desiring a more perfect deliverance.

In the strength of all temptation and in difficulties which appear very great, there has seemed before me a prospect, a power, able and ready to subdue all things to Himself.

In a fresh sense of pure love, I remain your friend

John Woolman

I send these by William Calvert with request
    to deliver them into your hand.

[Addressed] For Israel Pemberton, Philadelphia[22]

1763

• JW departs Burlington for mission to the Native Americans at Wyalusing on Susquehanna River, two hundred miles from Philadelphia. JW

---

21 *Ibid.*, p. 112.
22 Quoted by Gummere, p. 73.

accompanied by IP for first day and by John Pemberton as far as Bethlehem.[23] Upon his return, JW wrote IP as follows:

da   mo

Burlington, 27   6   1763   1 o'clock

Dear friend,

Through the mercies of the Lord my beloved companion and helpmeet B[enjamin] Parvin and I were helped to perform our journey to Wyalusing and came back to Bethlehem   on   seventh day night. Was yesterday at the Swamp Meeting and I lodged last night at John Cadwaleders and am now hasting home. Our journey though attended with much deep exercise has been greatly to our satisfaction. We were at seven religious meetings with the Indians, many of which people I believe were, in these troublous times, greatly comforted in our visit and they all appeared kind and loving to us. I saw nothing among any of them in that place which to me appeared like disaffection to the English, but our conversation was mostly with the soberer sort. The Moravian preacher [David Zeisberger (1721-1808)] who was there when I went and continued there while I stayed, appeared kind and courteous from first to last, and I believe his intentions are honest.

In a humbling sense of His goodness in whom my poor soul has trusted, I remain with kind love to you and family and all my dear friend

John Woolman

For Israel Pemberton in Philadelphia[24]

Several days later JW was visited at home by John Pemberton and his mother. Pemberton reported on the occasion to IP in this letter:

Burlington, 7mo. 2. 1763

Dear Brother,

Yesterday Mother and I spent with our friend John Woolman at his house. He looks better for his journey and is well satisfied that he went. I asked him several questions respecting the Indians, etc. and he gave me what accounts he could, but he found in the journey his mind closely engaged to attend to the concern he was engaged in, and cautious of questioning the

---

[23] *Journal*, pp. 124-25. This entry is the only time in the *Journal* any of the three Pemberton brothers is named.

[24] Quoted by Gummere, p. 91.

Indians. For prudential reasons he apprehended it might beget some jealousies in the minds of some and so close up his way, or some reasons might be alleged which he was not qualified to answer to, or that he could not say anything to, without casting some blame on the English. His companion B. Parvin used more freedom and can give better information. He allowed me the liberty to preserve his remarks on his journey, and to enclose them for your perusal, with this request: that you show them to no other person. . .and please to return them speedily. . .

John told me, if you desired it, he would come to town, but as he was particularly cautious of entering into inquiries, and heard little, he apprehended his intelligence would be of little service, and would rather avoid it. You may perceive from the enclosed that he was friendly received. In every place where they understood his errand, were rejoiced and very kind, and he did not perceive in any an evil disposition towards the English. He desired his love to you.

I am your affectionate brother,
John Pemberton[25]

1764
• JW, assisted by IP, John Churchman, Isaac Child, and Isaac Andrews, writes PYM Epistle to London YM. (See Appendix Text 8 herein.)

1768
• JW writes and publishes, after examination by the Overseers of the Press, "Considerations on Pure Wisdom and Human Policy etc." (Text 8 herein) which is concerned not only with the issues of slavery and war, but also with such matters as labor, education, and the proper use of resources, matters addressed in the reformed Queries adopted by PYM in 1755.
• N.B.: JW's "Serious Considerations on Trade" (Text 9 herein), which was intended as a part of Text 8, was not approved for publication by the Overseers of the Press and hence was not printed in JW's lifetime. The argument of the work seems brief and unfinished, and as it supports independent local economies over against excessive international trade, a question arises whether JW withheld it out of deference to the interests of eminent and wealthy fellow reformers engaged in international trade such as IP, John Reynell, and Samuel Emlen, Jr.
• JW assisted by two others writes PYM Epistle to London YM. (See Appendix Text 9 herein.)

---

[25] HSP Collection 484A, *op. cit.*, Vol. XVI, p. 109.

1770
• Publication of JW's "Considerations on the True Harmony of Mankind & how it is to be maintained" (Text 11 herein) after inspection by the Overseers of the Press.
• JW assisted by IP writes PYM Epistle to London YM. (See Appendix Text 10 herein.)

1771
• PYM directs that its Meeting for Sufferings take on the oversight of the press theretofore entrusted to Overseers.

1772
• JW prior to departing for England on 1 June writes "Conversations on the True Harmony of Mankind & how it may be promoted" (Text 12 herein) but does not submit it to the Meeting for Sufferings for either comments or approval to publish. IP would have been one of several close friends whom JW might have used as a model for "a man rich in money" and for "a thrifty landholder."
• JW writes "An Epistle to the Quarterly and Monthly Meetings of Friends" (Text 13 herein) as well as these two letters to IP regarding it:

> Beloved friend
> Thine by J[ohn] Comfort came to hand. It would be agreeable to my mind that the piece be handed to James [Pemberton, then the Clerk of PYM], and if no objection arise, to its being after opened to the Meeting for Sufferings that it be also opened there.
> As my mind has been more particularly drawn toward the northern parts of England, I do not yet feel settled to sail for London; but know not what may be as to that.
> Your loving friend,
> John Woolman[26]
> da   mo
> 15   4   1772

> Beloved friend
> I believe I may endeavor to see Joseph White soon. If you and such in this city who are careful to look over writings proposed to be printed, and to amend what may be imperfect, would employ a little time in correcting that piece, and afterwards let me see the prepared alterations, it would be acceptable to me to look over them.

---

[26] *Ibid.*, Vol. XXIII, p. 114.

Though I know not how it may be as to the sailing in this vessel, I am in care to endeavor to be in readiness soon.

Seventh day morning   John Woolman[27]

    for Israel Pemberton   (4 mo 1772)

The posthumous editing of the Journal

As noted, prior to his departure for England in 1772, Woolman had delivered his final manuscript of the first ten chapters of the *Journal* together with "other manuscripts" to John Pemberton as Clerk of the Monthly Meeting for Sufferings, the successor to the Overseers of the Press for reviewing works prior to publication. The other manuscripts undoubtedly would have included the "Epistle to the Quarterly and Monthly Meetings of Friends" (Text 13 herein) and the Memorial for Abner Woolman, including the testament to Abner's children (Appendix Text 11 herein).

The minutes of the Monthly Meeting for Sufferings held 15th day 4th mo 1773 officially record the meeting's first notification of the news of Woolman's death in England on the previous 7 October and provide the following information regarding a final service his friends and colleagues were to render him:

> Our Beloved Friend John Woolman having before his leaving us sealed up a Journal of his life to near that time together with some other manuscripts and directed them to John Pemberton in order that they should be communicated to this meeting if it should please the Lord to remove him from the stage of this life before his return, being now presented to this meeting, John Hunt, John Reynell, James Pemberton, Anthony Benezet, and Owen Jones are appointed to inspect them and communicate their sentiments thereon to a future meeting.

At the Monthly Meeting for Sufferings held 19th day 8th month three more members—Israel Pemberton, Samuel Emlen, Jr., and John Pemberton—were added to the original committee of five editors of Woolman's manuscripts. The minutes of the meeting for April 1774 reported that, the editors' work being finished, the *Journal* was in the Press and ready for subscription.

Of the eight members of the editing committee for the *Journal*, five of them had been colleagues as Overseers of the Press with Woolman

---

[27] *Ibid.*, p. 117.

since the 1750s: Israel Pemberton, Jr., Anthony Benezet, James and John Pemberton, and Owen Jones (1711-1793), who was appointed an Overseer in 1752, "(h)e served with distinction as Treasurer of the Province of Pennsylvania."[28] The other three persons appointed as editors were John Reynell (1708-1784) who then was Treasurer of PYM (1763-80), a shipping and commission merchant and sometime business associate of Israel Pemberton, Jr.; John Hunt (1712-1778), an Englishman, who, as Woolman noted in the *Journal*,[29] attended Philadelphia Yearly Meeting in 1757 as the war tax was being debated, and who emigrated to Darby, Pennsylvania in 1769; and Samuel Emlen, Jr. (1730-1799), a wealthy Philadelphian who traveled widely in the Friends' ministry and had sailed with Woolman to England.[30] It was Emlen who brought the manuscripts that Woolman had written during his time out of the country back to Philadelphia.

Postscriptum:
The capture and Virginia exile of the PYM leadership by the colonial Pennsylvania authorities, and the death of Israel Pemberton

There was still a signal—and suffering—ministry of Quaker witness that some of these beloved friends of John Woolman were to render on behalf of that testimony for peace in time of war which he had enunciated in the name of Truth. On 28 August 1777, the Continental Congress, meeting in Philadelphia, had recommended to the executive authorities of the states that it was

> necessary for the public safety at this time, when a British army has landed in Maryland, with a professed design of enslaving this free country, and is now advancing toward this city, as a principal object of hostility, that [named] dangerous persons be accordingly secured. . .[31]

In the Warrant issued on 31 August by the Supreme Executive Council of Pennsylvania in furtherance of the congressional recommendation, the following Friends, all but one of them an editor of the *Journal*, were named among the forty-one persons who, with their

---

28 Gummere, p. 514.
29 At p. 87.
30 *Journal*, p. 163.
31 Thomas Gilpin, *Exiles in Virginia: With Observations on the Conduct of the Society of Friends during the Revolutionary War* (Philadelphia: C. Sherman, 1848; 2003 reprint), pp. 71-72.

papers, were to be seized and secured: Israel, James, and John Pemberton, Samuel Emlen, Jr., and John Hunt, as well as Owen Jones, Jr., the son of another editor. The reason given was that these were persons "who have in their general conduct and conversation evinced a disposition inimical to the cause of America."[32] All of these men were apprehended and imprisoned except for Samuel Emlen who, as the arrest report of 3 September noted, was "confined to his bed; *we broke open his desk, but found no papers of a public nature.*"[33] On 5 September a Remonstrance addressed to the President and Council of Pennsylvania was signed by one hundred thirteen Friends, including these other editors of the *Journal*: William Brown, Anthony Benezet, Owen Jones, and John Reynell.

But all the protests and remonstrances of the prisoners and their friends were of no avail and on 9 September an Order in Council was issued by the Pennsylvania executive—without charges having been formally presented or hearings held—declaring the prisoners, who had "declined giving any assurance of allegiance to this State, as of right they ought," to have "renounce[d] all the privileges of citizenship" and, therefore, banished to Virginia.[34] The prisoners answered with another protest of the same date:

> In this resolve, contrary to the inherent rights of mankind, you condemn us to banishment *unheard.*
>
> You determine matters concerning us, which *we could have disproved*, had our right to a hearing been granted.
>
> The charge against us of refusing "to promise to *refrain* from corresponding with the enemy," insinuates that we have already held such correspondence, *which we utterly and solemnly deny.*
>
> The tests you proposed, we were by no law bound to subscribe, and notwithstanding our refusing them, we are still justly and lawfully entitled to all the rights of citizenship, of which you are attempting to deprive us.[35]

The prisoners journaled the commencement of their exile thus:

> 9th month, 11th—About five o'clock we were compelled, some by actual force, and some by force being admitted, to take seats in a

---

32 *Ibid.*
33 *Ibid.*, p. 265. No italics added.
34 *Ibid.*, pp. 111-12.
35 *Ibid.*, pp. 113-15, at p. 113. No italics added.

number of wagons, and were driven through the city, to the falls of Schuylkill—a spectacle to the people.

Thus, by the bold attempt of a set of men who had thrust themselves into power, there was accomplished an affair, which has no parallel in history. A people who had professedly risen up in opposition to what they called an arbitrary exercise of power, were in a little time so lost to every idea of liberty, as to see, without dreading the consequences, the very idea of freedom torn up. And men were found who would undertake the execution of the mandates of Council without inquiring into the justice of them.[36]

The Philadelphia Yearly Meeting met several weeks later and issued a Testimony on behalf of its exiled members in which it admonished those responsible for the banishment to "weightily consider the tendency of their own conduct, and how contrary it is to the doctrines and example of our Lord and Lawgiver, Christ Jesus; and do them that justice which their case requires."[37] PYM also appointed a committee to visit the commanding generals of the British and American armies, William Howe and George Washington, and to deliver copies of the Testimony and to give the reasons for it. Two of the six committee members were Samuel Emlen and William Brown who, with the other members of the committee, met with the generals and reported back to PYM the following year.

The ordeal for the exiles lasted over the winter of 1777-1778—while Washington's army was suffering at Valley Forge—until spring in 1778. On 10 March Congress received a request from the Council in Pennsylvania that the exiles be sent home because

the dangerous example which their longer continuance in banishment may afford on future occasions, has already given uneasiness to some good friends to the independency of these states.[38]

On 16 March Congress approved transferring the prisoners to the authority of Pennsylvania. Thereafter, the Pennsylvania Assembly directed the Council to bring the matter to an end, and in April the Council ordered the exiles

---

[36] *Ibid.*, p. 133.
[37] *Ibid.*, p. 59.
[38] Quoted in Arthur J. Mekeel, *The Relation of the Quakers to the American Revolution* (Washington, D.C.: University Press of America, 1979), p. 183.

brought back to Lancaster where they were "discharged to pass unmolested."[39]

Not all of the exiles came home, however. Woolman's friend John Hunt died in Virginia on 31 March. It was written of Hunt and another who perished in banishment that their deaths were "owing to some of the causes connected with their situation, and the anxieties which had from time to time affected them."[40]

And not all those who did come home survived for very long the rigors—including an unnamed epidemic—which they had endured in Virginia. One of the earliest to fall was Israel Pemberton, Jr. who in exile had written to his wife, Mary: "I am become a poor weak, old man. . ."[41] When at last he returned home he found Mary herself approaching death (she died in October 1778) and his personal wealth and estates greatly diminished in value. His own death occurred about a year after his exile had ended, on 22 April 1779. He was then 64 years of age.[42]

---

[39] Gilpin, *op. cit.*, p. 231f.

[40] *Ibid.*, p. 220.

[41] Quoted in Theodore Thayer, *Israel Pemberton: King of the Quakers* (Philadelphia: HSP, 1943) at p. 230.

[42] *Op. cit.*, pp. 207-33.

Table 1
John Woolman's missionary journeys
and his traveling companions

Year	Journey	Duration/Miles	Companion	Journal pp.
1743	East NJ	2 weeks	Abraham Farrington	34
1746	PA, MD, VA, NC	3 months/1500	Isaac Andrews	36-38
1746	NJ (seacoast)	22 days/340	Peter Andrews	38-39
1747	Long Island, New England	4 months/1650	Peter Andrews	40-42
1748	NJ, MD	6 weeks/550	John Sykes	42-43
1751	upper West NJ	9 days/170		45
1753	Bucks Co., Burlington MM	2+ weeks	John Sykes	45
1754-55 ca.	NJ various		John Sykes	47
1756	Long Island	24 days/316		51-53
1757	MD, VA, NC	2 months/1150	Uriah Woolman	58-74
1758	Chester Co., Philadelphia	2 weeks/200	Benjamin Jones	90
1758	Concord, Goshen		Daniel Stanton, John Scarborough, et al.	94-96
1759	Philadelphia, NJ	various	John Churchman, et al.	96-97
1759	Bucks Co.		Samuel Eastburn	101-102
1760	NJ, Long Island, New England	4 months	Samuel Eastburn	106-116

Year	Journey	Duration/Miles	Companion	Journal pp.
1761-63	Philadelphia, NJ		Benjamin Jones, Elizabeth Smith, Mary Noble	117, 122
1763	Indians at Wyalusing, PA		Benjamin Parvin	123-136
1764-65	NJ various		William Jones, John Sleeper, Elizabeth Smith, Benjamin Jones	143-144
1766	DE, eastern MD		John Sleeper	145-148
1766	upper NJ		Benjamin Jones	148
1767	western MD			149-151
1767	Berks & Philadelphia Cos., Mount Holly			151
1768	MD	5 weeks		151-152
1772	England			163-192

APPENDIX 2

Table 2
John Woolman's annual appointments to the PYM
epistle committees writing to other yearly meetings:

Historical Note:

From the inception of PYM in 1685, when it was agreed that there would be one yearly meeting of the Society of Friends for Pennsylvania and New Jersey and that the city of meeting would alternate each year between Burlington and Philadelphia,[43] it was the custom to receive and hear epistles from yearly meetings of Friends in London and, as they were founded, from those in Virginia, Rhode Island, Long Island, and North Carolina. (The names given to all yearly meetings herein are the same as those given in the source documents of PYM.) By means of these epistles PYM maintained a spiritual discourse in matters of Christian faith and Quaker order and shared the concerns of their common life with its mother church in England and its sister churches in the colonies. The minutes of PYM record the protocol during the years of JW's participation for hearing the epistles addressed to PYM read and for naming the members of the committees appointed to write the epistles issuing from PYM.

This Table shows the twenty-six consecutive epistle committee appointments JW received beginning in 1746 and the committee members with whom he served. There appears also to have been a protocol in the order of naming the committee members, the first named presumably being charged with drafting the epistle, the others assisting. As seen in JW's service, for the first ten years he assisted others in writing the several American epistles; following that apprenticeship, in the next eight years he drafted/authored seven of the American epistles. All the drafts for those seven epistles (**Appendix Texts 1 through 7** herein) are held in the PYM Miscellaneous Records at HC. Each is in JW's distinctive hand.

The most prestigious assignment was to the committee writing the epistle to London, and to that committee JW was assigned in each of his last eight years. He was the first named, and, as evidenced by the style and voice, the draftsman/author three times, in 1764, 1768, and 1770. These three London epistles (**Appendix Texts 8, 9, and 10** herein), as was the case with all epistles to London, were copied for their respective years into the PYM minutes.

---

[43] After the 1760 meeting in Burlington, it was agreed all subsequent meetings be held in Philadelphia.

Year	Yearly Meeting Addressed	Committee Members[44]

(a) [To American yearly meetings]

Year		
1746[45]	Virginia	Israel Pemberton, Jr. & JW
1747[46]	Rhode Island	Richard Smith, Jr. & JW
1748	Rhode Island	Samuel Smith & JW
1749	Virginia	Eben Large & JW
1750	Long Island	Abraham Farrington & JW
1751	Long Island	Jacob Howell & JW
1752	Virginia	William Hammanns & JW
1753	Rhode Island	Abraham Farrington & JW
1754	Virginia	Anthony Benezet & JW
1755	North Carolina	Thomas Carleton & JW
1756[47]	Long Island	JW & John Scarborough
1757[48]	Virginia	JW & Aaron Ashbridge
1758	North Carolina	JW & Samuel Smith
1759	North Carolina	Daniel Stanton & JW
1760[49]	Rhode Island	JW & Isaac Andrews
1761	Rhode Island	JW & Samuel Eastburn
1762	Long Island	JW & Benjamin Lightfoot
1763	Long Island	JW & John Pemberton

(b) [To London Yearly Meeting]

1764	London	JW, John Churchman, Israel Pemberton, Jr., Isaac Child, Isaac Andrews
1765	London	William Horne, JW, Joseph White

---

[44] The committee members are in the order listed in the PYM Minutes. It is assumed here that the first named is the principal author and that the after-named are assisting.

[45] After 1st southern journey made between 12th day 3rd month and 16th day 6th month 1746 (see *Journal*, pp. 36-38).

[46] After 1st New England journey made between 16th day 3rd month and 13th day 7th month 1747 (see *ibid.*, pp. 40-42).

[47] After Long Island journey made between 12th day 5th month and early 6th month 1756 (see *ibid.*, pp. 51-53).

[48] After 2nd southern journey of about 2 months beginning in 5th month 1757 (see *ibid.*, pp. 58-74).

[49] After 2nd New England journey made between 17th day 4th month and 10th day 8th month 1760 (see *ibid.*, pp. 106-16).

1766	London	Joseph White, JW, John Churchman
1767	London	John Hunt, JW, William Horne
1768	London	JW, Joseph White, George Mason
1769	London	Joseph White, JW, Geo Mason, Israel Pemberton, Jr.
1770	London	JW & Israel Pemberton, Jr.
1771	London	John Churchman & JW

Table 3
The PYM Overseers of the Press between 1743 and 1771:

Appointed   **Names**

1743   John Evans (1689-1756): minister
"   Michael Lightfoot (1683-1754): minister; Treasurer of
            Pennsylvania 1743-1754
"   Anthony Morris III (1682-1763): brewer; mayor,
            Philadelphia; member, Pennsylvania Assembly
"   William Morris (1695-1776): Trenton councilman;
            trader/merchant
"   Isaac Norris II (1701-1766): Speaker, Pennsylvania
            Assembly 1751-1764
"   Israel Pemberton, Jr. (1715-1779): Clerk of PYM 1750-1759;
            trader/merchant
"   Richard Smith (1699-1751): member, New Jersey Council;
            trader/merchant

1752   Anthony Benezet (1713-1784): abolitionist; teacher; author
"   Owen Jones (1711-1793) sometime Treasurer of
            Pennsylvania
"   Samuel Preston Moore (1710-85): physician; Treasurer of
            Pennsylvania 1754-1768
"   John Smith (1722-1771): trader/merchant; member,
            Pennsylvania Assembly
"   Samuel Smith, Jr. (1720-1776): trader/merchant; historian
            of colonial New Jersey
"   Mordecai Yarnall (1705-1771): minister

1756   John Armitt (1702-1762): elder
"   William Brown (nd-1786): minister, brother-in-law of John
            Churchman

"   John Churchman (1705-1775): minister, farmer, and
surveyor
"   William Logan (1718-1776): son of William Penn's Secretary
of Proprietary Affairs in Pennsylvania
"   James Pemberton (1723-1809): member, Pennsylvania
Assembly; Clerk of PYM
"   John Pemberton (1727-1795): minister
"   Joseph White (1712-1777): minister
"   John Woolman

Historical Notes:
(1) The PYM Overseers of the Press

The presentation of Truth in publications faithful to the principles of the
Society of Friends "of Pennsylvania, East and West Jersey, and of the
adjacent Provinces" was always a matter of high concern for PYM, but
especially so in the time of such a divisive issue among Quakers as slavery,
wherein a number of eminent Friends were slave owners, and others were
committed abolitionists. In 1709 PYM institutionalized its concern
regarding publications by creating the precursor of the Overseers in the
following action:

> The care of the Press being recommended to the care of
> Philadelphia Monthly Meeting, [to appoint] a committee of eight
> Friends, any five of whom are desired to take care to peruse all
> writings or manuscripts that are intended to be printed, before
> they go to the Press, with power to correct what may not be for
> the service of Truth; otherwise not to suffer anything to be
> printed.[50]

By 1718 the problem of unapproved publications—especially anti-slavery
tracts—stirred PYM to adopt this resolution:

> This meeting, seeing occasion to renew to the notice of Friends,
> our ancient care and practice in the case of publishing books and
> writings, now recommend to the Monthly and Quarterly
> Meetings, that such be dealt with as shall write, print, or publish
> any books or writings tending to raise contention, or occasion

---

[50] Michener, p. 30.

breach of unity among brethren, or that have not first had the perusal and approbation of the Friends appointed by the Yearly Meeting for that purpose.[51]

In the following year, PYM adopted *The Book of Discipline, 1719* in which the Overseers were officially given their title as well as their responsibilities for broad governance, including that over the Press:

(I)t is the business of the Overseers or other weighty Friends to speak to and deal with. . .Such as write, print or publish any books or writings tending to raise contention or occasion breach of unity among Brethren, or that have not first had the perusal and approbation of the Friends appointed by the Yearly Meeting for that purpose.

And in 1722, two years after JW's birth, PYM adopted a resolution "that what writings are approved of by the overseers of the Press for printing, shall be done at the charge of this meeting." This, then, until 1771, was the Quaker governance regarding the "Press" during JW's mature years as an author, an author whose first vocation was to write on behalf of Truth against slavery.

But governance never operates in a vacuum; it can only be administered through the agency of governors. In 1746, when JW wrote his first major work, "Some Considerations on the Keeping of Negroes" (Text 1), it was the slave-owning Friends who ruled in the Overseers of the Press and so JW withheld his work from their review. In the early 1750s, however, more and more of those governors were departing their offices and being replaced, during the time of Israel Pemberton's leadership of PYM, by reformers who reflected PYM's growing condemnation of the evil practice. With the PYM appointment of six new Overseers in 1752, Quaker abolitionists and reformers came into the ascendancy, and, after years of patient waiting, JW was at last able to present his first major essay to the Overseers, receive their approval, and have it published in 1754. And there were eight more new Overseers—including James and John Pemberton and John Woolman—appointed by PYM in 1756.

The Overseers who came to the fore during this critical change in the governing control in PYM, were a unique company of weighty Quakers. They included merchant princes of Philadelphia, leaders in the provincial government, civic philanthropists, writers and educators, traveling

---

[51] *Ibid.*

ministers and preachers.[52] Together they formed a circle of influence, and increasingly of reform, that reached not only into the leadership of PYM but into the consciousness of American and British Quakerism. For JW, who became an Overseer in 1756, many of these men remained, throughout his ministry, intimate colleagues and confidants, advisers and companions, in the wider world beyond Rancocas, Mount Holly, and Burlington.

In 1771, upon the recommendation of PYM, the supervision of publications was transferred from the Overseers of the Press to the Meeting for Sufferings of Philadelphia Yearly Meeting, a body PYM had created in 1756 to serve those distressed in times of oppression and war. It was this body that approved JW's "1772 Epistle to the Quarterly and Monthly Meetings of Friends" (Text 13). Curiously, in 1770, the year before the Meeting for Sufferings assumed the role of the Overseers of the Press, JW's "Considerations on the True Harmony of Mankind" (Text 11) was first published after having been read in the Meeting for Sufferings.[53]

(2) Woolman's submissions to the Overseers of the Press

From the beginning of his career as an author, JW was scrupulous in having his essays officially reviewed by the Overseers. As the record shows, he sought and received the Overseers' approval for "Some Considerations on the Keeping of Negroes" (Text 1), "Considerations on Keeping Negroes: Part Second" (Text 5) and "Considerations on Pure Wisdom and Human Policy &c" (Text 8). He sought but failed to receive such approval for "Serious Considerations on Trade" (Text 9), and as a result withheld that work from publication. There is no record that he either submitted "A Word of Remembrance & Caution to the Rich &c" (Text 6) for approval or offered the work for publication in his lifetime.

---

[52] See Jean R. Soderlund, *Quakers & Slavery: A Divided Spirit* (Princeton, NJ: Princeton University Press, 1985), pp. 194-99.

[53] Gummere, p. 438.

Appendix Text 1

The Epistle of 1756 from PYM to Long Island Yearly Meeting

Editor's Introduction

After ten years of officially assisting others in their appointments as principal authors of the annual PYM epistles to the several American Quaker yearly meetings, Woolman here takes on the authorial responsibility of such an epistle for the first time. He was well prepared for this work not only by his prior appointments as assistant but also by having traveled during the 5th and 6th months of 1756 into Long Island and there attending many meetings, including the yearly meeting at Flushing. He wrote of that mission in the *Journal* thus:

> My mind was deeply engaged in this visit, both in public and private; and at several places where I was, on observing that they had slaves, I found myself under a necessity in a friendly way to labor with them on that subject, expressing as way opened the inconsistency of that practice with the purity of the Christian religion and the ill effects it manifested among us.[1]

In writing this pastoral epistle—which omits reference to the evil of that enslavement he had recently seen on Long Island and alludes instead to the "sorrow and calamity" of war and to the difficulties of maintaining the discipline of the church, being other issues of the day—Woolman was assisted by his fellow minister John Scarborough (1704-1769) whom, in a later year, he would join on visits to slave-owning Friends elsewhere. The text is modernized from the MS of this document held at HC.[2]

+++

Text

From our yearly meeting held at Burlington by adjournments from the 16th of the 9th month to the 24th of the same inclusive 1756, to our friends and brethren at their next yearly meeting at Flushing on Long Island.

---

[1] *Journal*, p. 52.
[2] In Box 46, PYM Miscellaneous Records, Document #13 of 1756, HC Call # D 2.5 (1754-1759).

1   Dear Friends: In a degree of pure love, which through the continued mercies of God have at this time been renewed in the hearts of the humble, we salute you. Though the voice of his righteous judgments were louder and louder and scenes of sorrow and calamity appear to be increasing, yet in deep reverence we acknowledge as that which we in some measure learned, that the meek in spirit find an inward support on which alone we desire to rely, that in all times of trial we may in patience possess our souls. Your epistle of the present year was here read, and we freely continue our correspondence defining that lively evidence of cementing love and sympathy with each other in the manifold difficulties attending a Christian perseverance which would enable us mutually to communicate matters tending to strengthen each other therein.

2   By accounts from our several Quarterly Meetings we are informed that love and unity are preserved in a good degree among us, our meetings for worship and discipline kept up and in general pretty well attended, and a mighty concern rests on the minds of many by which they are laboriously engaged that in the pure wisdom of Truth our discipline may be supported.

3   And, dear friends, feeling the necessity of being inwardly turned from that friendship which is of the world in order to be the friends of Christ Jesus, in clearness to distinguish those things which pertain to his sanctified and peaceable flock from those which do not, our desires are that we may all join impartially to try our foundations, lest by too strong a desire after the things of this life we be insensibly drawn from that happy station where the faithful find refuge in affliction, for although on the upright in heart who dwell in humility the signature of the everlasting covenant of peace becomes imprinted, yet where there is a secret reservation in following the guidance of that unction which leads from the ways and spirits and love of the world, the hands waxing feeble and the ears dull of hearing and the clothing of heavenly fortitude not being experienced, there is then not only a turning from the Rock of the Righteous but an additional weight of trouble brought on those who through deep and painful labor feel their minds engaged, that God's testimony according to the pure nature of it may be supported in this declining age.

In gospel love we remain your friends and brethren.

Appendix Text 2

The Epistle of 1757 from PYM to Virginia Yearly Meeting

Editor's Introduction

In the 5ᵗʰ and 6ᵗʰ months of this year Woolman made his second mission into Maryland, Virginia, and North Carolina. He journeyed without a ministerial colleague, although he had the companionship of his businessman brother Uriah until reaching North Carolina where they parted. While in Virginia, Woolman attended the yearly meeting.[1] As in the 1756 Epistle to Long Island this gentle letter does not reflect the anguish of spirit Woolman experienced in witnessing the plight of enslaved humanity in the South; rather it dwells on mutual concerns over wartime suffering and the condition of the church.

In writing this epistle Woolman was assisted by Aaron Ashbridge (1712-1776), a Chester County farmer who served as Justice of the Peace between 1749 and 1757, in which year a complaint was brought against him in the Governor's Council for both refusing to attest recruits brought before him for militia service and discouraging men to take on such service.[2] The text is modernized from the MS held at HC.[3]

+++
Text

From our yearly meeting held at Philadelphia for Pennsylvania and New Jersey by adjournments from the 17ᵗʰ day of the 9ᵗʰ month to the 24ᵗʰ of the same inclusive 1757

To Friends at their next yearly meeting for the Province of Virginia

---

[1] *Journal*, p. 70.
[2] Gummere, p. 585.
[3] In Box 46, PYM Miscellaneous Records, Document #16 of 1757, HC Call # D 2.5 (1754-1759).

Dear Friends:

1   We salute you in brotherly love and hereby inform you that our meeting has been large and through divine favor made comfortable and edifying. Your epistle of the present year was now read and we are glad to hear that a faithful remnant are in care for the cause of Truth and should rejoice if that concern were become more general among us as a people everywhere, being a cause most weighty and worthy to be cared for.

2   We understand by accounts from our several Quarterly Meetings that a good degree of love and unity subsists among us, our meetings for worship and discipline kept up and pretty well attended, and many are concerned to labor honestly that our Christian testimony in all its branches may be supported agreeable to the intent and design thereof.

3   We find by the Minutes of the proceedings of our Meeting for Sufferings now laid before us that sundry suffering cases have occurred, and, among others, several families of our Friends reduced to straits (occasioned by the calamitous circumstances of the frontiers) whose necessities have been ministered unto.

4   We are heartily glad that some of your young men were freely given up to endure affliction for the sake of that noble testimony which we are called to bear against wars and fightings, and trust it will be their joy and rejoicing that they were accounted worthy so to suffer. And as it is evident that the faithful suffering for the Truth has ever had a tendency to promote the work of God in the earth, it would be agreeable to us as proposed by you to have a brief narrative of their sufferings and others of the like nature and if such happen sent with your next epistle, or at such other time as you may find most convenient, to our Meeting for Sufferings. Yet we desire you may not thereby be induced to decline from your usual practice of sending an account of your Meeting for Sufferings to the Yearly Meeting of London.

5   And, dear friends, finding by experience that deeply attending to the pure divine principle in the mind is the only way to be qualified to stand firm in the day of trial, we are truly desirous that you and we may enough consider it and wait to know that in us mortified, which would lead to things which the great master does not own, having learned that whenever we too much consult our own ease and convenience and thereby shun the cross of Christ we add to our difficulties, and distrust and

doubtings come upon us, but in the humble resignation of our minds to the divine, wise refuge is found in the day of trouble.

6   We most affectionately sympathize with you in regard to the small number of the faithful as mentioned in your epistle, yet as it is not by the greatness of numbers only that the work of God is carried on in the earth, but by humbly standing in his counsel, we hope the upright among you may not be discouraged. That which supported Enoch to walk with God [Gen. 5:22,24] among a declining people, and fortified Noah to hold fast his integrity in opposition to the stream of customs in an age when "the earth was filled with violence and all flesh had corrupted their way" [Gen. 6:11,12], the same everlasting arm is now as near and as strong to uphold those who really trust in [the Lord] through all their deep trials and baptisms.

We conclude in true love your Friends and Brethren

Appendix Text 3

The Epistle of 1758 from PYM to North Carolina Yearly Meeting

Editor's Introduction

Here Woolman is writing to Quakers whom he had visited in their several monthly meetings during his southern missionary journeys of 1746 and 1757. In this epistle he was assisted by Samuel Smith (1720-1776), his close friend and contemporary, who prospered in both Burlington and Philadelphia as a merchant trader and also distinguished himself as the historian of colonial New Jersey. The text is modernized from the MS held at HC.[1]

+++

Text

From our Yearly Meeting

To Friends and Brethren at their next Yearly Meeting in North Carolina

Dear Friends

1   We salute you in true love and hereby inform you that our meeting has been large and through the great goodness of God the upright-hearted have been comforted. It appears that our meetings for worship and discipline are kept up, and that many are careful steadily to attend and that a weighty concern rests on minds to put our discipline in practice.

2   Your epistle of the last year was read in this our meeting. We are glad to hear that you were favored with the blessings of divine love and fervently desire that all of us may unfeignedly turn unto our heavenly Father who in infinite mercy has not utterly rejected us. He deals with us in mercies and in judgments that we may be weaned from perishing treasures and thoroughly devoted to his work here on earth. And how necessary it is that we attend to his visitations and diligently perform what he requires of us, though contrary to the will and wisdom of the creature.

---

[1] In Box 46, PYM Miscellaneous Records, Document #18 of 1758, HC Call # D 2.5 (1754-1759).

To follow the moving of his Spirit leads to a stability and peace otherwise unattainable. Nor was this desirable situation ever more precious to mankind in any past ages than it is to the upright-hearted at this present time, and in some fresh experience of it we most affectionately desire that the very least in the family may be encouraged and strengthened and in true humility may stand steady in every trial.

3   Though such who live in the pure life, separated to the gospel of Christ may be few in number, mistreated here and there on the earth, yet the Lord our God is mighty and such who trust in him with all their hearts, do and will find him a strong tower in the sharpest conflicts and a sufficient helper under all difficulties.

With brotherly love we remain your friends

Appendix Text 4

The Epistle of 1760 from PYM to Rhode Island Yearly Meeting

Editor's Introduction

In the 4th to 8th months of 1760 Woolman made his second missionary journey into New England. He attended the Rhode Island Yearly Meeting at Newport where he felt "bowedness of spirit" because of the extensive Quaker involvement in the slave trade there, an exercise upon which he reflected in his *Journal*.[1] His ministerial traveling companion was Samuel Eastburn (1702-1785) of Bucks County, a fellow opponent of war taxes.

Assisting in the preparation of this epistle was Isaac Andrews (nd-1775), Woolman's ministerial companion on the first mission to the South made in 1746. The text is modernized from the MS held at HC.[2]

+++

Text

From our yearly meeting at Burlington held by adjournments from the[3]

Dear Friends:

1   We salute you in true love and hereby inform you that this meeting has been large and comfortable and by reports from our several Quarterly Meetings it appears that Friends in general are preserved in a good degree of love and unity and many Friends are laboriously exercised to maintain that Christian testimony the Lord has given us to bear.

2   Your epistle of the present year was read in this meeting. We are glad to hear that there is a lively concern on many of your minds for the cause of Truth and it is our sincere desire that this heavenly work may more and more spread among us, that our habitation being in meekness and humility we may know the Lord to be our refuge and fortress in every

---

[1] *Journal*, pp. 108-12.
[2] In Box 47, PYM Miscellaneous Records, Document #12 of 1760, HC Call # D 3.1 (1760-1765).
[3] [JW did not complete this sentence in his draft, presumably leaving it to the scrivener of the official document to insert the dates of the commencement and conclusion of the meeting.]

trial and have our minds drawn from a dependence on help from the powers of this world. In ceasing from the imaginations of our hearts and singly trusting the almighty we feel the treasures of the divine life opened and the powerful effects of his voice who says now, as formerly, behold, I make all things new [Rev. 21:5]. In this new and heavenly life walking in self-denial and resignation we experience our Redeemer to bring us from that state which is polluted and feelingly understand that there is a rest prepared for the people of God.

3   And, dear friends, as the Lord our God has been gracious in his visitation to us may we prize the day of our mercies and manifest our love and gratitude to him and our regard to the real good of the succeeding generations that as we frequently mention the example of our predecessors in instances of self-denial when following the pure openings of Truth they parted from outward conveniences of life and were despised of the world, so we in the greatest difficulties attending in our several conditions may manifest to our children and succeeding generations that our outward interests and things of this world we have freely given up when the cause of Truth requires it.

4   May we weightily consider the changes and uncertainties of this life, the dangerous tendency of a desire to outward wealth and greatness and that for our children to be the children of the Lord walking before him in the plainness and simplicity of the gospel is their true promotion, their greatest riches and a situation above all others to be desired.

In true love we remain your friends.

Appendix Text 5

The Epistle of 1761 from PYM to Rhode Island Yearly Meeting

Editor's Introduction

Woolman, together with his fellow minister Samuel Eastburn, had travelled in Rhode Island the previous year and later the same year had written the epistle to the yearly meeting. In writing this epistle, the MS of which is held by HC,[1] Woolman was assisted by Eastburn.

+++
Text

From our Yearly Meeting held at Philadelphia for Pennsylvania and New Jersey from the 26th of the nine month to the 30th of the same inclusive 1761.

To our Friends and Brethren at their next Yearly Meeting at Rhode Island.

Dear Friends and Brethren,

1   We salute you in the love of our heavenly Father whose kindness we gratefully acknowledge has been manifested to the sincere-hearted in several sittings of this meeting. Though the spirit of this world too much prevails with many under our name, yet a lively concern and engagement remains to support our Christian testimony in the several branches of it. And we have the comfortable prospect of many of our youth being rightly sensible of the importance thereof and zealously concerned to maintain it on its primitive foundation.

2   Your epistle of the present year was now read, and in true brotherly love we are concerned to continue our correspondence, sincerely desiring that we and you may improve every opportunity of divine favor to our lasting advantage. That as our Lord Jesus Christ said to his followers, "I have called you out of the world" [John 15:19]; and is graciously pleased by his Spirit to continue this call to us, let a sense of the dangers which

---

[1]   In Box 47, PYM Miscellaneous Records, Document #14 of 1761, HC Call # D 3.1 (1760-1765).

attend us in this life be deeply impressed on our minds, and engage us carefully to consider the greatness of this favor, and to attend to his heavenly language, that being clothed with his wisdom we may be supported to stand steadfast in his cause whatever difficulties we may meet with. Thus in the exercise of our several gifts and by the spirit of our conduct we may labor to draw the minds of others toward that inward heavenly life in which alone is true safety and felicity. "The Lord is my portion" [Lam. 3:24], was the language of one formerly, and some in this age who have tasted a variety of the things of this life, have had experience of those outward pleasures which their minds naturally inclined to, and through the long sufferings of our gracious God have passed through sundry dispensations can testify, that to be properly weaned from the love of things outward and gratefully and contentedly to accept of that use of the creatures which the Creator intended for them and to have our love settled on that fountain of felicity in which there is no change nor disappointment, the joys whereof the power of death will not lessen, is of all things most worthy the name of a portion.

3   May the youth be encouraged seriously to consider the snares and dangers which attend a too familiar converse with a libertine people and the sorrowful consequences that frequently follow it, and wisely lay hold on early visitations to devote the flower of youth to the service of our Creator, that standing in the meekness of wisdom they may remain unshaken in times of trial, and choose rather to suffer affliction with the faithful than to decline from the precious testimony, that the fruits of this inward heavenly principle may from age to age be manifested through a people crucified to the world, and the immoveable constancy of those among you now called to the Lord's work incite generations to come to trust in that almighty Being who is a refuge for his people and never fails to help those whose hearts are devoted to him, is the fervent desire of your Friends and Brethren.

Signed on behalf of our said meeting.

Appendix Text 6

The Epistle of 1762 from PYM to Long Island Yearly Meeting

Editor's Introduction

Woolman had most recently visited Friends on Long Island in 1760, outward bound on his second missionary journey to New England. He had been there in 1747 on the first New England mission and again in 1756 when he traveled to Long Island for that yearly meeting. Benjamin Lightfoot assisted in writing this epistle, the MS of which is at HC.[1]

+++

Text

From our Yearly Meeting held at Philadelphia for Pennsylvania and New Jersey by adjournments from the 25ᵗʰ day of the 9ᵗʰ month to the 1ˢᵗ day of 10 month inclusive 1762

To our Friends and Brethren at their next yearly meeting at Flushing on Long Island

Dear Friends

1   In a renewed sense of heavenly kindness we salute you and hereby inform you that your epistle of the present year was read in this meeting and the lively concern you express for the good of the church in general and your laborious endeavors to discourage the practice of slave-keeping in particular is matter of comfort to us. And our sincere desires are, that being rightly redeemed from the spirit of the world and clothed with true charity our labors in the meekness of wisdom in this and every other branch of discipline may search the pure witness in the hearts of such for whose good we are exercised.

---

[1] In Box 47, PYM Miscellaneous Records, Document #13 of 1762, HC Call # D 3.1 (1760-1765).

260

2   By accounts from our several Quarterly Meetings it appears that love and unity in good degree subsists among us. Our meetings are generally kept up, and though some under our profession too little attend to the pure spirit of wisdom and do not come forward in the lively exercise of an inward spiritual life, yet there is a hopeful prospect of youth in some places, and a laborious concern on the hearts of many that the pure testimony of Jesus may be supported according to the true design of it.

3   And dear friends as the Lord who is yet pleading by his righteous judgments does in long suffering and tender mercies preserve from those grievous calamities which are felt in many places, a remnant are bowed in spirit with desires that in all our concerns and business we may live and walk in that Spirit "which breathes peace on earth and good will toward all mankind" [Luke 2:14]. That so the uprightness and weightiness of our conduct may afford examples of deep instruction to our children, tending to wean them from the desire of worldly show and greatness, and to their furtherance in that humble self-denying life so much and so powerfully recommended by our Redeemer.

4   May the youth whose hearts are at times touched with the tendering power of Truth weightily consider that this inward acquaintance with our Lord Jesus Christ is the most precious of all treasure and carefully avoid the ensnaring enticements of such company who are carried away with the vanities of this world. Some who have tasted that the Lord is gracious and felt the humbling operation of his love on their souls, by shunning the cross in small matters and mixing with those of a more unsavory conversation, have been estranged from that peace and sweetness which accompanies true obedience and sorrowfully wandered into a dark disquieted condition. Let the lambs in the flock who have heard and understood the voice of the shepherd prize these days of divine visitation that they may stand in the strength of the Lord and be serviceable in his church when the elders are removed.

5   This our meeting was large and though the faithful witnessed some laborious seasons yet through the extendings of divine kindness the heavenly wing was experienced to be measurably stretched forth under a sense whereof the affairs of the church were transacted in a good degree of brotherly love.

In gospel love we salute you and are your Friends and Brethren

Appendix Text 7

The Epistle of 1763 from PYM to Long Island Yearly Meeting

Editor's Introduction

Woolman wrote this epistle, assisted by his friend and fellow minister John Pemberton, just three months after conducting his mission among the Native Americans at Wyalusing. Concern for the Indians is here carefully expressed in paragraph 2. Pemberton, along with his brother Israel, had accompanied Woolman in the first hours of his perilous journey. Benjamin Parvin "fastened" himself to the mission and stayed with Woolman for the entire journey. This MS is at HC. [1]

+++

Text

From our Yearly Meeting held at Philadelphia for the Provinces of Pennsylvania and New Jersey from the 24th day 9th month to the 30th day inclusive 1763

To Friends at their next Yearly Meeting to be held on Long Island

Dear Friends

1   Your epistle of the present year was received by us in brotherly love in which we are concerned to continue our religious correspondence. This our meeting has been large and we have to acknowledge that the Lord in his tender mercies is yet manifesting himself for our help, a sense whereof bows the hearts of a remnant in awfulness before him, with strong desires that as he is graciously continuing to move in our hearts by his Holy Spirit, we may reverently regard these heavenly instructions thereby communicated, and come forward in a faithful obedience thereto, that our minds being thus leavened with divine love, we may look with compassion over those who are wandering from this heavenly principle, and in meekness and patience labor earnestly for their good as individuals, and for the good of the church in general.

---

[1] In Box 47, Miscellaneous Records, Document #14 of 1763, HC Call # D 3.1 (1760-1765).

2   And, dear friends, may such among us who have plenty of this world's goods so attend to the power of Truth as to be true followers of him who is meek and low of heart, and so apply our treasures to charitable and benevolent purposes that we may truly honor God with our substance, and that those in low circumstances among us, being treated with tenderness, may have less temptation to seek settlement on lands which have not been properly purchased of the natives. The discouraging of our members from selling lands so circumstanced having been the weighty care of friends now assembled.

3   By accounts received from our several Quarterly Meetings it appears that a good degree of love and unity subsists among Friends in general, that our meetings for worship and discipline are kept up, and a care is maintained for the exercise of our Christian discipline.

4   Finally, dear friends, may our attention be so fixed on our Lord Jesus Christ that he being unto us wisdom and righteousness we may be strengthened to go through the service intended for us individually in our several stations and omit nothing in our power which may tend to prepare the minds of the youth to love and serve him when we are removed, that he may be their friend and their comforter in all the troubles attending them in this life and administer an entrance to them in endless felicity when time to them shall be no more.

We salute you with brotherly affection and remain your friends and brethren.

Appendix Text 8

The Epistle of 1764 from PYM to London Yearly Meeting

Editor's Introduction

For every year from 1764 to 1771 Woolman was assigned to the committee writing the annual PYM epistle to London Yearly Meeting, and for three of those years—1764, 1768, and 1770—he was the first named member and, thus, the principal author. Those named to assist him in 1764 were John Churchman (1705-1775), a farmer and Justice of the Peace in Chester County, Pennsylvania, a renowned Quaker minister, missionary, and journalist; Israel Pemberton, Jr., (1715-1779), Philadelphia merchant trader and the 'King of the Quakers,' Woolman's close friend, and the reforming Clerk of PYM from 1750 to 1759; Isaac Child (1734-1769); and Isaac Andrews (nd-1775), Woolman's traveling companion on his first southern mission. The 'tossings and tempests' and the 'trials and difficulties' referred to in paragraph 1 of this epistle included the ongoing problems of abolishing enslavement, securing peace, reforming the church, and, as herein described, the involvement of Quakers in the government of Pennsylvania at a time when the Assembly had requested the King to take control of the province from the Proprietors.

The text is modernized from the fair copy of the epistle recorded in the minutes of PYM for 1764 held at HC.[1]

+++

Text

To our Friends and Brethren at the next Yearly Meeting at London.

Dear Friends:

1 Being now, through the merciful providence of Almighty God, assembled from our several places of abode, the hearts of many among us have been baptized into a feeling of the various entanglements and perils which attend us in this life, and inward cries have been raised that he in whom the fatherless find mercy may forgive us as individuals our

---

[1] PYM Minute Book (1747-1779) pp. 203-05, HC Call # A 1.3. Also available on film at HC and SC.

trespasses and preserve us from the cunningly devised snares of the enemy. Under this exercise the Lord our Redeemer who laid down his life for us has in some of our sittings together graciously condescended in the subjecting our wills to renew our hopes in him that amid the manifold tossings and tempests we may be conducted safely to that rest which he has prepared for them who are truly his people. And an earnest engagement is revived in the minds of many to pass the time of our sojourning in fear, and to feel after his help from day to day. As the trials and difficulties which the sincere-hearted meet with tend to loosen their minds from the friendships which are not on the true foundation, and to beget longings to be wholly redeemed from self-will in all its workings, that Christ the Prince of Peace may have the whole government of them, so these dispensations though least agreeable to nature are made the most profitable blessing to those who patiently continue under them. And in feeling the sanctifying power of Christ, preparing our hearts to serve him faithfully we are made to rejoice in him our Redeemer though he proves us in the furnace of adversity.

2   Your printed and written Epistles of the present year, and your last Epistle to our Meeting for Sufferings, were read to our help and encouragement. The true brotherly sympathy which you manifest towards us is very comfortable, and we doubt not the continuance thereof in every respect as the pure Truth opens your way therein. The hearts of many among us are deeply bowed with fervent desires that in the present commotions and stirrings there may be an inward gathering to that sure habitation where we may experience that "the Lord is our strength and our fortress, our refuge also in the day of our affliction" [Jer. 16:19].

3   Thus exercised, we have had weightily to consider the present state of our religious society, and been engaged to administer such advice and instruction as in the openings of Truth have appeared necessary.

4   By the minutes of our Meeting for Sufferings we find some account has been given to yours of divers matters which have been and are the occasion of much painful concern to the faithful. The conduct of those of our profession who deviated from our principles by bearing arms in the late commotions in Philadelphia² appear to be under the notice and care of

---

² [A reference to the march on Philadelphia in January, 1764 by the Paxton Boys, estimated to be from 600 to 1500 frontiersmen, mostly Scots-Irish immigrants, identified with the village of Paxton near Harrisburg. They were protesting the failure of the Provincial Assembly to protect their settlements from Indian raids. Some two hundred Philadelphia Quakers took up arms in self-defense before the

Friends there, and after much deliberation thereon we have now been deeply baptized into the suffering state of that Monthly Meeting and hope strength and confirmation will be administered to them to persevere in the discharge of their duty with holy zeal and Christian charity in that spirit of meekness and wisdom you have so affectionately and lovingly recommended.

5   The controversies between the Governor and Assembly of Pennsylvania having issued in a resolution of the Assembly to request the King to take the government into his own hands,[3] some Friends considering this as a matter of a civil nature, from this and other motives which then appeared of weight with them, have without waiting for the united sense of the brethren on this occasion, signed some of these petitions addressed to the King.

6   This subject has deeply impressed the minds of many at this time, and as our repeated endeavors have not been so effectual as to prevent a considerable number of our profession from accepting of seats in that House of Assembly,[4] we have been desirous every occasion should be avoided of ministering grounds to our adversaries to charge us as a body with a connection with them. And this proceeding having contrary to the intention of those Friends who signed the petitions been interpreted in that manner, we find it necessary to acquaint you that, after deliberate and weighty consideration, this meeting does not find freedom to join therewith, believing it to be most expedient for us in this time of probation, as much as may be, to be still and quiet. But should the measures already taken be likely to bring the matter to issue, we desire you would interpose with your influence for securing our liberties and privileges as Truth may open the way.

---

threat to the capitol was withdrawn. See Jack D. Marietta, *The Reformation of American Quakerism, 1748-1783* (Philadelphia: University of Pennsylvania Press, 1984), pp. 189-92.]
3 [*Ibid.*, pp. 197-201]
4 [*Ibid.*, pp. 195-97]

Appendix Text 9

The Epistle of 1768 from PYM to London Yearly Meeting

Editor's Introduction

Assisting Woolman in writing his second epistle to London YM were Joseph White (1712-1777), a Bucks County, Pennsylvania, minister and missionary; and George Mason.

The text is modernized from the fair copy of the epistle recorded in the minutes of PYM for 1768 held at HC.[1]

+++

Text

From our Yearly Meeting, held at Philadelphia for Pennsylvania and New Jersey, by adjournments from the 24th day of the 9th month 1768 to the 28th of the same inclusive.

To our Friends and Brethren at their next Yearly Meeting in London.

Dear Friends:

1   Under a fresh renewing of the baptizing influence of Truth, of which a remnant have been made partakers together, we at this time affectionately salute you, and have reason to acknowledge, with thankfulness, the deep obligation we are under, by the abundant condescension of our heavenly Father to renew our covenant and walk reverently and circumspectly before him, whose eye penetrates through every covering, and his heart-searching power is trying and will try every foundation, and bring to desolation every false building, until the alone sure rock of ages, the foundation and safety of the righteous, be established and exalted above all, to the enlargement of his spiritual kingdom, and the completion of his gracious purpose, that his dominion shall be from sea to sea, and from the rivers to the ends of the earth.

---

[1] PYM Minute Book (1747-1779) pp. 252-53, HC Call # A 1.3. Also available on film at HC and SC.

2   On reading the Epistles from your last Yearly Meeting, the remembrance of brotherly kindness was sensibly renewed, the advice and counsel therein contained being seasonable and truly edifying, and we freely concur with you in fervently desiring that our correspondence may be accompanied with sensible impressions of divine love.

3   And, dear friends, notwithstanding it is a season wherein we have occasion to bow in thankfulness for the continuance of mercies vouchsafed to us, so on the occasion of the revolt of many by joining with the restless and fluctuating state of the world, it is a time of painful travail of spirit to the sincere in heart, under which a remnant are bowed in humble prostration for the restoration of those who are gone astray, and also on their own account that they may be preserved from falling into the same or any other snare, and that they may endure with patience the furnace of affliction, and pass willingly through the baptisms allotted, in order to qualify them truly for their respective services; and that therein they may act as faithful stewards of the manifold grace of God, and as watchmen upon the walls, discover the approach of the enemy under all his artful disguises and dissembling transformations, and may give timely and faithful warning under the direction of the captain of our salvation, that in the day of inquisition they may be found clear of the blood of all men.

4   May the children of the family who have felt each other in the life, and whose hearts have been circumcised to receive the instructions of our heavenly Father, dwell near him and resignedly accept of the cup he appoints for them.

5   Our blessed Redeemer, when the most pinching time of his sufferings for our sakes approached, endured the grief and has left a pattern of resignation for us, saying: "The cup which my Father has given me, shall I not drink it?" [John 18:11].

6   There are [those] who at times rejoice under his humbling dispensations and are strengthened in a belief that he will purify a people and work through them in repairing the waste places. And O! that we in our respective stations, where the Lord of the harvest has placed us, may stand separated from the world and its spirit, and walk in that real humility where our minds may never be clouded nor our services interrupted by any cares relating to this life which he by his Holy Spirit does not lead into.

7   By the reports from our several Quarters we find a good degree of care subsists for the maintaining love and unity, and the exercise of our Christian discipline, and our Meeting has at this time been large and the manifestation of divine favor therein graciously continued to us, under a sense of which the affairs of Truth have been transacted with much brotherly love, and we now in the fellowship of the gospel, remain

Your Friends and Brethren

Signed on behalf and by appointment

of the Yearly Meeting   By James Pemberton Clerk to the
Meeting this year

Appendix Text 10

The Epistle of 1770 from PYM to London Yearly Meeting

Editor's Introduction

It seems appropriate that as Woolman began his service on the PYM epistle-writing committees in 1746 by being the only assistant to Israel Pemberton, Jr. in preparing the epistle to Virginia YM, so in this 1770 epistle to London YM Woolman ends his authorial responsibilities with the sole assistance of Pemberton. They have come full circle through their shared reforming issues together. The epistle's concern for both the aged and the youth of the Church now appears prophetic.

The text is modernized from the fair copy of the Epistle recorded in the minutes of PYM for 1770 held at HC.[1]

+++

Text

From our Yearly Meeting held in Philadelphia for Pennsylvania and New Jersey, by adjournments from the 22nd day of the 9th month 1770 to the 28th of the same inclusive.

To our Friends and Brethren at their next Yearly Meeting in London.

Beloved Friends,

1   Your printed and written Epistle were read in this Meeting, attended with a concern in some of our minds that the purity of life in them pointed out, may be carefully and earnestly labored after by us.

2   As the piously concerned from various parts meeting together, and in reverent attention to him who has laid his yoke upon them, do in simplicity and godly sincerity, open that feeling he has given them of the state of our religious society, it tends to strengthen individuals under those burdens they frequently bear in their more retired habitations, so one branch of the Church thus assembled, communicating their feeling to their

---

[1] PYM Minute Book (1747-1779) pp. 272-73, HC Call # A 1.3. Also available on film at HC and SC.

brethren in other parts we find by experience does frequently contribute to the same end, and to confirm our desires that in all these communications the counsel of him who teaches us to profit, and leads in the way that we should go, may be reverently attended to.

3   Through the gracious continuation of heavenly regard, a living exercise remains among us, that we as a people may feel the heavenly instructor near us, and know the pure separated from the vile in our own minds, not only in our Meetings for Solemn Worship, but also in those for supporting the testimony of Truth, and there is a salutation of pure love to that seed which the Lord has blessed among you, with desires that we may all be preserved in true humility before him, and in the leadings of his Spirit find our way opened through the various difficulties that may attend us, to labor faithfully in the present age in maintaining that testimony he has given us to bear to a life of righteousness and purity.

4   And as too many under our profession, not being sufficiently baptized into that state where the voice of the Shepherd is clearly understood, do sometimes in the affairs of this life depart from the footsteps of the flock, and increase the trials of those who are sincerely exercised, may our minds be gathered to the inward habitation of safety, where we may feel the mind of Christ, and experience him to put us forth in all our proceedings.

5   A remnant among us being sensible of the weight of that holy calling wherewith we are called, and that where those who are active in discipline do manifestly depart from the Truth as it is in Jesus, their example operates against the pure principle of righteousness, and tends to leaven the minds of others into a disposition to look for rest in that which is distinguishable from perfect purity. May the sense of these things be livingly impressed upon us, that all who have experienced the purifying work of the Holy Spirit, by patiently abiding under it, may not only be preserved from doing anything against the Truth, but know an inward preparation for those services in the Church which the Father of mercies intends for us while we remain in this state of probation.

6   May the aged among us, who have often experienced the refining operation of Truth and the sweetness of an inward sanctification, carefully dwell under that which has helped us, and like fathers lead the younger in that humble exemplary walking wherein there is peace and safety, that while we look toward the day of our outward dissolution and are waiting till our change come, the purified state of our minds may have a savor of

life in it and ardent desires for the prosperity of Zion evidently accompanying our declining age.

7   May the minds of the youth be turned towards him who has preserved many from the enticements and snares of the enemy and whose tender mercies are yet extended, that many more may become the children of his family. And may your hearts, dear youth, be humbled before him, that you may often seek for that precious situation where prayer in true resignation of soul ascends to his throne, and amid the various temptations in this life you may feel the seasoning virtue of Truth to preserve you chaste before him and prepare you for precious services in the Church.

8   The minutes of our Meeting for Sufferings for the last year have now been communicated to us and tended to excite in many of our minds near sympathy with them in the laborious exercise, which in these times of difficulty they are necessarily subjected to, in the faithful discharge of their duty. The services of that Meeting appear to be more extensive than were generally expected at the first institution thereof, and as their correspondence with your Meeting for Sufferings has been maintained to mutual edification and satisfaction, we desire it may continue, that thereby such of the affairs of Truth, as may render a mutual communication to each other necessary, when it would not be expedient to wait for the time of our annual meetings, may be duly attended to.

9   The accounts now given us of the circumstances of Friends, and the affairs of Truth in our several Quarters, and the Epistles from all the other Provinces, tend to confirm our faith and hope that, notwithstanding many sorrowful instances appear of a declension from the simplicity and integrity of our ancestors, a godly care and concern is maintained by a considerable number of Friends in most places, that our Christian discipline may be supported, and that our conversation and conduct may evince to the world the excellency of the divine principle we profess to follow.

10   This Meeting has been attended by a greater number of Friends than usual, many of whom though young in years appear to have a living concern for the prosperity of Truth, and we humbly trust that the gracious manifestations of divine regard with which we have been favored will tend to strengthen, establish and settle them in these pious desires which have been raised in their minds, to fill up the vacant places of divers worthy

Friends lately removed from among us by death, who were bright and shining lights, and whose memory is precious to us.

11   That love which is the bond of our Christian fellowship, having presided in our solemn deliberations on divers weighty affairs, we have abundant cause to acknowledge with thankfulness the continuation of divine goodness, and in the sense thereof we salute you with true affection, being in the nearest relation

Your Friends and Brethren

Signed on behalf and by appointment

of the Yearly Meeting   James Pemberton Clerk this year

Appendix 3

John Woolman's memorial concerning his brother Abner addressed to the Meeting for Sufferings at Philadelphia

Written by 1772; not printed

Editor's Introduction

Eleven months and three days before his own death on 7 October 1772 in York, England, far from family and home, John Woolman sat at the bedside and recorded the death of his brother Abner, the third of the seven Woolman brothers, John being the first. Abner was forty-seven years old as of the previous 20 July and the father of a daughter and four sons (one of whom had died in infancy, another of whom the journalist addressed as "John Woolman, Junr"[1]). Abner lived in Mansfield, West Jersey, about twelve miles northeast of the family seat in Rancocas and about nine miles north-northeast of John's home in Mount Holly.

By his own account, Abner had suffered illness and pain for a number of years,[2] and in the final months of his life he was confined first to his home and then to his bed. As John recorded:[3] "I was sundry times with him within the last three months of his time. . ." In these visits John heard Abner's desires to have his writing concerning the West Indies trade (Part III hereafter) circulated among Friends at Wilmington and to have kept in circulation among Friends at the Burlington Monthly Meeting another of his writings (Part II hereafter). John felt that these desires laid on him a trust, and "with some exercise of mind" he sent, under his own transmittal letter (Part I hereafter) which was simply dated "1772," to the Meeting for Sufferings in Philadelphia for their consideration, those two documents as well as a third (Appendix Text 11 herein), addressed to "My dear children," which John captioned "Some writings left by Abner Woolman."

Concerning the writings addressed to Abner's children, John wrote in his transmittal letter to the Meeting for Sufferings:

---

[1]   See Introduction, p. xxvii herein.
[2]   Appendix Text 11, chaps. I, VII, XXIX, XXX, XXXIII, XLII.
[3]   Appendix Text 11, after chap. XLII.

[I] have also collected the substance of sundry short chapters, part from a stitched book, and part from loose papers which I found in said book, and propose to send them herewith.[4]

In gathering together these various writings to Abner's children during a time of their grieving as well as his own, it undoubtedly was necessary for John to impose some order and structure upon the contents of the "stitched book" and "loose papers." It also seems likely John would have, with an intentional sensitivity, prepared them as a testament of the spiritual legacy from a devoted father to his children and as a memorial worthy of presentation to the Meeting for Sufferings.

John certainly shaped Abner's testament to his children. There are even some signs and indications that the testament was in considerable measure John's own work. What form the shaping took and the measure of John's actual contribution cannot now be precisely fixed, but the entire record indicates that John was revealing much of his own inner being in these chapters.

Both in the *Journal* and in his general writings John was a very private person in family matters. He only referred by name in the *Journal* to his father, his wife, his eldest sister, and two paternal aunts, and each of them he named only once, except for his sister Elizabeth Woolman, Jr., whose name appears three times. The names of his mother, his daughter and his son, his other five sisters, and his six brothers do not appear. Only one brother is even mentioned by reference in the text, the reference being to the companion whom John scrupled whether to take with him on the second southern journey. That brother, Uriah, who at the time was a Philadelphia businessman, was going because of "outward affairs" unrelated to John's inward exercise concerning the enslavement issue.

Notwithstanding this tender protection of personal and family privacy, it is evident that John had a close and ongoing relationship with his family, and in the case of all his brothers the closeness is demonstrable in the running accounts he kept with each of them in his business records. Both *Ledger B 1753* and *Account Book 1769* show John schooling some of their children, making their clothes, and selling them both merchandise from his shop and trees from his orchard.

Regarding Abner, the record suggests that he and John had an extraordinary closeness. There was the matter of the real estate that John inherited from Eber, his youngest brother (the inheritance resulting from Eber's death during minority), that Eber in turn had received under their father's Will in which Abner was not even named. To rectify what John

---

[4] Part I.

must have perceived to be a wrong, he negotiated with his other brothers—Asher, Jonah, Uriah, and Abraham—to consent to the release to Abner of the real estate interest that John by law was to receive from Eber; and with their verbal consents John then drafted the written legal agreement, which the brothers executed.

Also marking their closeness, John schooled and boarded in his own home both Abner's son John in 1767 and Abner's daughter Sarah in 1768 and 1769. John even suggested in his ledger that some credit toward Abner's expenses for tuition and boarding was given for "Jonathan's work about [the premises]." Further testimony to John's affectionate regard for Abner is the following letter:

Dear Brother

I have remembered (since I left home) thee and thy family very often with much warmness of love.

We are at Newport and expect to go for Nantucket soon, if way open. We have been fellow feelers with the afflicted, nor is any affliction too great to endure for the Truth. This I own, and am labouring daily to be found in that resignation.

I am pinched for time, but wanted to let thee know I often thought of you.

John Woolman

da. mo.

17 6   1760   For Abner Woolman

As shown in the testament to Abner's children, Abner had large concerns on the issues of slavery, Native Americans, and alcoholism, concerns shared with John and on which John had written frequently and eloquently. As well as being brothers, it may also be that the two were soul mates, sharing feelings for all those who are afflicted, knowing the personal surrender and sacrifice necessary in the cause of Truth. John undoubtedly was an inspiration and role-model for Abner as he labored in the active ministry among Friends. And Abner would have modeled for John a quiet dignity and spiritual fortitude both during years of poor health and finally as he approached death and the end of earthly life.

This testament is akin to a confession as well as to the wisdom literature and psalms of personal lament in the Bible. The testament is artfully composed by one of mature thought and expression. Yet when it is compared with the style and content of Abner's two known works (see Parts II and III), the question naturally arises whether the testament is from the same author's hand.

Giving weight to that question is the meaning of the phrase found in Chapter XXXIX of the testament, which John has highlighted with separated underscore marks and has noted in the margin as "Abner's own words": *the approaching danger and calamities which threaten these neighboring provinces*. The certain implication of John's marginal note must be that not all the words in the testament are Abner's own. And if not Abner's, then most certainly they are the words of John.

The Memorial to the Meeting for Sufferings at Philadelphia is divided into four parts. Each part was written by John, who states in Part I that the original papers in Abner's handwriting "I have by me and am free to send. . ." The text has been modernized based upon John's holographs which are held at HC (PYM-Meeting for Sufferings Miscellaneous Papers [1766-1773], folder 1772 Item 15a, Call # B.5.1).

- **Part I**: John Woolman's letter to the Meeting for Sufferings transmitting his memorial concerning Abner Woolman
- **Part II**: Abner's letter to members of the Burlington Monthly Meeting regarding slavery
- **Part III**: Abner's essay on the West Indies trade
- **Part IV**: [For the testament to Abner's children (Chaps. I to XLII), and John's endnote on Abner's death, see **Appendix Text 11**: **The testament to Abner Woolman's children**]

[Part I: John's transmittal letter]

To the Meeting for Sufferings to be held at Philadelphia:

Beloved friends –

About three months before the decease of my brother Abner he expressed in my hearing a desire that a piece he had written concerning trading to the West Indies might be handed about among Friends at Wilmington. And near his departure, having had a particular desire to speak to me, he then told me that he felt a desire that a piece he had written directed to the active members of Burlington Monthly Meeting, which he had handed about to a considerable number, might be continued to be handed about among Friends of said meeting.

This trust thus laid on me has been attended with some exercise of mind, under which I have believed it best for me to offer the said pieces to the consideration of the Meeting for Sufferings; and have also collected the substance of sundry short chapters, part from a stitched book, and part from loose papers which I found in said book, and propose to send them herewith.

The original papers in his handwriting I have by me and am free to send, or bring them, if the Meeting for Sufferings desire it.

From your loving friend John Woolman

1772

[Part II: Abner's letter to Burlington Monthly Meeting]

To the active members of Burlington Monthly Meeting, Dear Friends, the unhappy case of the slaves for some years at times has been livingly on my mind, and were the weight of their sufferings laid upon us, were we fully acquainted with all the painful thoughts connected with slavery, saw our minority spent without being acquainted with the scripture, that at full age we felt ourselves in a state of slavery, and knew of no crime we had committed, or agreement made by us that were the cause of it, nor could our masters give us any satisfactory reason why they kept us as slaves, that we saw people in general take but little notice of us, and when we heard of any pleading for our liberty, they were often advised not to carry it too far, that the law is such as makes it difficult to set the Negroes free, that when we incline to marry, we consider slavery entailed on our offspring, that from year to year we observed the family we labored for were often paying visits to their friends, and their friends returning visits to them, and we as inferiors commanded to wait upon them, that in sickness we had nobody to call upon, but those who considered themselves as our superiors, and sometimes felt ourselves suffering for want of careful tender nursing, that some of us had not been permitted to live with our wives and children, and now in the decline of life, saw them in a helpless condition, heard their complaints but were not able to relieve them, from one year to another find our appetite and strength to fail, and have nothing at command to help ourselves with, at length through age and weakness become unable to labor, and considered by those who have the care of us, as a charge to their estates, and feel the warmth of nature very much to abate, yet in cold winter nights are obliged to lie by ourselves, often feel chilly, and thinking on our own unhappy condition, joined with that of our children, desire to sleep but cannot, were we sensibly to pass through all this, then the case of slaves I believe to many of us, would appear very different from what it now does.

Last Spring was three years a sorrowful exercise came upon me, which continued some months, small intervals excepted, concerning slaves and those who keep them. In the forepart of this exercise, it opened in my mind that there were estates in the Jerseys and Pennsylvania that were advanced by slaves, but the scales were now on a turn, that in future those in these two Provinces who keep them with a desire of profit and ease, in general would be disappointed and pass through great difficulties which otherwise they might have been clear of. In the latter part of this exercise I became settled in my mind, that if those whose estates were advanced by the labor of slaves would give up freely to have the case examined and equity put in practice and continue in that mind, it would be pleasing to Providence and add to their happiness even in this life. Now my beloved Friends, I am more and more settled in a belief that the Lord is acquainted with all our ways, and is of purer eyes than to behold iniquity with the least degree of approbation, that at this present time there are Negroes among us who have monies justly due to them from members of our monthly meeting, and I feel a tender desire that we may unite together in Christian love and weightily consider whether it is not needful that their case should be examined to the bottom without partiality or respect of person, in order that justice may be done to those who as slaves have labored among us.

From your loving Friend   Abner Woolman   9th month 1770

[Part III: Abner's essay on the West Indies trade]

It has sometimes come in my mind that the great trade which the Americans have to the Sugar Islands has not been fully considered even by men who are desirous to live clear from any connection with oppression. The produce which we send there is chiefly flour and pork and in raising and gathering of this how often do we see creatures and some times men oppressed. The return which we have is chiefly rum, sugar and molasses and it often has been as a query in my mind: Is rum as it is used by us of any real service to the inhabitants of America? How often do we see people deprived of their reason by drinking too freely of it and many have so far given way to it that it has been the cause of their own and their families poverty and that which is more dreadful it unfits the soul for that glorious kingdom prepared for the righteous from the foundation of the world. We may further consider that the return which we have from these islands is chiefly the labor of slaves, that those slaves are often oppressed and through oppression they have been vexed and raised in opposition to the white people. After those slaves have been subdued some of them by the white people have been burned to death, others hung up in irons till they have starved to death. All this barbarity and a great deal more is done to a people who were placed in a part of the world not in a condition able to disturb us but the English nation has by force boldly taken these people from their native land, from all their dearest enjoyments, and used them as above expressed.

Now the cry of David comes before me *Search me, O God*. And is not a deep impartial search needful for every one of us. *Search me, O God* and give me to understand and obey that which is right. Do I stand clear from any connection with the above oppression or has my example in trading with those oppressors made their hearts more hard and is some means of having the oppression of the oppressed continued.

The blessings which Providence has bestowed upon the children of men are numberless. If we look on the face of the earth we may see great variety of pleasant healthful fruits and the innumerable sorts of plants and herbs which in the beginning the great Creator of the whole universe desired man in a state of innocency should subsist on. But alas, by giving way to selfish desires, how is he degenerated and alienated from his Maker and in this dark fallen state what vast havoc does he make with the Creation? What numberless number of animals are oppressed and destroyed by man, and how often do men oppress and afflict each other? O my soul, think on the above hints, and in deep humility strive daily to experience a returning to your Maker and a living in the same innocency and uprightness which man in the beginning was created in.

There is a Spirit which, if men give way to, will humble and calm the mind, and make man who is frail by nature, content with that which is only useful, and I believe if this Divine Gift is strictly attended to, it will appear and prevail more and more until the oppressed go free, and the voice of the oppressor shall no more be heard in the land.

+++
Text

Appendix Text 11

The testament to Abner Woolman's children

Some writings left by Abner Woolman:

My dear children, the following lines were written in tenderness, and the chief part of them in the night when you, my dear children, were asleep.

Some of you are sensible in some measure of those afflictions which have for a number of years attended me in a state of bodily weakness; and my gracious God was pleased often in the night season to touch my heart with his love, and sometimes matter arose fresh in my mind which I believed it my duty to write, and have found satisfaction in writing it, now a little, and then a little, for whose sake I know not, but am easy to leave it to you as a legacy, and desire that you may read it in the same spirit in which it was written.

Chapter I I believe it may be useful to make some mention of the dealing of the Lord with me in my youth who often reproved me for sin and folly, and caused me to walk mournfully when as yet I knew not what it was which thus affected my mind; but after some time I became more acquainted with his ways, which were pleasant, and I was made willing to forsake the pleasures of sin for the sake of his favor, which to me was very precious. And I being then an apprentice was exposed to vain company which was a burden to me, and I often in the evenings was alone in the fields and other places in prayer to God who often favored me with comfortable opportunities. And while I was upon my watch I found peace of mind; but through carelessness I fell from this good state and ran again into folly, which caused me great sorrow. O that all may be careful to watch over the vain desires of their hearts, and be obedient to the voice of God in their hearts, lest they perish in the dark howling wilderness which I in some measure then was in, for I ate my bread with sorrow and often in the night my sleep went from me, and I could take little or no delight in any thing for at times I was ready to despair in my mind of ever obtaining salvation. But day and night I cried to the Lord to look down upon me with an eye of pity, and have mercy on me, or I should perish. And glory be to his great Name he was pleased to be gracious to me and comfort my heart in that needful time.

The above account was written when I was a young man, and now looking over it, it seemed to be a means of bringing former visitations to my remembrance, and in deep humility found my mind engaged to acknowledge that I have often sinned and fallen short of glorifying God as I ought to have done by a holy life and conversation. And he in his great goodness has been pleased to afflict me very sore, yet in judgment he hath remembered mercy, and his kindness to me is beyond expression. 1760.

Chapter II I feel a desire to leave some further hints of the favors and mercies of the Lord toward me, for he is the best master that ever I served, and I am not able to set forth his goodness to his servants to the full. But I entreat you to strive daily to be his faithful servant, and in faithfulness you will be in love with him, and the higher you draw to him the more you will experience of his goodness. He will give that peace and comfort which you will find more precious than any outward enjoyment.

You who are a stranger to him, O come and taste of his goodness! Why will you for a little worldly pleasure miss of that great and lasting salvation which he has appointed for all those who love and serve him.

Chapter III I have been afflicted from a lad upward, leaving my dear father's house, and part of several summers I worked in the pines beyond the inhabitants, helping to build saw mills, often with vain company who were disagreeable to me, which was a trial so deep that I believe I did not mention it to anyone for some years. My heart with comparison was often led with sadness, yet I not being fully subjected to the leadings of Truth, did sometimes endeavor to remove this sadness by mirth.

The ways of the Lord are deep, and he often afflicts the children of men that he may bring them near to him.

O my son! My daughter! While I remember the state I was then in, my heart is open toward you, and I feel desires that you may listen to one who has gained experience through various exercises. In all your troubles and distress seek to feel Truth in your inward parts, and there keep peace; and in prosperity remember your Creator with awfulness, and be obedient to his voice in your soul.

Chapter IV Some things happened the latter part of my apprenticeship, and soon after I was free, which were very afflicting, and which most of my intimate friends are yet strangers to. The Lord alone then knew my distress, and heard my cry when deeply beset, and so hedged about, that had he not had mercy upon me, I had been overwhelmed in total sorrow. And after I was married and had a family, I was so weakly that I could work but a little, and had no outward help, but what I hired, and help being then scarce and dear, I labored under many difficulties, and the world seemed to frown upon me. Then was I overwhelmed with troubles, yet the Lord arose, the floods vanished, and the mountains disappeared, for I can truly say that in my great afflictions, these words did often rise fresh in my mind with joy. I shall yet see your habitation, O Lord! Which I verily believe was a favor to me from the Almighty.

O that you and I may humbly abide under his protection! Then in the most piercing and trying times, when all outward help and comfort does vanish, there will be an anchor to the soul, with a belief that after the miseries of this life are over, we shall enter into everlasting rest.

Chapter V I feel love in my heart to all mankind, and in tenderness entreat after divine love, the enjoyment whereof is our greatest happiness. It is a hidden treasure which the carnal mind knows not of.

O forsake vanity and cleave to the Lord! For this divine sweetness is to be found in inward stillness, in waiting upon the Lord to appear in your heart as a light to enlighten the dark understanding, to give you to see and taste of the glorious riches which he has in store for those who love and serve him.

Chapter VI In the Spring of the year 1760 as I stood near our door, I saw soldiers coming up the road toward our house, at which sight an awe came over me. I felt inwardly weak, but felt earnest desires to be preserved faithful.

Soon after several of them came to our house and wanted to buy cider, but I not feeling freedom to sell nor give them any, they went away, and soon after their captain and doctor came. The captain asked me if I would hire my light wagon to him to go as far as Cranberry, but I endeavored to put him by. Then he asked me if I could read and showed me a press warrant from their commander-in-chief to empower his officers to press wagons and horses to help them on their march. I told him that I looked upon the life of a man to be precious, and could not consistent with my religious principles do anything to forward them on their march. The captain replied, you understand I have power to press; but I had rather have your wagon and horses without pressing, for it may be pressing them will make you angry. I told him I believed it would not, however, I could in no wise consent to hire them, and if he pressed them I could take no pay for them, as it was on a religious principle that I was against his having them.

In the forepart of this discourse the captain appeared warm, but grew more pleasant, and then solid, and said that I differed from all other men that ever he had conversed with, and as from a religious principle I was not easy to help them on their march, it was not easy to him to press my wagon and horses, and so went away on foot without showing any signs of resentment. After they were gone the love of my heavenly Father was sweet to my soul and I was thankful in my heart that I had been preserved in a good degree of faithfulness.

Chapter VII In the 8th month 1760 I went to the seashore partly for my health's sake, and there was taken with a fit of my old disorder, the phthisic,5 which was very afflicting to me, but that which was heaviest of all, was this, I felt destitute as to divine help, and could not feel the Comforter, and my belief and trust in the Almighty were very weak.

I believed that in times past I had looked upon the visible part of the Creation in a degree of the same light and power in which it was made, but now it was hidden from me. I beheld with my outward eyes the raging of the great deep, which I had not seen before, and on the shore I saw great variety of shells curiously fashioned, which with many other things do wonderfully show forth the works of divine providence to the mind under the influence of the Holy Spirit. But without this, things appear almost natural, as they did then to me. In which state I mourned for days together, and yet under this poor mournful condition I felt a concern to visit a certain poor woman who lived near where I made my home, but being under discouragements I did not feel my mind settled to go, till near the time of setting off for home, and the exercise then grew more and more heavy, and as I was inwardly waiting on the Lord for help, this language arose fresh in my mind, *thou knowest not but that for this service thou wast brought here*, then I gave up and went and had a little seasonable opportunity in a religious way which was kindly taken by the woman, and I felt easy in my mind, and so departed without entering into any conversation on temporal things, believing that where we go on business of this nature, much other conversation is hurtful. After this I returned home, and in an inward thankfulness I shed tears of joy, being glad that I was again brought back to my wife and family, and an inward sweetness lay on my mind day after day.

Chapter VIII In a few weeks after the before mentioned journey, I was at our yearly meeting at Burlington part of the time, though weak in body, and the meeting was comfortable to me. And one evening as I was returning from meeting, the love of God was exceeding sweet to my soul. Then I endeavored to ride alone, and now I remembered the adverse state which I passed through at the seashore, and in this sweet frame of spirit it rose fresh in my mind that some of the inhabitants near where I was in that journey were in part in a like condition to that which I passed through among them; but with this odds, that I did not see them mourning for want of God. Then in love to their souls my secret prayer was that they might taste of his goodness, and know him to be a safe hiding place.

Chapter IX For some years past I have been thoughtful about the payment of money which was made sometime before to defray military

---

5 [A progressively wasting or consumptive condition, esp. pulmonary tuberculosis.]

expenses, and in the year 1758 was sinking by a tax, and my exercise was at times very great and I often looked round about, and thought no one's state is like mine, neither did I know who to converse with. I often was alone, endeavoring to have my mind still, and after some time it looked most clear to decline paying the money thus appointed to military uses, and when the officer came to my house to demand it, I told him that I was most easy to decline paying of that tax. And the state I was in the night following is at this time fresh in my mind.

In the evening I was weary and lay down to sleep, and in the night I awoke and thought of the state which Jacob was in, with greater clearness than ever I had before, when he left his father's house and was traveling from his acquaintance and native land, and on the way the God of his fathers appeared to him in a dream which gave him fresh encouragement to trust in the mighty Jehovah, for he awoke and said with awfulness, *surely the Lord is in this place and I knew it not.*[6]

O when men are favored with a sense of his presence! How awful, how dreadful does he appear? What heart is too hard to melt before him? Here I remembered how of old time the law was written on tables of stone, but the substance of the new covenant was now fresh in my mind, that covenant in which the Lord immediately reveals his will in the hearts of his people, and it looked to me then and continues to look so, that the Lord in this our day is calling to some, and in tender love drawing their minds towards him, to leave their acquaintance and kindred which they once took delight in, and follow the leadings of his unerring Spirit in some things which were not opened to our forefathers.

And some whose hearts are touched with the love of God are brought like little Jacob to enter into covenant with him, that if he will be with them and keep them in the way that they go, and give them bread to eat and raiment to put on, then the Lord shall be their God and they will serve him.

Chapter X O Lord, when you hide your face from me, then am I troubled, and fear and anguish beset me.

Be pleased, O Lord, to look down upon me with an eye of pity, and give me rest.

Is it for the sins of my youth that you are pleased to afflict me so very sore?

All your judgments, O Lord, are righteous and your ways exceeding deep. Mercy and loving kindness are your delight, and you do not willingly afflict the children of men.

---

6 [Gen. 28:16]

O Lord, forsake me not, for in you alone is my hope. You have done great things for me; my heart that was like a stone for hardness you have softened and melted into tenderness, and prepared to receive your heavenly instruction.

Weakness and poverty is mine; but strength and fullness is in thee, O God.

Chapter XI The language of Truth as it opened in my heart.

In sickness when your health was taken from you, then you were low in your mind and your greatest desire was to be found in the way of your duty. You then also desired that the Lord might be pleased to restore you to health. Now the Lord has granted you your desires. O remember how you then desired above all the pleasure and delights of this world to be found in the way of your duty! O may this good desire continue with you now in your health! Then may your latter end be happy, and the day of your death more joyful than the day of your birth.

Look upon this as a kind of invitation from heaven and be careful lest you forget the mercies of a merciful God who has waited long to be gracious to you.

Chapter XII I dreamed that I, with one of my brothers, went to a public house, and I, asking him if he would drink some beer, he said no, not at this time. Then I called for a pint of beer, and the woman of the house was displeased because I called for so little. I told her it was enough for one man. There being a company of men, one of them began to talk to me in a scornful way, then I went and sat near to him, and looking earnestly upon him spoke to him in the face of the Lord, and the power of Truth coming over him, he spoke to me no more, but turned away, upon which I awoke and wrote this dream, and what follows, part thereof with tears, for it settled in my mind that great wickedness is often committed in public houses, and that frequenting them proves dangerous to many who are thereby led astray and ruined.

That people do often provoke one another to excess and vain conversation, and in the time thereof those who have the prosperity of Truth at heart are often treated with contempt.

Now if one who is generally well inclined does in any degree join with them it tends to weakness, but if our lives throughout are agreeable to Truth, and we steadily keep to the Truth, the Lord preserves us, and gives power over evil spirits.

O you wasteful drinker who enflames yourself with strong drink! Flatter not your self, the day of judgment is at hand, and O that you may repent before it is too late.

Chapter XIII It is a great pity that any should be scattered like sheep without a shepherd.

My beloved, my desire is that each of us may strive earnestly that we may enter into the fold of everlasting rest.

When death comes, if we are not prepared, O how shall we feel then! If we have time to think we shall then have mournful thoughts!

O that I had in the days of prosperity been diligent in seeking after and serving the Lord.

Death sometimes comes suddenly and may not be put by. My mind has been deeply affected with the thoughts of it.

O that we may more and more seek to be acquainted with God and serve him faithfully!

Chapter XIV How shall men confide in one with whom they are not acquainted? O that we may be rightly acquainted with God, then may we put our trust in him.

In ages past his faithful servants have spoken well of him. They have by experience found him a gracious helper in a needful time.

Chapter XV There is a treasure which the world knows not of. It is the gift of God to mankind and is to be enjoyed in the denial of self and in the forsaking of the vanities of this world.

It is pure and inward. O my soul, seek for it.

Chapter XVI What have we done for the natives of this land? Have we been careful to instruct them in the principles of that pure religion which Jesus Christ is the author of?

O how necessary it is that our example before them be agreeable to these heavenly doctrines!

How sorrowful is it that they should be encouraged in drunkenness by the professors of Christianity?

How sorrowful is it that they should learn profane and wicked language from the professed followers of Christ?

May the kindness of their fathers to our fathers when these provinces were first settled be remembered, and may we in our conduct toward them bear in mind the small price they set on these lands which we now possess.

Chapter XVII When the world smiles upon you, remember to keep to plainness and let moderation appear in all your conduct and actions. Be exceedingly careful lest your mind be lifted up and carried away with deceitful pleasures. Remember that this world is not your proper home; you ought to be a stranger in it, your business is to do good with what divine providence has entrusted you with, and above all things to strive daily to be prepared for your last change.

All things below are changeable and uncertain; it will therefore be your greatest wisdom and happiness to have your mind fixed on God, and serve him with all your strength, then you may safely rely on him.

If you attain to old age and have bodily weakness, he will be your comfort, even when your appetite for the pleasant things of this life is gone. But if you forsake him, so great and good a master, and fix your mind on things here below, then as David said, *He will cast you off forever*.[7] O lamentable state indeed!

Chapter XVIII The trees and visible part of the Creation may afford us an innocent pleasure in this life, if the mind be fully subdued, and above all things delighted in adoring the great Creator. Thus we may see his works and with admiration behold things in their proper time and place; but for want of giving diligent heed to the true and inwardly taught, true comfort is missed of, and that innocent pleasure which the visible part of the Creation might afford us, we in a great measure are strangers to.

Chapter XIX A Christian spirit is a spirit of love, and they who live in it live in love for they cannot live otherwise. The happy effect which it has on those who rightly attend to it is very admirable; it works out and delivers from all malice and desire of revenge.

Chapter XX At one of our fourth day meetings my mind was released from earthly objects and my inward man strengthened in my silent sittings. Then heavenly treasure appeared exceedingly beautiful and desirable, and there was a language in my heart. *O my beloved, seek for it.* And after meeting on my way home, tears of joy ran down my cheeks, and I felt a fresh confirmation that it is profitable, and likewise my duty, to endeavor to attend weekday meetings, which by many are neglected, and the consideration of so great a neglect has at times caused me to mourn.

Chapter XXI In the beginning of the year 1763 the winter was very cold, and corn and hay scarce with me and many more, which at times caused a sadness in my mind, yet at times my mind was drawn heavenward, and melted into tenderness which caused me to praise the

---

7 [Ps. 44:23]

great Governor of the world, and to consider the saying of the apostle, *that all things work together for good to them who love God.*[8]

One day with you, O Lord, is as a thousand years, and a thousand years as one day. All your judgments are righteous; neither do you willingly afflict the children of men.

Chapter XXII The Most High in the beginning created man in his own image, and gave him power over the inferior part of the Creation, and commanding him to be merciful said by his servant Moses, *thou shalt not muzzle the ox which treadeth out the corn,*[9] but innocent men he gave not power one over another, so far as to enslave one another, and as man through disobedience fell from that state which he was created in, into a state of sin and death, the mercy of the Most High was such that he forsook not man, but strove with him, and to redeem him from this sorrowful fall, he gave his only son who tasted death for every man, then certainly for the poor Negroes. And dare you who profess to believe in Christ have the boldness to keep that man in slavery for whom Christ died? O you that have eyes but refuse to see, and ears but refuse to hear, know you of a truth that God is no respecter of persons.

Chapter XXIII 2nd day 2nd month 1764 on my way home from Burlington it revived in my mind that to spend a little time in a Christian way, in visiting the aged, the sick, and the afflicted, and to assist the poor under their difficulties is more pleasing to the Almighty than to lay up riches for posterity, or lay out money in dyed colors, and it opened in my mind that the Most High at this time is calling to some and moving upon their hearts to forsake some of their acquaintance and the use of costly apparel, and dyed colors, which once they delighted in.

The ways of the Most High are wonderful and as the children of men give way to the leadings of his Spirit, he teaches them all things needful to be understood, but when they forsake his leadings they forsake their own mercies and wander in a dark way which is unprofitable to themselves and to others.

My heart is concerned for the happiness of mankind, and it is sealed on my mind that it does not depend on customs approved by men, but on obedience to the Spirit of Truth.

---

[8] [Rom. 8:28]
[9] [Deut. 25:4]

Chapter XXIV The love of God which unites in true brotherhood is a treasure of all others most desirable, and is a blessing beyond expression. O the sweetness of it! Is your heart hard and shut up against the cries of the afflicted, this divine love as you seek after it and delight to feel the movings of it on your mind will soften and melt your heart into tenderness. Then you will find no narrowness of heart.

The desire of revenge which is very afflicting will be removed from your mind, and you will experience an increase of love to flow toward all your fellow creatures. O the happy effect of the love of God! It is beyond expression. O my soul seek after it and live in it. Without it there is darkness and misery, but in it is all true happiness.

Chapter XXV O Lord, what is man without thee! Or what are the treasures of this world without thy presence!

Man is a poor frail creature, and the treasures of this world are not sufficient to make him happy. His imaginations and conclusions are vain and foolish, but thy ways, O Lord, are pure and deep and thy presence is more than life.

Chapter XXVI I beheld the Christian path and it was so narrow that there was no room for self to speak or move. It appeared as if self should drop down and hide, and let Truth arise and bear sway. O my soul, choose Truth for your companion! Prize it as your bosom friend! Then you may walk in the Christian path with a secret delight, but take care lest self arise.

Chapter XXVII Keep honesty and humility for your constant companions, then in times of trial, when the friendship of the world passes away, as you keep Truth for your bosom friend it will be as a wall and bulwark[10] round about you, and will give you that peace which the world cannot take away.

Chapter XXVIII You may deck yourself with silver, and array yourself in fine linen and costly apparel, but the time is near that of these your imaginary ornaments, you must be stripped and stand bare before the Almighty Judge. Then the ornament of a meek spirit, of a dove, lamblike innocence and uprightness, these will be the ornaments which in the sight of God will be of great price.

---

[10] [Isa. 26:1]

Chapter XXIX Near the end of the seventh month 1766 I had a fit of the asthma, and when the extremity of the pain was over, some of my dear friends who have departed this life revived in my memory, who I believe are entered into the mansions of glory. Then all earthly treasures and enjoyments, crowns and scepters, appeared no more than bubbles on the water, and there was an earnest longing in my mind that I might so spend my time as to be rightly prepared to meet with the faithful in the glorious kingdom, where the wicked cease from troubling, where all tears shall be wiped away, and where the soul shall continually rejoice, and sing praise to the Redeemer, world without end.

Chapter XXX O Lord, through long and sore affliction my flesh and strength are wasted! My spirit is covered with sadness, and my life is afflictive to me! O Lord, my mind is turned toward you! Be pleased I beseech you in the multitude of your mercies, to remember me.

Chapter XXXI O heavenly Father, as a righteous judge you were near me in the days of my youth, when darkness covered my mind, and thick darkness was over my understanding. Then in tender mercies did your glorious light shine and you did often draw my mind to forsake earthly vanities and cleave to you, the fountain of life and peace.

O the sweetness of your love to them that seek you in contrition of spirit and yield obedience to you!

Chapter XXXII Being often afflicted I have been led to consider this vast globe. The lights in the firmament, the depth of the sea, the many sorts of grain, plants, and herbs, all these set forth the power of an almighty being.

I considered multitudes of birds with a pleasant harmonious voice, and beheld them singing of his praise. I considered great numbers of four-footed beasts in fatness and delight who are fed by him. And while my meditations have been on the wonderful works of the Almighty, all-wise, powerful, and merciful Creator among his creatures, a serious consideration has arisen in my mind: why men, the most noble part of this visible creation, should be so grievous afflicted?

These considerations have attended my mind year after year, and I have felt an earnest desire that I might be acquainted with the true cause of my own afflictions. And in these awakening times it often arose in my mind that man was created in the image of God; and through disobedience fell from it into a state of sin, and death to the soul, where he is endeavoring to please himself with creaturely delights, and too much neglects to seek after a return to his maker. Thus he is craving the treasures of this world, seeking after greatness and costly apparel with almost innumerable unnecessary things, which cause abundance of needless labor and unprofitable cares. These things though common among the children of men and approved by many, do hinder us from seeking diligently to return to our maker.

Now in these times of my sore affliction, I believed that the time is come wherein the Almighty is visiting some home! Sometimes bringing them near to the gates of death, making life afflictive to them, that they may feel of the distress which the oppressed go through, both man and beast, preparing their hearts to receive instruction, to learn a new lesson, such an one as would be hard to learn in outward prosperity. That they may leave off oppression and cease to have fellowship with the oppressors and worldly-minded men. That they may be delivered from narrowness of heart and leave off seeking for advantage over others. That they may come out of all things which would lead themselves or others into hurry. And with hearts full of love, call to others to come out of these things and live a new life. A life sympathizing with the oppressed and others in their afflictions. To deal their bread to the hungry, and consider the whole of mankind as brothers and sisters.

To love the Lord with all our hearts, and our neighbors as ourselves.

Chapter XXXIII Third month 1768 this winter I passed through pains and weakness of body and was confined chiefly within doors. In which state the former sufferings for the cause of Truth, which Friends patiently went through, and the present sufferings and oppression of the Negroes under us, were often in my mind. Now if a true history of the oppressions of the Negroes, together with an account of the costly apparel, household furniture, and high living of many among us, were published, how evidently would it appear that there is a grievous backsliding and degeneracy from that uprightness and simplicity which in time past appeared among Friends.

Chapter XXXIV After recovering a little from the before mentioned weakness, I wrapped myself in warm clothes and went to one of our religious meetings. I sat near the fire but I felt very chilly and had many reasonings in my mind how I should get home without taking fresh cold. I thought in myself that I was a weak and helpless creature, and the remembrance of the great pain which I had lately endured increased my fear, in the height of which it suddenly came in my mind that the Lord is a powerful God. Then there was no room for doubts or fears for I was sure that this was the Truth. My heart was warmed and immediately I felt inward comfort which is a treasure superior to all the delights of this world, and through the renewed mercies of the Lord I returned safe home.

Chapter XXXV When you think on the poor, when you deal with the poor, then let tenderness come over your mind. When you undertake the management of young, or other, creatures, O then remember the innocency of man, when the Almighty gave him dominion over the inferior part of the Creation! And labor for that innocent state, therein to govern with tenderness and mercy.

When you take away the life of a creature, let awfulness cover your mind, let the execution be quick and with as little pain as is possible, always remembering that the Lord has a regard for every part of his Creation, and that you as a steward must account to him for all your conduct toward them.

Chapter XXXVI Our habitations remain undisturbed, and our land yields plenty, while many of us under this outward quiet do too much neglect our duty, and are pleasing our palates with the fruits of the labor of an oppressed people.

While we as a nation in fullness of bread do knowingly make merchandise of the labor of oppressed slaves, it gradually tends to lessen that inward tenderness which ought to be in our minds toward the oppressed. *When the time called Christmas came, while others were feasting themselves, I looked out poor widows from house to house, and gave them some money.* G. Fox Journal page 4.[11] In this sympathizing spirit the poor and the afflicted are often in our remembrance, and a care maintained to do nothing to strengthen those bands under which our fellow creatures are oppressed.

If we would be acquainted with that which belongs to our everlasting peace, we must look from the world, and get down into the valley which is unknown to the world, and in humility and abasement of self wait to hear the voice of the true Shepherd, and when we hear, be careful to obey.

Chapter XXXVII There are several sorts of people who have but little of the treasure of this world. Some widows who are left with small

---

[11] [George Fox (1624-1691), *A journal or historical account of the life, travels, sufferings, Christian experiences and labour of love in the work of the ministry, of that ancient, eminent and faithful servant of Jesus Christ, George Fox* (London: printed for Thomas Northcott, 1694)]

children; some weakly people; some aged people; some in these conditions labor hard, rather beyond their ability, and yet are straitened for the necessaries of life. There are others who live at ease, in worldly greatness and fullness of bread. When I have thought on these things, my heart has been sorrowful. That which the latter lay out in superfluities being rightly applied, might be a means of help and relief to the former.

Chapter XXXVIII In the days of my youth I was in the practice of using sugar and other West India produce, without thinking much on the manner of its being raised and made, but within twelve years past I have been repeatedly and credibly informed that the labor is chiefly performed by slaves who are under oppression, many of whom were taken by violence from their native land, which with me is a sufficient reason to decline using the West India produce.

Chapter XXXIX At a time when vanity and oppression is increasing among the inhabitants of the land, it becomes us, who profess to be led by the Spirit of Truth, to experience our hearts cleansed and our minds enlightened with the light of Christ, that we may see the *approaching danger and calamities which threaten these neighboring provinces*[12] and stand like faithful watchmen on the wall, uniting together in example and Godly labors to convince the youth of the danger there is in conversing with such whose lives and practices are contrary to the doctrine of Christ.

Chapter XL In a time of mourning, when my heart was exceeding sorrowful, it opened in my mind that while the rich men live in greatness and demand interest at seven percent, weekday meetings will be small; and while the members of our Society are engaged in promoting the bringing so much rum into this land, the Society will not be clear from the great sin of drunkenness.

Chapter XLI I have experienced the mercies of the Lord to be greater than what I have words to express. With his good gifts I have been fed all my life long. He has given me of his own good Spirit, which has instructed me to do justly, to love mercy, to walk humbly, and to deal equitably with all my fellow creatures, without seeking for advantage over any, and to oppress nothing—and so far as I have been obedient he has given me peace. And this morning, the thirteenth day of the eighth month

---

[12]   [JW has noted in the left margin along the highlighted text: "Abner's own words."]

1771, under a fresh sense of his wonderful mercies, in my lonely condition I have shed tears of joy.

Chapter XLII Under a long continuance of bodily weakness, and my strength gradually wasting, I generally felt a concern, on meeting days, while I was able to walk to the door without outward help, to give my attendance in dry weather, at our religious meetings, and to take the greatest part of my family with me. And through the renewed mercies of the Lord I thought that the last meeting I was at, was one of the sweetest to me that ever I was in. 20th day 8th month 1771.

It does not appear that he made any notes in writing after the last date, several of his last being found on pieces of paper and probably written when he was unable to attend meetings. And as I was sundry times with him in the three last months of his time, I had some opportunities of hearing him express the state of his mind. He once told me that since his strength was so gone that he could not attend meetings, his concern to attend them ceased, and that his mind was made easy in his present condition.

At another time when he had during some days been under great distress of body, I went to see him, and he said that under the most trying times he had a trust in the mercies of the Lord, and that these afflictions to him were a great blessing for which he was very thankful.

That he was sensible of many imperfections which at times had attended him, but found the mercies of the Lord flow forth like the opening of a fountain, and that he had no trust in anything, but in this only. He made mention of a sense he had of the greatness of God's love which to him had appeared as a boundless ocean, and again repeated his sight thereof in a manner which manifested an inward awfulness of soul.

After this he gathered bodily strength a little so that he sometimes rode out, and one pleasant day as he rode on a slow walk, he in a reverent manner made mention to me of the beauty of this visible creation, and signified that as men came to be restored to perfect uprightness in living, they might enjoy sweetness and innocent delight in things pertaining to this life. After this he soon grew weaker again, and I going to see him got there, I believe, about five hours before he departed. He appeared in a quiet state of mind and was glad to see me, having before expressed a desire of an opportunity with me. And we being left in private, he said, It has been the most humbling time that ever I passed through, and I find nothing to trust in but in the mercies of the Lord, and I believe the Lord will prepare a place of rest for me. He signified that through divine love his heart had been brought into very great tenderness, and sympathizing love with his fellow creatures. Then he expressed a lively concern that the active members of our Society might keep to the Spirit of Truth in their living and outward concerns, and that he having been much exercised in an inward sympathy with the oppressed, felt that concern still to live in his mind.

He appeared apprehensive that his change was now near, and said he had no desire to live longer in this world. Soon after this he was in much bodily pain and said I have greatly desired a support that I may bear these heavy pains with patience, and said I have felt many pains in my life but these pains are different from any that I ever felt before. Which petition the Lord was mercifully pleased to grant, so that no signs of murmuring appeared on him. His speech soon after failed, under the pangs of death, and at length he did not appear to have much pain; but to outward appearance breathed quiet and easy for half an hour or more, and departed like one going to sleep, on the 4th day 11th month 1771 in the evening aged about 47.   John Woolman

A

Account Book 1769. See Woolman, John, *Account Book 1769*
Adanson, Michel, 46
Andrews, Isaac, 1, 111, 234, 241, 244, 256, 264
Andrews, Peter, 224, 225, 241
Arscott, Alexander, xiii, 7
Armitt, John, 245
Ashbridge, Aaron, 228, 244, 251

B

Babylon, 152
Barclay, Robert, 184, 190
Benezet, Anthony, 181, 226, 227, 236-37, 238, 244-45: *A Caution and
    Warning to Great Britain*, 93; on trading of enslaved in Guinea, 94; on
    treatment of enslaved, 95: in America, 96; Barbadoes, 96; West Indies,
    98-99
Bible, vii, xii-xiii, xv, xvii, xl, 276
Bosman, Willem, 46
Bradford, John, 153
brotherhood, 4, 7, 11-12, 66, 67, 83
Brown, William, 111, 181, 227, 228, 238, 239, 245
brute creatures, use of, xxviii, 44, 280, 293
Buchanan, George, 49
Burlington (NJ) Monthly Meeting, 109, 129, 220
Burlington (NJ) Quarterly Meeting: and John Woolman, 220

C

Cadbury, Henry J., xxvii, xxxv
Carleton, Thomas, 244
Catholic Church, the, 31
Cave's Primitive Christianity, 149
charity, spirit of, 28, 32, 42, 48, 64, 67, 107, 260, 266; estrangement from,
    176
Child, Isaac, 234, 244, 264
children: care of, 45; Christian education of, 9, 28, 119, 129, 202; concern
    for schools, 120; concern for succeeding generations of, xxiv, xxviii-
    xxix, xxxi, 71, 72-74, 75, 106, 198-99, 211; love of, 3; message to, 22;
    role of parents, 120; setting examples for, 3, 9, 21; spiritual life of, 185
Christ Jesus: blessings of, 21; as example, 105, 154-56; glorification of, 161;
    love of, 185; obeying spirit of, 114; as servant, 153; sufferings of, 185-
    86; teachings of, 5-6, 7, 75; as treasure, 178; work of, 103-04, 121-22,
    161, 162, 205, 207, 209, 210, 212

Christian life, the, 75-76, 78, 101, 105, 112, 121, 125-26, 128, 147, 148, 173-74, 198, 199: alienation from, 13-14, 81-82, 268; compassion, 262-63; diligence in, 123, 156, 162, 193, 199, 254, 259, 261, 262, 265, 272; and earthly treasures, 23, 196-97; equity, 13; fellowship, 13, 122, 268, 272-73; gratitude, 163, 188-89; humility, 122, 162, 268, 271; justice, 13, 154; longings for, 122; meekness, 149, 205, 250, 256, 266; moving away from, xxiv, 27, 250, 266; obedience, 200; patience, 102; peace,162, 191, 192; persecutions for, 187-88; purity, 19, 35, 60, 73, 78, 82-83, 100, 106, 109, 112, 115, 123, 152, 153-54, 157, 178, 180, 182, 184, 185, 188,189, 190, 200, 210, 212, 228, 232, 270, 271, ; queries for, 191, 192; right use of things, 210-211, 212, 250, 257; righteousness, 13, 271; and discouraging enslavement, 260; simplicity, 210; wisdom, xxiv, 193; and worldly pursuits, 78, 123, 148-49, 178, 197-98, 257, 261, 268; and youth, 259, 261, 263, 272

church, the visible gathered: benefits of, 21; concern for, xxviii; discipline, 182; disownment, 182-83; gratitude, 188; humility, 190; obedience to teachings of the Holy Spirit, 183; responsibility, 187, 188, 189, 191; right order, 190; silent worship, 189-90; Spirit of Truth, 189; spiritual rebellion, 192-93; unfaithfulness, 180, 187;and wisdom of the world, 180; worship, 183, 215

Churchman, John, xiii, 111, 222, 227, 228, 230, 234, 241, 244-46, 264

Comfort, George (JW's great-grandson), xxxiv

Comfort, Ira (JW's grandson), xxxiii

Comfort, John (JW's son-in-law), Woolman's business records, xxix, xxxiii

Comfort, John (JW's grandson), xxxiii-xxxiv: birth, 185

Comfort, Joseph (JW's grandson), xxxiii-xxxiv

Comfort, Maj. Samuel (JW's great-great-grandson), xxxiv, 102

Comfort, Mary Woolman (JW's daughter), 185: birth of, xiv; children, xxvi; marriage, xxvi

Comfort, Samuel (JW's grandson), xxxiii-xxxiv, 102

Comfort, Stephen (Mary Woolman Comfort's father-in-law): as trustee of Woolman's land, xxix-xxx, xxxiii; will of, xxxiii

Comfort, Stephen (JW's grandson), xxxiii-xxxiv

Comfort, William (JW's grandson), xxxiii

Cowpland, Caleb, 111

creation, the, 31, 280, 288, 291, 295: tenderness toward, 195

Crisp, Stephen, xv

D

Dewsbury, William, 162

disciples, the, 103, 212

divine admonitions, 163-65

divine love, 83, 204

Dudley, Elizabeth Comfort Lawrence, xxxiv

E

earth: care of, 106, 147; defilement of, xxvi, 164-65
earthly treasures: 79, 113, 191, 195-97, 290, 291-92; dangers of, 18, 21, 63,
    65, 83, 114, 126, 127, 176,179, 200, 211, 263; hoarding of, 154, 196; and
    true heavenly principle, 3, 80, 167, 199, 208, 254
Eastburn, Samuel, 241, 244, 256, 258
education, 118-20, 129-45. *See also* children: Christian education of;
    Philadelphia Yearly Meeting: committee to establish schools among
    Friends
Ellis, Sarah. *See* Woolman, Sarah Ellis
Emlen, Samuel Jr., 234, 236-37, 238, 239
enslaved, the: assumptions about, 6; children of, 34, 201; concern for, 20;
    conditions of, 6; hospitality toward as strangers, 7-8; as individuals,
    44; integrity of heart, 7; intelligence of, 46; responsibility toward, 8;
    treatment of, 8, 34, 56, 201, 202-03, 204-05
enslavement: and Christians, 70, 97, 99-100; and color distinction, 46-47;
    causes of, 32, 48; concern for reformation of, 98, 99; effects on
    enslaved, 30, 45, 69-71, 96, 100-01, 117, 118; effects on enslavers, 22-
    23, 30, 43, 44-45, 49, 60, 69; effect on Woolman, 1, 4; and guilt, 3;
    repentance from, 100; and torture, 43; enslavers: and inner state, 67;
    and need for repentance, 71-72, 96
"Epistle of Caution and Advice, Concerning the Buying and Keeping of
    Slaves," xiii, 2, 226-27
Evans, John, 111, 245
expensive customs, effect on Woolman, 105-08

F

Farrington, Abraham, 241, 244
Fearon, Peter, xxi, 29
Fothergill, Samuel, 111, 227
Fox, George, 209-10, 293
Foxe's Actes and Monuments, 54, 153, 162
French and Indian War, 87: and Canada, 15; consideration of among
    Friends, xiv, xv, 228; and England, 15; Philadelphia Yearly Meeting
    epistles (1755), xiv-v; (1759), xvii, 15, 24; and Treaty of Paris, 15
Friendly Association for Regaining and Preserving Peace with the Indians
    by Pacific Measures, 229

G

God's judgment, 5, 27, 80, 106
God's providence, 5, 9, 10-11, 25, 32, 45-46, 60-61, 65, 74, 79: opposition
    to, 60, 65, 66; submission to, 8, 83-84, 192, 196

God's will, discernment of, 33
God's work, 152, 253
gold: evils of, 178; and merchandizing, 175, 179; and power, 176; and vanity, 176; and war, 166-67, 179
Golden Rule, the, 67. *See* Scripture Index, Matt. 7:12
gratitude, xxix, 42, 48, 122, 156, 188

H

Haines, Samuel, xxi
Hammanns, William, 244
harmony, xi, xxxii, 12-13, 49, 96, 121, 126, 146, 154, 167, 178, 197, 199
Harvey, Elizabeth Woolman, xxvii
Harvey, Peter, death of, xxvii, 109
Haverford College, Quaker Collection, xxxiv-xxxv
Hinde, Mary, xxx, 194
Historical Society of Pennsylvania, xxi, xxxiv-v, 102, 222
holographs: dating of, 62-63; final disposition of, xxxiv-v; missing, xxxv, 16, 24, 30, 111, 217-19
Holy Spirit: waiting for, 160; work of the, 25-26, 182-84, 186, 190
Horne, William, 181, 244-45
Howell, Jacob, 244
humility, 10, 21, 27, 75, 78, 115, 119, 122, 149, 152, 158-59, 190, 199, 201, 250, 255, 257, 268, 271, 280, 281, 290, 293
Hunt, John, 236-37, 238, 240, 245
husbandry, 81, 168, 171, 173: and country compared with city life, 148

I

idleness, 116, 176, 203; and children, 10
idolatry, Jacob's example, 110
ingratitude, 5
integrity of heart, 7, 9, 82, 88, 89, 197, 253
inward tenderness, 67, 68, 69, 154, 186, 195, 207, 208, 283, 286, 288, 290, 293, 296
Isaiah, on the impoverished, 150
Israelites, the: prophets' reproach of, 33-35, 40, 203; corruption of Mosaic law, 39-40; as enslavers, 36-39; treatment of servants, 39; Babylonian captivity as punishment, 35-36, 40-41; year of Jubilee, 79. *See also* prophets of Ancient Israel, the: and idolatry; and oppression

J

John Woolman's Book 1769. See Woolman, John, *Account Book 1769*
John Woolman's Book of Executorship, xxi

Jones, Benjamin, 241, 242
Jones, Owen, 236-37, 238, 245
Jones, Owen, Jr., 238
Jones, William, 242
Journal of John Woolman: writing of, xvi, 1

K

Kinsey, John, 225

L

labor: benefits of, 116; dangers of excess, 116-17;
Large, Eben, 244
Latey, Gilbert: epistle, (1660), 209; self-denial, 209
Latimer, Bishop Hugh, 161-62
Ledger B 1753. See Woolman, John, *Ledger B 1753*
Library of the Society of Friends in Britain, 130
light of Christ, attention to, 127, 149, 187
Lightfoot, Benjamin, 244, 260
Lightfoot, Michael, 245
liquor, dangers of, 69-71, 279, 286
Logan, James, 109
Logan, William, 228, 246
London Yearly Meeting, 264-73
Long Island Yearly Meeting, 249-50, 260-63
Lord, Joshua, 111
Lundy, J. Wilmer, xxxiv

M

Mason, George, 245, 267
merchandizing: blatant immorality in, 157; and exports, 173, 174-75;
    moderation in, 156-57
missionary journeys of John Woolman, (Table 1, 241-42): apprenticeship
    journey (1743), xii, 224; Bucks County, PA (1753) xiv; (1759) xvii;
    Connecticut (1747), 225; Delaware (1748), xiv; England (1772), xxx-
    xxxii: preparation for, xxvi, xxix-xxx; Long Island (1747), xiv, 225, 260;
    (1756), xv, 228, 249-50, 260; (1760), xvii, 230, 260-63; Maryland
    (1746), 1, 225; (1757), 20, 30, 228, 251; (1766), xxiii, 147; (1767), xxiii,
    147; (1768), xxiii, 147; New England (1747) xiv, 30, 62, 225, 244, 260;
    (1760), xvii, 30, 62, 230, 244, 256-59, 260; New Jersey (1743), xii,
    224; (1746), xiv; (1748), xiv; (1751), xiv; (1754), xv; (1759), xvii; (1760),
    xvii; North Carolina (1746), 1, 30, 62, 225, 254; (1757), xvi, 20, 30, 62,
    228, 251, 254-55; Pennsylvania (1746), xii, 1; (1758), xvi; (1759), xvii;

Wyalusing, PA and Native Americans (1763), xix-xx, xxii, 62, 91, 232-34, 262; Virginia (1746), xii, 1, 30, 225; (1757), 20-21, 30, 228, 251-53
Mohammedans, 100-01
Moore, Samuel Preston, 245
Morris, Anthony III, 245
Morris, William, 245
Mount Holly, New Jersey, xi
Mount Holly Preparative Meeting, 220

N

Native Americans, 11: Christian outreach to, 81; relationships with, 80-81, 263, 287; trade with, 81. *See also* missionary journeys of John Woolman
New-England Primer, the: 129; contrasted with *A First Book for Children*, 129-30
New Garden (NC) Monthly Meeting, xvi, 20; epistle to, (1757), xxxv, 20-21
New-Jersey Association for Helping the Indians, 229
Noble, Mary, 242
Norris, Isaac II, 226, 245
North Carolina Yearly Meeting, 254-55

O

Overseers of the Press, (Table 3, 245-48), xiii, xviii, 1-2, 30, 111, 125, 147, 167, 224-28, 230, 234-36

P

Parvin, Benjamin, 233, 234, 242, 262
peace, spirit of, 122-23, 127, 128, 148, 192
Peace Testimony, the: "An Epistle from our General Spring Meeting of Ministers and Elders" (1755), xiv-xv, 15-19; "From our Yearly Meeting held at Philadelphia" (1759), xvii, 24-29; in time of war, xx, 16, 237; threats to, 27
Peaceable Kingdom, 16, 18, 122, 157
Pemberton, Israel, Sr., 221-22
Pemberton, Israel, Jr., xviii, 91, 181, 220-40, 244-45, 262, 264, 270; and Overseers of the Press, 247
Pemberton, James, 181, 221, 222, 228, 235-37, 238, 246-47
Pemberton, John, xxx, xxxiii, 91, 222, 223, 227, 228, 233-34, 236-37, 238, 244, 246-47, 262
Pemberton, Mary, 240
Pemberton, Phineas, 221

Pennsylvania: abolition acts of (1780) and (1847), xiii; French and Indian War, xiv, xvii, 15, 16, 24; Peace Testimony, xx, 16; Pennsylvania Abolition Society, 222

Philadelphia Quarterly Meeting, 222, 226

Philadelphia Yearly Meeting: adoption of queries (1743), 224, (1755), 228; American Quaker reform, 220-21, 223; capture and exile of leadership: by colonial government, 237-40, and PYM response to, 228, 239; committee to establish schools among Friends, 226; committee to revise the queries (1755), 111, 225, 227; committee for visiting Quaker enslavers (1758), xiii, xvi-xvii, 230; committee of press overseers formed (1709), 246; ethical concerns (1755), 111; expensive customs during, 107; French and Indian War, xiv, xvii, 15, 24; Meeting for Ministers and Elders, 107, 220, 227, 228, 234, 247; Meeting for Sufferings, 235, 236, 248, and creation of, 228; posthumous edition of *Journal*, 236-37; resolution on printing (1718), 246; right order in business meetings, 107; statement on defense in war (1758), xv; and John Woolman, 220-21: appointments to epistle committees, (Table 2, 243-45), 225; appointment to committee to establish schools among Friends, 226. *See also* "Epistle of Caution and Advice, Concerning the Buying and Keeping of Slaves"; Overseers of the Press; Woolman, John, reform of Philadelphia Yearly Meeting

Polycarp, 161

poor, the: attitudes toward wealthy, 68; concern for, 106, 213-14; condition of, 68-69; and envy, 200; hardships of, xxviii, 198, 213; humility, 199; mistreatment of, 65-66, 195; response to fair treatment, 66; rights of, 83; sympathy with, 153-54

prophets of Ancient Israel, the 160, 162, 208: and idolatry, 207-08; and oppression, 207

Provincial Assembly of Pennsylvania, 225: and James Pemberton, 222

pure principle, the, 59-60, 252

R

Rancocas Meeting for Worship, 220

redemption, 116

Reformation, the, and effect on worship, 215

religious hypocrisy, 106

religious liberty, xxix

Remarks on Sundry Subjects, xxx, 194

repentance, 27, 74, 157

Reynell, John, 181, 224, 234, 236-37, 238

Rhode Island Yearly Meeting, xvii, 256-59

righteousness, 65, 113, 158-60, 179: threats to, 84-86; work of, 23

Rutgers University, xxxv, 91

S

sailors, 211-14
Scarborough, John, xiii, 228, 230, 241, 244, 249
self-love: effects of, 7, 27, 42-43, 48-49, 76-77, 82; and natural affection, 2; and the soul, 73-74
simplicity: 81, 82, 83, 106, 107-08, 149, 177-78; departure from, 149-50; Friends' repudiation of, 208
Shinn, Thomas, xxi
Shotwell, Joseph, 111
sin, retribution for, 26, 203
Sleeper, John, 242
Smith, Elizabeth, 109, 242
Smith, Humphrey, 201
Smith, John, 109, 245
Smith, Richard, 244, 245
Smith, Samuel, 111, 229, 244, 245, 254
Some Considerations Relating to the Present State of the Christian Religion, xiii, 7
spiritual darkness, effects of, xxxii, 6, 27, 74, 100, 123, 161, 199, 291
spiritual life, the, and perfection, 82
Stanton, Daniel, xiii, 230, 241, 244
stillness, inward, 22, 122, 189, 215, 283
strangers, treatment of, 96, 204; and Israelites, 8, 10-11, 38-39, 41
Swarthmore College, Friends Historical Library of, xxxiv
Sykes, John, xiii, 241

T

thieves, encouragement of, 105-06
Thompson, Jonah, 111
Tilton, Nathan, 111
trade, international, 125-28, 147, 212
trading of the enslaved: concern for, 55, 56-59, 208, 211, 256; conditions on ships, 52; evils of compared to sufferings of early Christians, 53-55, 100; in Guinea, 50-51, 54-55; queries about, 206-07; tyranny of, 206; and war, xxxvi, 94, 112-13, 206, 227, 234
Truth: concern that Friends wait and live in it, 20-21, 208; deviation from spirit of, 19, 199, 200-01; living in the spirit of, 153-54, 172; professors of, xv, 184-85; and pure principle of equity, 100; standard of, 2; waiting for spirit of, 18, 107, 123, 200; walking contrary to, 186

U

useful trades, 81, 173

V

violence, xxvi, 40, 42, 56, 95, 100, 113, 150, 164, 202, 204, 211, 294
Virginia Yearly Meeting, 20, 251-53

W

walking: falling away from, 148-49; in pure light, 113, 162, 198; and
    spiritual harmony, 8, 114, 123,146, 148, 153-54, 156, 162, 184, 191, 267,
    271; as used in scripture, 78, 103, 151, 159; Woolman's theology on, 146
war: as antithesis of Christian life, xiv, xxiv, 16, 18, 27, 78, 79, 112, 123, 128,
    151-52, 157, 191-93, 205; dream of, xxiii, 91-92; and enslavement, 53,
    55, 94-96, 206-07; parable against, 87-90; preparations for, 77, 166,
    179; refusal to participate, 89; seed of, 197; and taxes for, 16, 89, 237,
    256, 284-85
wealth: burdens of, xxx-xxxi; misuse of, xx, xxiv, xxvi; pursuit of, 48-49,
    74, 112, 166, 202; and beasts of burden, 63-64; and charity, 11, 64; and
    dangers of, 9, 12, 63, 127, 151-52; effects on children, 35, 150-51, 177;
    effects on the church, 189-90; effects on impoverished, 169-70;
    Ezekiel's parable on, 172; and interest on land, 167-69, 172; and labor
    practices, 171, 195-96; and oppression of the impoverished, 176, 177,
    179; and power, 75, 176, 198; and repentance for, 170-71; and seeds of
    war, 78-79; and spiritual life, 109-10, 114, 115; and temptations,109,
    177; and threat to family, 126; virtue versus vanity, 64-65
wealthy, the: consciences of, 67; queries for, 205-06; responsibility of, 66;
    spiritual life of, 80; Woolman's prayer for, 115
Wharton, Florence Elizabeth Dudley, letter of, xxxiv
White, Joseph, 111, 235, 244-46, 267
White, Josiah, 224
Whitefield, George, 221
Woolman, Abner (JW's brother): Christian life, the, 287-89, 290-91, 294;
    concerns on alcoholism, 276, 279, 286, 294; enslavement, and Native
    Americans, 276, 278-79, 289, 292, 293; death of, xxvii, 274, 296;
    dream, 286; essay on West Indian trade, 279-80; on God's presence,
    280, 285-86, 295; on God's providence, 281-82, 284, 290, 292-93,
    294-95; on the impoverished, 289, 292, 293-94; on leadings, 284,
    289; letter to Burlington Monthly Meeting, 278-79; memorial for, 236,
    277; obedience, 289; refusal of military requests, 283, 284-85; self-
    denial, 287; on taking away the life of a creature, 280, 293; testament
    to his children, xxviii, 236, 280-95; visible Creation, the, 280, 288,
    291, 295; on waiting for God, 283; on West Indies produce, 277, 279-
    80; on worldly treasures, 291-92
Woolman, Abraham (JW's brother), xxv, 276
Woolman, Asher (JW's brother), 230, 276
Woolman, Eber (JW's brother), 275-76

Woolman, Elizabeth Jr. (JW's sister), xxi, 275

Woolman, John: *Account Book 1769*, xxii, xxv, xxix, 129, 218, 275; business records, xxi-xxii, xxv, xxxii, 218; childhood, xi; children of (Mary. *See* Comfort, Mary Woolman; William. *See* Woolman, William); death of, xxv, xxx, xxxii, xxxiii, 236, 274; deathbed prayer, xxxii; dreams, xviii, xxxii, 91-92; employment of, xi, xii; grandchildren of (Ira Comfort, xxxiii; John Comfort, xxxiii-iv, 185; Joseph Comfort, xxxiii-iv; Samuel Comfort, xxxiii-iv, 102; Stephen Comfort, xxxiii-iv, William Comfort, xxxiii); illness, xxv, xxxii, 109; *Ledger B 1753*, xxi-xxii, xxv, 218, 275; letters of: to John Aaronson Woolman, xxvii; and to Israel Pemberton, Jr., 230-33, 235-36; literary activity for Abner Woolman, xxvii-xxviii, 274-96; and reform of Philadelphia Yearly Meeting, 220-21, 223; relationship with family, 275, 276; as teacher, 129. *See also* holographs; *John Woolman's Book of Executorship*; *Journal of John Woolman*; missionary journeys of John Woolman; Philadelphia Yearly Meeting: and John Woolman

Woolman, John Aaronson (JW's nephew), birth of, xxvii, 276

Woolman, Jonah (JW's brother), 276

Woolman, Mary (JW's daughter). *See* Comfort, Mary Woolman

Woolman, Samuel (JW's father), xi, 222, 223; death of, xiv

Woolman, Sarah Ellis (JW's wife): death of, xxvi, xxxiii; marriage of, xiv; will of, xxxiii

Woolman, Uriah (JW's brother), 20, 241, 251, 275-76

Woolman, William (JW's son), birth and death of, xiv, xxvii

worldly spirit: conformity to, 107; temptations of, 154, 212-13

Wyalusing, PA, 232-33, 262

Y

Yarnall, Mordecai, 245

Z

Zeisberger, David, 233

A

Acts 1:8	6
Acts 8:33	155
Acts 10:34	160
Acts 11:18	5
Amos 6:13	80

C

1 Chron. 1:9, 10	87
1 Chron. 21:13	8-9
Col. 1:24	114, 186, 187
Col. 3:3	78, 179, 191, 200
Col. 3:4	199
Col. 3:11	32, 196
Col. 3:14	146
Col. 3:17	121
1 Cor. 1:30	197
1 Cor. 3:19	123, 197
1 Cor. 6:19-20	156
2 Cor. 1:5	200
2 Cor. 5:1	160
2 Cor. 5:7	200
2 Cor. 5:15	157, 196
2 Cor. 5:17-18	196
2 Cor. 6:1	162
2 Cor. 6:14	210
2 Cor. 6:18	198
2 Cor. 11:3	105

D

Deut. 1:17	31
Deut. 7:2	36
Deut. 10:19	11
Deut. 20:10-11	37
Deut. 20:16	36
Deut. 21:6	164
Deut. 25:4	289
Deut. 27:19	8
Deut. 28:43-44	38
Deut. 32:29	14

E

Eccles. 7:7	6
Eph. 1:22	187
Eph. 5:11	123, 210
Eph. 5:20	163
Eph. 5: 25-27	185
Eph. 6:4	119
Exod. 3:2	37
Exod. 18:19	37
Exod. 21:6	39
Exod. 21:16	40
Exod. 23:2	159
Exod. 23:7	207
Exod. 23:9	11, 68, 69
Exod. 23:13	157
Exod. 23:32-33	36
Exod. 40:12, 15	39
Ezek. 2:6-7	34
Ezek. 9:4, 9	203
Ezek. 13:22	207
Ezek. 16:49	203
Ezek. 18:2	34-35
Ezek. 18:1-3	35
Ezek. 18:20	35
Ezek. 28:18	158
Ezek. 34:17-22	172
Ezek. 34:18	69
Ezek. 47:22-23	41

G

Gal. 2:20	183, 187
Gen. 3:20	4
Gen. 5: 22, 24	253
Gen. 5:32	87, 88
Gen. 6:10	87, 88
Gen. 6:11	164
Gen. 6:11, 12	253
Gen. 7:13	87
Gen. 9:18, 22	87
Gen. 9:18, 23, 26-7	88
Gen. 10:1, 6-9, 20	87
Gen. 11:4	152
Gen. 13:15	80
Gen. 18:19	38
Gen. 23:6	10
Gen. 28:16	285

Gen. 32:10	10	Isa. 53:4, 7	155
Gen. 35:1-5	110	Isa. 53:5	156
Gen. 35:12	80	Isa. 53:12	161
Gen. 48:15	10	Isa. 54:14	207
		Isa. 55:4	199
H		Isa. 57:14	105
		Isa. 58:11	199
Hab. 3:17, 18	19	Isa. 60:21	208
Heb. 11:10	9, 28	Isa. 61:8-9	205
Heb. 13:5	17	Isa. 62:12	157
Heb. 13:8	185	Isa. 65:5	5
Heb. 13:14	28	Isa. 65:25	90
Hos. 10:12	211	Isa. 66:18	160
Hos. 10:13	208	Isa. 66:24	77
Hos. 14:3	75		
I		**J**	
Isa. 2:4	18, 113,	James 3:17	112
	122-23	James 5:7	102
Isa. 2:5	123	Jer. 1:8	33-34
Isa. 3:12, 15	150	Jer. 2:17, 19	164
Isa. 5:1-7	19	Jer. 2:19	26
Isa. 5:8	80	Jer. 2:34	164
Isa. 10:18	189	Jer. 6:14	39
Isa. 17:11	79	Jer. 6:15	158
Isa. 24:5	164	Jer. 7:3, 5-7	40
Isa. 26:1	9, 290	Jer. 7:18	207
Isa. 26:8	160	Jer. 8:8	40
Isa. 26:12	199	Jer. 8:11	39
Isa. 28:6	183	Jer. 9:24	13
Isa. 32:17	23	Jer. 11:15	158
Isa. 33:14-15	159	Jer. 16:19	265
Isa. 33:14-17	147	Jer. 17:7	113
Isa. 33:15	159	Jer. 22:1, 3, 5	40
Isa. 33:16	159-60	Jer. 23:6	158
Isa. 33:16-17	160	Jer. 26:2	34
Isa. 33:17	160	Jer. 34:11-22	41
Isa. 35:8	154	Jer. 34:15-20	41
Isa. 40:15	160	Jer. 49:11	76
Isa. 40:15, 22	17	Jer. 50:34	18
Isa. 40:31	159	Job 16:4	205
Isa. 43:24	xxvi, 165	Job 31:14-15	12
Isa. 45:24	199	Joel 2:25	163
Isa. 49:6	161	John 1:4	199
Isa. 49:15	148	John 1:9	119
Isa. 52:5	183, 201	John 2:10	104

John 3:21 113
John 5:2-9 103
John 6:15-21 103
John 8:31 7
John 10:16 5-6
John 12:35 199
John 13:34 212
John 15:7 183
John 15:9 150
John 15:10 196
John 15:14 148
John 15:19 258
John 18:11 268
1 John 1:7 151
1 John 2:5 182
1 John 2:6 153
1 John 2:16 123
1 John 3:8 156
1 John 5:3 183
1 John 5:12 199
Jon. 2:8 26
Josh. 5:13 37
Josh. 9:7 37
Josh. 9:14, 15 36
Josh. 9:19-21 36
Josh. 9:23 37
Josh. 9:25 37
Judg. 2:12, 19 35
Judg. 10:16 13

K

1 Kings 17:4, 6, 14 74
2 Kings 5:26-27 162

L

Lam. 3:24 259
Lam. 5:7 35-36
Lev. 3:17 39
Lev. 10:3 185
Lev. 19:17 207
Lev. 19:33, 34 8
Lev. 25:23 79
Lev. 25:45-46 38
Lev. 25:45 39
Lev. 25:46 39
Lev. 26:39 193

Luke 2:14 261
Luke 6:31 170, 191
Luke 6:37 183
Luke 11:34 111,113
Luke 11:50-51 193
Luke 14:28 191
Luke 16:13 154
Luke 17:27, 28-29 203
Luke 18:22, 25 75
Luke 22:27 153
Luke 22:42 155
Luke 23:34 156

M

Mal. 1:11 160
Mal. 2:10 204
Mark 3:35 186
Mark 6:45-52 103
Mark 10:14 118
Mark 10:21, 25 75
Matt. 5:5 192
Matt. 5:8 160
Matt. 5:9 127
Matt. 5:14 178, 191
Matt. 5:18 79
Matt. 5:23-24 186
Matt. 5:29, 30 150
Matt. 6:8 123
Matt. 6:9-10 183
Matt. 6:19 114, 196
Matt. 6:22 111, 113
Matt. 6:24 154
Matt. 6:26 116
Matt. 6:32 123
Matt. 6:33 3
Matt. 7:1 183
Matt. 7:12 67, 170, 191
Matt. 10:25 76
Matt. 10:29 78
Matt. 12:48-50 3
Matt. 14:22-33 103
Matt. 15:6 40
Matt. 17:21 72
Matt. 18:17 182
Matt. 19:19 197
Matt. 19:21, 24 75

Matt. 23:5 — 119
Matt. 23:9 — 192
Matt. 25:40 — 4
Mic. 4:3 — 18
Mic. 5:6 — 87
Mic. 5:7 — 147
Mic. 6:9 — 26

N

Nah. 1:7 — 23
Neh. 6:16 — 113
Num. 27:21 — 37
Num. 35:33 — 203

P

1 Peter 1:12 — 161
1 Peter 1:15 — 157, 184
Phil. 2:4-5 — 154
Phil. 3:10 — 114
Phil: 4:8-9 — 28-29
Prov. 12:18 — 157
Prov. 14:34 — 26
Prov. 16:5 — 207
Prov. 29:24 — 42
Ps. 2:8 — 160
Ps. 9:9 — 118
Ps. 44:23 — 288
Ps. 50:12 — 79
Ps. 50:18 — 207
Ps. 91:9 — 114

Ps. 115:16 — 79
Ps. 116:12 — 26
Ps. 133:1 — 151

R

Rev. 8:1 — 190
Rev. 18:3, 4 — 152
Rev. 21:5 — 257
Rom. 2:14 — 32
Rom. 2:24 — 183
Rom. 6:3 — 185
Rom. 8:28 — 289
Rom. 12:2 — 190
Rom. 12:16 — 146
Rom. 14:4 — 12
Rom. 15:5 — 146

T

1 Tim. 1:10 — 40
1 Tim. 3:15 — 187
1 Tim. 5:22 — 106, 210
Titus 2:14 — 123

Z

Zech. 4:6 — 17
Zech. 9:10 — 18
Zeph. 3:3-4 — 39
Zeph. 3:9 — 152

Lightning Source UK Ltd.
Milton Keynes UK

172035UK00001B/120/P